LIVING A HOLY LIFE IN UNHOLY TIMES

WEAPONS OF THE Spirit

SELECTED WRITINGS OF FATHER JOHN HUGO

EDITED BY DAVID SCOTT AND MIKE AQUILINA

Our Sunday Visitor Publishing Division
Our Sunday Visitor, Inc.
Huntington, Indiana 46750

The editors and publisher are grateful to all copyright holders without whose material this book could not have been completed. If any copyrighted materials have been inadvertently used in this book without proper credit being given in one manner or another, please notify Our Sunday Visitor in writing so that future printings of this work may be corrected accordingly.

International Standard Book Number: 0-87973-608-9
Library of Congress Catalog Card Number: 96-70439

Cover design by Kathi Hilaski
Printed in the United States of America

608

To Cecilia Marie Hugo,
sister of Father John
and keeper of the true fire
of his teaching,
this book is lovingly dedicated.

Acknowledgments

Thanks to Greg Erlandson, editor-in-chief of Our Sunday Visitor, a good friend and colleague, who had the vision to make this book a reality. Thanks, too, to Jim Manney of Our Sunday Visitor for his friendship and editorial advice on the manuscript.

Thanks to Sarah and Terri, our wives, and all our children, who gave us the time and the support we needed to pull this book together.

Special thanks to those who testified in their lives and words to the spiritual "fruits" of Father Hugo's teachings — Sister Peter Claver Fahy, M.S.B.T., Bob Corcoran, Ed Kelly, Sister Rita Brocke, R.S.M., Lane Core, J.F. Powers, Msgr. Joseph Meenan, Father Francis Ott, Father Edward Farina, Sister Janice Fulmer, C.S.F.N., Sister Virgilyn Lukaszewicz, C.S.F.N., Daniel Lyons, Father Marian Casey, and Scott Hahn.

A special note of thanks to Pat Bartos for her prayers and invaluable assistance.

Thanks to Philip Runkel, head of the Dorothy Day-Catholic Worker Collection at the Marquette University Archives, and to Frank Donovan of the New York Catholic Worker, for permission to quote from the correspondence of Father Hugo and Dorothy Day.

Thanks finally to the Hugo family, especially Rosemary Hugo Fielding for her prayers and encouragement and her flawless typing. Thanks, too, to Michael Hugo.

Thanks most of all to Cecilia Marie Hugo. This is really *her* book, the fruits of her years of "sowing." Her friendship remains a great grace and treasure in our lives, and one we know will "continue in eternity."

David Scott and Mike Aquilina
October 1, 1996, Feast of St. Thérèse of Lisieux

A Note on Scripture Translations

Father Hugo was first and foremost a preacher. He drew on various Bible translations, his favorites being the Revised Standard Version and the Douay, although he also made use of the Jerusalem Bible and the translation of the Confraternity of Christian Doctrine. His command of the Scriptures was thorough, and he moved easily from translation to translation, sometimes even within the same text. In the editing process, we have chosen, for the most part, to leave his Scripture quotations as they appear in his original manuscripts.

Contents

The Hidden Life of Father John Hugo: An Introduction 11

I — A Higher Calling: God's Plan for Our Lives 23
*A Goal for Your Life . . . How to Be a Perfectionist . . . What We
Have to Do . . . No Spiritual Double-Standards . . . Two Ways to
Be Religious . . . Pinocchio and the Mystery of God . . . Adam's
Choice and Our Lord's . . . Eve's Choice and Our Lady's . . . The
Christian Manifesto . . . Born in God . . . Repentance, the Other
Face of Love . . . The Gospel and the Grain of Wheat.*

II — Bread of the Strong:
The Christian Life as Call to Heroism 56
*Avoidance of Sin Is Not Enough . . . Three Steps on the Way . . .
Worldliness Makes Us Lukewarm . . . Detachment Is Not Optional
. . . Seeing God in Creation . . . From Attachment to Addiction
. . . No Christianity Without the Cross . . . The Price and Measure
of Love . . . A Cautionary Tale from History . . . We Want to Be
Heroes . . . Positively Penitential . . . Infinitely Better than Choco-
late and Mozart . . . Falling Away . . . Mary in Action.*

III — Prayer and Practice: The Life of the Saint 76
*The Prayer of the Busy . . . Lack of Prayer Is Lack of Love . . .
Conditions for Prayer . . . An Eastern Remedy for Western Activ-
ism . . . Distractions in Prayer: A Ladder to God . . . Resisting
Temptations . . . How to Discern God's Will . . . Make Frequent
Confession . . . Three Reasons to Go to Confession . . . The
Place of Spiritual Direction . . . What to Look for in a Spiritual
Director . . . How to Find the Best Books . . . What Is Meditation?
. . . Breath of Prayer, Touch of God.*

IV — Believing in the Church: Discipleship in Time of Division .. 93
*The Spiritual Condition of Our People ... Practical Priests ...
Bad Homilies ... The Scandal of Bingo ... Pharisees — Cause
of All Conflict in the Church ... 'Why Does the Truth Call Forth
Hatred?' ... Faith in the Church ... Who's in Charge? ... 'We
Have Powerful Enemies Everywhere' ... My Bishop's Hands ...
'Religion Without Obedience Is Simply Self-Delusion' ...
'Progressives' and 'Conservatives' Are Both Irrelevant ... The
Church Did Not Begin with Your Generation.*

V — Mysticism in Action: Catholics in the Public Square............. 125
*The Failure of Christian Effort ... A Religion of Our Own Stan-
dards ... Death of a 'Practical' Catholic ... Spiritual Aptitude
Test Scores ... The Illusion of Christian Effectiveness ... Nero's
Fiddle ... The Fatal Delusion of Our Times ... There Is No
Such Thing as Personal Ethics ... Your Own Private Revolution
... The Only Reason to Act ... Mystics in Action ... The Work
of the Apostolate ... Supernatural Living ... Detachment and
Turning ... The Radical Cross ... Dying to Self ... Our Lady,
Queen of Apostles ... God's Law and the Law of the Land ...
Dorothy Day, Apostle of the Industrial Age.*

**VI — How to Fight a War:
Conscientious Objection and the Nuclear Age 150**
*Catholics and War ... Nations and the Moral Law ... War in
Scripture and Tradition ... The Law of Love ... The Evil of the
Draft ... After the Bomb ... A Christian Manifesto on War ...
The Impractical Weapons of the Spirit ... Our Lady, Queen of
Peace ... The Leaven of the Beatitudes.*

VII — Virgins and Lovers: Is the Church Obsessed with Sex? 196
*Celibacy and Sex . . . Wedded Bliss . . . Visions of Loveliness . . .
Unsafe Sex.*

VIII — The Sense of Suffering:
The How and Why of Human Pain 208
*Why Must I Suffer? . . . Pruning: Reflections Under Trial . . . For
the Sake of Joy . . . Destiny Draws You On . . . Everything to
Gain . . . Look to Glory . . . The Eucharist of Our Lives.*

Epilogue: The Art of Living 225

Sources 226

Index 228

The Hidden Life of Father John Hugo:
An Introduction

Father John Hugo's life seems to have been written with invisible ink, the passing years having erased all but a trace of him from even the footnotes of the history of the Catholic Church in America.

Perhaps this is as it should be. Father Hugo was not well understood during his lifetime (1911-1985), and he took as his credo those obscure and frightening lines from Jesus' farewell to His disciples: "Truly, truly, I say to you, unless a grain of wheat falls into the earth and dies, it remains alone; but if it dies, it bears much fruit. He who loves his life loses it, and he who hates his life in this world will keep it for eternal life" (Jn 12:24-25).

He lived this maxim well. Through almost fifty years of priesthood in the Diocese of Pittsburgh, he went where he was sent — inner-city missions, rural and suburban parishes, prison chaplaincy, college teaching, even street preaching. He labored quietly and occupied no glory pulpits. Father Hugo was a retreat master who wrote prolifically but published little, and almost exclusively for a small circle of his friends and devotees. Yet his teaching somehow reached and influenced some of the most influential figures and movements in the twentieth-century American Church.

Dorothy Day, the founder of the Catholic Worker movement and one of the most challenging Christian witnesses of the twentieth century, called him her spiritual director, and she traced her "second conversion" to a retreat under his direction. As she lay on her deathbed in 1980, Day was reading one of Father Hugo's retreat notebooks. "I'm still sowing," she told a close friend who was visiting, speaking of her life in terms that Father Hugo had taught her — as a grain of wheat that must be sown in order to reap the abundant harvest of new life in Christ.

Cardinal John J. Wright, head of the Vatican Congregation for the Clergy through the 1970s, commissioned Father Hugo to write a book clarifying St. Augustine's teaching on sexuality (and the Church's teaching) in the years when both Augustine and the Church were subject to caricature by some of the world's leading theologians.

Father Hugo was also a guide for the nascent charismatic renewal movement and he was one of the midwives of authentic liturgical renewal in the years before the Second Vatican Council. He had a key role in writing one of the first adult catechisms of the post-Vatican II era, and he served as father confessor to two generations of conscientious objectors, from World War II through the invasion of Grenada.

The writings in this volume reflect the variety of Father Hugo's gifts, though they are only small samples. Some come from books that bear imprimaturs from important leaders such as Cardinal Francis J. Spellman and Archbishop John F. Noll. Others come from fading typescripts.

His words burn with urgency even today. The cost of discipleship has not fallen since the 1940s. He wrote with penetrating, prophetic insight into struggles that are ever contemporary: war and peace, sex and love, justice and mercy. In a way, Father Hugo speaks more clearly and forcefully in death than he did during his life, when his ideas were so new and radical as to frighten even the leaders of the Church.

⚜

John Jacob Hugo was born of second-generation American Catholics on April 20, 1911, and was baptized at St. Pius V Church in McKeesport, a steel town near Pittsburgh, Pennsylvania.

His mother, the former Mary Caulfield, was Irish Catholic and worked as a secretary for a steel company. His father, Lawrence, was an orphan of French and Welsh lineage, and he ran a fairly successful insurance and real estate business.

In a memoir written in his last year, Father Hugo described a happy childhood. He was the firstborn of four. Along with his two sisters and brother, he attended Benedictine schools. John was a voracious reader. His parents led him to read the classics in literature and philosophy. In his memoir, Father Hugo recalled that his parents encouraged him as he discerned his priestly vocation, but they never pressured him. He felt, rather, that God was tugging at him:

> I fall back on the word *attraction* used by older spiritual writers, that is to say, the attraction of God's grace or, better, God Himself. That makes sense; after all, marriages begin in an attraction that grows until it becomes irresistible. Dorothy Day, in her autobiography, speaks of being haunted by God even in her unlikely girlhood. I recall no such experience, although God was always high and bright in my universe, but like a distant star. . . . If I may use a figure, it would be a magnet, subtle, at first unfelt, but growing in force until it became all but overpowering. So perhaps it is simpler and truer just to compare it to falling in love.

Through his seminary years in the early 1930s, John Hugo acquired a reputation as an esthete, an intellectual, and a *bon vivant*. One classmate recalls him in those years as "proud" and an elitist, associating "only with the brainy guys. . . . He would go to New York with them to see shows. He knew authors we hadn't ever heard of. He was always in the library."

He was ordained by Bishop Hugh C. Boyle of Pittsburgh on June 14, 1936, at the basilica church of his seminary, St. Vincent Archabbey in Latrobe, Pennsylvania. His ordination photo shows a handsome man with bright, piercing eyes set above strong cheekbones.

His intellectual gifts earned him an early post as a college chaplain and an opportunity to study at the University of Chicago. Yet it was not until two years after his ordination that Father Hugo's particular vocation would become clear to him. It was in Baltimore, in September of 1938, that he made the retreat that would change his life. He would later recall it as his "first real religious experience."

Such experiences were, perhaps, becoming more common as the Church was in the midst of what is today remembered as the great "retreat movement" of the mid-twentieth century, a movement urged on by Popes Pius XI and Pius XII. It was part of the Church's contribution to the whole-sale reevaluation of the human condition that the world seemed to be undergoing in this period, a period that had witnessed "total war," Auschwitz, the gulag, and the atomic bomb.

While some answered with grand new ideologies and mass movements — everything from psychoanalysis and existentialism to neoimperialism, Marxism, and nationalism — the Catholic Church issued a much humbler, yet far more radical call for individuals to seek holiness in the little things of everyday life.

The Church's answer might be traced back to "the little way" of a saint who would profoundly influence Father Hugo in the succeeding years, St. Thérèse of Lisieux. At the dawn of the modern era, as if anticipating the way the human person would be degraded by technology and ideology in this era, St. Thérèse had stressed the God-given dignity of each person and the potential for divine significance in our every act. Father Hugo liked to quote these lines of Thérèse: "The holiness to which we should aspire does not consist in notable deeds or special favors from God, but in the sanctification of all works, no matter how humble, of human living."

Father Hugo was a well-trained priest when he arrived for that retreat in 1938. He was steeped in St. Thomas Aquinas. He had read the major moderns, such as Jacques Maritain. He breathed deeply the same Catholic cultural air that produced modern saints like Frank Sheed and Dorothy Day, and influential movements such as Catholic Action, Opus Dei, and the Catholic Worker.

Like others involved in this mid-century Catholic "renaissance," he believed that the resolution of the modern crisis, perhaps even the survival of the human race, demanded nothing less than a generation of saints — holy men and women living only for the love of God and the building of His kingdom.

And this was the intuition Father Hugo made his own on that autumn retreat in Baltimore: God wanted John Hugo to be a saint, nothing less; and God wanted this for everyone else as well.

The messenger that week in Baltimore was one of the most renowned (and controversial) retreat masters on the continent, the Canadian Jesuit Father Onesimus Lacouture. The eight-day, silent Ignatian retreat focused on the themes of radical conversion, repentance, and the following of Jesus Christ. Father Lacouture preached this retreat some 132 times to 5,400 priests in Canada and the United States.

One of Father Hugo's companions on the Baltimore retreat summed up Father Hugo's experience: "He found out the life he'd been living was a good natural life, but it was not supernatural; the emphasis was not on spirituality. That moment was his turning point. He no longer wanted to do the things his friends did."

Father Hugo was shaken and thrilled by the radical demands of Father Lacouture's teaching: that each of our daily acts must be done solely for the love of God, apart from any "natural" motives, and that even our slightest attachments can be obstacles to loving God. Father Hugo later recalled:

> Religion as a complete act of self-surrender to God, I did not know. This I was to learn, or to begin to learn. Henceforth God was to be in the center of my life, and at the front. In fact, He was to become the whole of my life. He was to dominate the entire horizon. . . .
>
> Henceforth there was only one thing important, only one thing necessary: God. Everything had its value in the measure of its capacity to lead to God. Everything was to be used only in reference to Him, to serve Him, to glorify Him, to bring me closer to Him. Everything that did not lead to Him was to be forgotten, neglected, renounced, cut out of one's life at whatever cost. . . . Religion was henceforth for me not a paying of one's duty to God; it was the giving of everything to God, knowing, of course, that God would return to me, and with good measures overflowing, whatever I needed for my life.

In very practical terms, as Father Hugo would write in the 1940s, there were some adjustments to make — in his style of living: "When I returned home and reentered my pleasant apartment I saw it with different eyes than when I had left it."

He surveyed the racks and racks of books and record albums, the comfortable furniture, his collection of pipes, and shelves of bric-a-brac. He saw that many of these, though good in themselves, were for him "attachments" that he had allowed to distract him from God and even to take the place of God in his life.

He quit smoking then and there. He rid himself of hundreds of volumes of poetry, drama, essays, novels. Again, he did not believe that these things in themselves were evil. For others, they might be harmless; they might even be used for God's glory. But Father Hugo knew himself and he knew the spell these comforts cast over him. "They were a key and a doorway into a magic world," he said. But the bottom line came from Jesus: "Whoever of you does not renounce all that he has cannot be My disciple" (Lk 14:33). If Father Hugo chose to continue ownership of these goods, he knew, the goods would increasingly come to own him.

He could not keep this realization to himself. Since the call to sanctity was meant for everyone, Father Hugo dedicated his life to taking this message to others. He began preaching Father Lacouture's retreat, not only to priests (as Father Lacouture did), but to lay people as well. During the eight days of the retreat, retreatants were forbidden to speak or to read anything other than the Bible. Amid the silence, they attended three retreat conferences each day, as well as Mass and spent long periods in mental prayer.

Father Hugo's conferences offered spiritual riches from the Catholic tradition: the Fathers of the Church, the saints, and the popes. At the core of it all was Jesus' simple and direct call to holiness, from the Sermon on the Mount: "You, therefore, must be perfect, as your heavenly Father is perfect" (Mt 5:48).

Father Hugo found this message borne out through all the Scriptures — "Strive for . . . holiness without which no one will see the Lord" (Heb 12:14), "This is the will of God, your sanctification" (1 Thes 4:3). And again: "You shall be holy, for I am holy" (1 Pt 1:16, cf. Lev 11:44). And: "He chose us in Him before the foundation of the world, that we should be holy and blameless before Him. He destined us in love to be His sons through Jesus Christ" (Eph 1:4-5).

He heard the same call to holiness echoed in the spiritual classics, especially in the works of St. Francis de Sales, St. John of the Cross, St. Teresa of

Ávila, and in *The Imitation of Christ*. Among the moderns he called frequently upon St. Thérèse of Lisieux and Cardinal John Henry Newman.

And just as the call awakened in Father Hugo a desire to be a saint, so he strove to awaken that desire in others. Often he succeeded. Dorothy Day said that hearing Father Hugo preach a retreat was like "hearing the Gospel for the first time." Through Father Hugo, she said, she came to see Scripture as "a love letter" addressed personally to her. While on retreat with Father Hugo, she wrote:

> I think to myself with a touch of bitterness, the ordinary man does not hear the Word of God. The poor do not have the Gospel preached to them. Never have I heard it as I hear it now, each year in retreat, and with the sureness that it is indeed the Gospel.
>
> The average Catholic is baptized, instructed for his first holy Communion, then confirmation, and then, Sunday after Sunday, the short Masses repeat themselves, with inadequate sermons, all the announcements, appeals for money.
>
> The shepherds are not feeding their sheep. But they themselves have not been fed. And the sad part is, the people are poor and do not know they are poor. Poor, undernourished, even starving as far as spiritual nourishment goes. The priest too. One has to make an attempt to know God before we can love Him and serve Him. Or try to know the Unknowable. The search goes on as long as we live.

In the same period, Father Hugo was a periodic contributor to Day's newspaper, *The Catholic Worker*. In the midst of the "Good War," World War II, pacifism was at best an unpopular position among American Catholics and the American hierarchy; at worst it was thought treasonous.

But Father Hugo believed it was an extension of the theology of his retreat — "completing the obligation to seek holiness." His writings helped some in their conviction that participation in the war effort was immoral. One was the novelist J.F. Powers, who credits Father Hugo with influencing his decision to be a conscientious objector. Powers tells an amusing story of attending a retreat on his way to jail for draft resistance.

> I first saw Father Hugo at a priests' retreat, preached by him, in the summer of 1943 at St. John's Abbey, Collegeville [Minnesota], to which I'd received an invitation and train fare from an old friend, a priest in the St. Paul diocese.

I knew I was going to prison and so I was in the mood for Father Hugo (unlike one elderly retreatant, I remember, who, on learning there would be no group picture, checked out). I remember seeing Father Hugo off at the Minneapolis-St. Paul airport, all of us kneeling on the tarmac for his blessing. . . . I admired and liked Father Hugo, his mind, heart, wit, courage.

Father Hugo's message was not for the faint of heart, and it was a reproach to the direction that much of the American Church was taking. After the war, he found himself at odds with the growing affluence and comfort-seeking in the United States, especially among Catholics. In the World War, Catholics had proven that they were loyal Americans. Having fought and died beside their Protestant countrymen, they had finally overcome nativist, anti-Catholic suspicion and were now ready to take their place in the mainstream of American life.

But Father Hugo saw in this confident assimilation a watering down of Catholic identity. Catholics seemed to him to be growing daily more American and less Catholic. He criticized priests and Catholic fraternal organizations for promoting an increasingly less demanding version of the faith, one more conformable to the spirit of American individualism, pragmatism, and pluralism. This brand of Catholicism downplayed rituals and beliefs that distinguished Catholics, demanding only that Catholics live up to minimum middle-class standards of virtue — to be courteous, temperate, to go to Mass and avoid egregious sins. Father Hugo called this bland creed "pious naturalism" or, more severely, "paganism," a betrayal of Christ and His saving message.

Father Hugo's teaching did not sit well with his brother priests. They circulated rumors that he was a fanatic, a rigorist, a puritan, and — worst of all — a "Jansenist" who believed that our thoughts and deeds were so ruined by our sinfulness and lusts that we were incapable of doing anything good. His followers were taunted as "Hugonuts," a derisive play on the name used to describe sixteenth-century French Calvinists ("Huguenots"). His teaching of detachment was caricatured as masochistic self-hatred and hatred of creation.

One of Father Hugo's closest friends now recalls those years as a major trial of his own priestly life: "When priests would gather, at funerals and ceremonies, others would avoid us. . . . It was a very difficult period, to be in a sense ostracized by your fellow priests. It seemed to me that what we were saying was just what we were reading in Scripture and the classics."

That was, in fact, the great irony. The teachings of the retreat were rooted in the oldest spiritual traditions of the Church, and yet those teachings had so fallen out of fashion that they were barely recognizable to even some Church leaders at the time. And even today, Father Hugo's teachings will strike many as too severe, so accustomed have we become to spiritualities based, not on the radical demands of Christ, but on the supposed needs of the "self" for "affirmation" and "healing."

Though Bishop Boyle considered Father Hugo "a very helpful irritant," the rumors and the dissension increased among the clergy, and they began to have serious consequences. At one parish function, the bishop reportedly pulled out a cigarette, then hesitated, looked at Father Hugo and said: "It's okay, isn't it?"

Priests put steady pressure on the bishop and, in the late 1940s, suddenly and without warning, he withdrew the permission Father Hugo needed to give retreats in the Pittsburgh diocese. A routine and promised imprimatur for one of Father Hugo's books was abruptly canceled. Finally, Bishop Boyle ordered him to stop preaching retreats and transferred him to a remote rural parish.

It was a campaign of whispers. No formal accusations were ever lodged against Father Hugo. He received no opportunity to respond to insinuations of wrongdoing or to defend himself against veiled charges of heresy.

He could take no comfort in the fact that similar purges were waged against the "new theologians" of Europe, such as Henri de Lubac, Hans Urs von Balthasar, Yves Congar. Like Father Hugo, they poured new wine, a bit much for old wineskins to contain, and they were silenced for it.

Like them, Father Hugo broke from the empty formalisms that had reduced Catholic spiritual life to a sort of rigorous application of certain minimal rules and rituals. Like them, he favored a return to contemplative prayer and reading of the Scriptures along with the Fathers and Doctors of the Church. He spoke of the "high adventure" of the spiritual life and the great holy things that God expects of each one of us.

There was a misperception by some in the Church leadership that such ideas were divisive and a threat to Church authority and Catholic identity. Father Lacouture's retreat had indeed provoked splits within the Jesuits and other clergy in Canada, and this led to a crackdown on the retreat initiated by the Pope's apostolic delegate to Canada. Father Lacouture, in his turn, would be silenced and assigned to remote missions among Native Americans. His discipline went so far as to include suspension of some of his priestly faculties.

Father Hugo was singled out as the most influential agent of "Lacouturism" in the United States. The papal delegate to the United States,

Archbishop Amleto Cicognani, was reportedly charged with stamping out the movement. Father Hugo, it seems, made some mighty enemies.

He drew sustained fire from two influential American theologians, Father Joseph Clifford Fenton and Redemptorist Father Francis J. Connell. As professors at Catholic University of America, these men had trained a generation of U.S. Church leaders and were frequently consulted by bishops and clergymen. With close ties to the Vatican, they were widely assumed to reflect "the mind of Rome" when they spoke of the American Church.

Father Fenton was editor of the *American Ecclesiastical Review* from 1944 to 1963. He and Father Connell contributed hundreds of articles to the influential journal — including articles attacking Father Hugo, whose teaching they deemed "pernicious" and a threat to the Church. Never ones for understatement, the pair charged that if Father Hugo's teaching gained currency, it would lead to a "situation seriously disadvantageous to Catholicism in the United States."

Again, Father Hugo was not alone. Other voices, today considered prophetic, were roundly trounced in the journal. Fathers Connell and Fenton would later become notorious for their efforts to stem the influence of Jesuit Father John Courtney Murray, whose teachings on religious liberty and the civil order helped shape some of the thinking of the Council Fathers at Vatican II.

Since Father Hugo's attackers agreed with him in the most fundamental matters of doctrine, the points on which they disagreed became flash points, and the attacks grew more intense and even personal. To the nonspecialist, the critiques and Father Hugo's book-length responses can seem like so much theological hairsplitting.

But the concern was genuine: Critics seemed worried that Father Hugo's teaching, with its emphasis on personal holiness, would lead to a devaluation of the role of the institutional Church. As Father Hugo drew believers into a more personal faith, a closer union with the Risen Lord, and as believers began to see their everyday actions as holy offerings, wouldn't they also experience a corresponding decrease in their fervor for the Church, its authority, and its traditional devotions? They charged further that, following Father Hugo's teaching, one could surmise that membership in the "visible" Catholic Church was unnecessary. This, they believed, would accelerate Catholics' slide into religious indifferentism and would hasten their homogenization with the Protestant mainstream.

But the proof against these charges was the witness of Father Hugo himself. Religious indifferentism was precisely the spiritual disease he had set out to cure. As for respecting the institutional Church, when Father Hugo was silenced, he submitted. When asked by his bishop to stop distributing one of his books, he and his sister Cecilia, his lifelong personal assistant, drove a carload of copies to the dump and threw them in.

Father Hugo seemed to welcome this "dying," as a grain of wheat, even though it meant being forbidden from preaching his beloved retreat for nearly twenty years. His brother priests, even those who disagreed with Father Hugo, say that he was "never gloomy," always cheerful, even when he was under the most severe trials.

There was a supernatural reason. He would later recall that he and his close friend Father Louis Farina (who was also disciplined for his role in the movement), "together one evening at St. Anthony's chapel, and following the example of St. Thérèse of Lisieux, . . . had both offered ourselves as victims to God's merciful love."

This is hardly the reaction of a self-styled, self-appointed reformer. Father Hugo issued no denunciations, called no press conferences, started no petition drives to stir up dissent. "True faith means also believing in the Church as coming from God," he said. And if he privately disagreed with some whom he called his "petty inquisitors," he never questioned the authority of the institution of the Church to protect and defend the integrity of the faith. He trusted that the teachings of the retreat were not his own, really, but were God's, and God could advance their cause, if need be, without the public witness of John Jacob Hugo.

"Since I had once placed my hands within my bishop's and promised obedience," he later wrote, "I . . . was never seriously tempted to do otherwise. It was to God that I had committed my spirit."

Like other "reformers" in the pre-Vatican II church, Father Hugo was ahead of his time and he suffered for it. But in due course he was rehabilitated, as were the "new theologians" of Europe. Father Hugo's long silence came to an end with the naming of a new bishop in Pittsburgh in 1959. Bishop John J. Wright recognized him as "for many years a seeker after means of realizing the fullest possible potential for the sanctification of the faithful, lay and clerical."

He made Father Hugo a confidant and adviser. Through the years, Father Hugo would assist Bishop Wright in nurturing the emerging charismatic movement, in introducing the Mass in English, and in establishing a diocesan theological commission (of which Father Hugo was founding director).

In Cardinal Wright's Rome years, Father Hugo was invited to collaborate in writing a catechism for adults, the still popular *The Teaching of Christ*, edited by Cardinal Wright's successor in Pittsburgh, Bishop Donald W. Wuerl. Cardinal Wright also called upon Father Hugo to write the 1968 book, *St. Augustine on Nature, Sex and Marriage*, a defense of the Church's constant teachings on sexuality and contraception (which was then *the* controversial issue). The cardinal wrote the book's introduction as well.

But more than by Bishop Wright, Father Hugo was vindicated by the Second Vatican Council. The fifth chapter of the council document *Lumen Gentium* once and for all confirmed the universal call to the perfection of holiness. All the baptized are called to be saints. "The Lord Jesus," the document states, "divine teacher and model of all perfection, preached holiness of life (of which He is the author and maker) to each and every one of His disciples without distinction."

But "victory" mellowed Father Hugo not a bit. Age softened his appearance, but in his final decade he put forth just as strong a challenge to the baptized. He stood by the Church in its increasingly unpopular teachings on sexuality and family life. At the height of the nuclear disarmament campaigns, he wrote a "manifesto" on peace, distributed throughout the world in several languages. And he continued to preach the retreat until the last month of his life — his voice still penetrating, his mind as alert as ever, his wit even more biting.

He was writing, too, until his very last weeks, putting the finishing touches on *Your Ways Are Not My Ways*, a two-volume work that is part history of the Father Lacouture retreat, part memoir, and part spiritual testament. In a conclusion, he wrote:

> It is a great happiness to be spared to present this parting gift to the Church that I love and have served faithfully throughout my life. At the start, I dedicated this work to the Church as the bride of Christ, praying that what I then undertook to do would help to remove those spots and wrinkles marring her beauty, of which St. Paul speaks and which it is indeed the duty of all Christians to hate and seek to purge in order that she may be seen in splendor, holy and without blemish (Eph 5:27).

Though his faith in the Church never diminished, his early battles had left him scarred. Even in his last years, Father Hugo remained wary of those he perceived to be in positions of "power" in the Church. Yet he never confused his own suspicions, or even the faults of certain leaders, with the legitimate expression of Church authority. He spoke out against those Catholics who ventured to put forward a "new morality" that flatly rejected the "old" one taught by Jesus and the tradition of the Church.

His "retirement" years were spent as chaplain to the Sisters of the

Holy Family of Nazareth in Bellevue, Pennsylvania. He continued to preach the retreat and to give himself generously to friends and seekers. Until her last, Dorothy Day remained close, writing in *The Catholic Worker* about her "very old and precious friend" and "brilliant teacher." She credited his spiritual teaching, which she called "the bread of the strong," with being the motive force for her activism.

In quarters messy with papers, Father Hugo welcomed frequent guests. He kept his status as "the least skilled" in his priestly foursome of golfers. He told corny jokes just to make people smile. He liked to treat friends and family to Chinese dinners at the Bellevue Tea Garden and take breezy walks through Pittsburgh's North Park.

Though he had long since renounced his attachment to poetry (at least in intention), he never imposed his mortification on others. To his friends' delight, Father Hugo would read aloud Hilaire Belloc's more raucous poems and move easily to the stanzas of St. John of the Cross. God made the good things of the world, Father Hugo knew, for His greater glory, and they were to be given in charity.

Father Hugo died in an automobile accident on a rainy, windswept road near Greensburg, Pennsylvania, on October 1, 1985, the feast of his beloved St. Thérèse of Lisieux.

He had, just two days before, finished giving his last retreat. And, at the moment of his death, he was discussing the Scriptures with his close friend, Father Francis Ott, in whose car he was a passenger. It was a conversation, Father Ott said later, "to be continued in eternity."

Father Hugo was buried on the feast of another of his favorite saints, Francis of Assisi, October 4, in a simple grave on the grounds of the convent of the Sisters of the Holy Family of Nazareth.

Like the grain of wheat in Christ's parting words, Father Hugo, after a lifetime of sowing and self-sacrifice, fell into the earth and died, surely to bear a rich harvest of spiritual fruit. Today, his retreat is carried on in Pittsburgh and elsewhere, and the list of those who consider themselves his spiritual "godchildren" continues to grow quietly, even as his memory remains "hid with Christ in God" (Col 3:3).

More of us need to hear Father Hugo today, to learn from him how to live a holy life in these unholy times, to learn to die like our Lord's grain of wheat. That we may say with St. Paul, in words cherished and lived by Father Hugo — "as dying, and behold we live" (2 Cor 6:9).

I
A Higher Calling:
God's Plan for Our Lives

A Goal for Your Life

*The outstanding breakthrough in spirituality in this century has been
the rediscovery of the truth that Jesus Christ extends to each and every one
of us a personal call to perfection and holiness, a personal invitation to
share in the divine love-life of the Trinity.*

*Father Hugo was an early pioneer in the rediscovery of what has
come to be called, since the Second Vatican Council, the "universal call to
holiness." The texts in this section are essentially meditations on the Scriptures, read as if they are love letters written by the Lord to each of us —
telling us about God's surpassing love for us and the great plans He has
for our lives.*

Standing on a hillside, a little above the multitude who were listening
to Him, Jesus said to them: "You therefore must be perfect, even as your
heavenly Father is perfect" (Mt 5:48).

Such words could have been spoken by one demented, or by one divine; but by no one else. For they tell us to do what, every day, we say
cannot be done by men and women, or even expected of us — they tell us to
be perfect.

They prescribe this, moreover, without limitation or mitigation of any
kind, and imperatively. They are spoken, as it appears, almost casually, with
no special vehemence or any indication that Our Lord expected his hearers
to be surprised at His extraordinary demand.

And since we know the speaker was not demented, but divine, we
must conclude that His words are to be taken seriously — as seriously as
when He said, "This is My Body; this is the chalice of My Blood."

In a word, this command of Jesus fixes the life goal of the Christian:
perfection. Henceforth, the end of all human life and all human effort can
be no other thing than holiness. For the perfect person is the complete person, the whole person.

From this moment, made unforgettable by the awful challenge of the
God-man, those who claim to be His followers, that is, Christians, will be
distinguished from all other people by this — that laying aside or at least

23

rigorously subordinating all other ends whatsoever, they shall give themselves up to a unique quest for sanctity.

God from all eternity desires that we should be holy. He desires that we should live in love and union with Him, and to do this we must be holy: "And everyone who has this hope in him [of entering into happiness with God] *makes himself holy, just as He is also holy*" (1 Jn 3:3).

It is to sanctify us that God sends His only-begotten Son into the world: "This is the will of God — your sanctification" (1 Thes 4:4). And in establishing His Church, Jesus has made it "holy and without blemish" (Eph 5:27), that it might continue the work of sanctification in souls. He will send the Holy Spirit, who will abide with us forever — to sanctify us.

It could not be otherwise: God is holy, and we must likewise be holy. The sufficient reason for this enormous demand made upon us is given by God Himself, briefly and finally: "You shall be holy, because I am holy" (1 Pt 1:16).

The words of Jesus tell us also what kind of holiness we are to seek. Every day we hear people say things like this: "God does not expect us to be saints" or "We cannot be like angels."

But study the teaching of Our Lord. He does not, assuredly, say that He expects us to be as holy *as Carmelites*, or *as priests,* or *as monks*, or *as angels*. He tells us to be holy *as God is holy.*

"Impossible!" you say. Yes, impossible to attain the infinite degree of God's holiness, but not impossible to possess the same *kind* of holiness. Better yet, it is not impossible to *share* in the divine holiness. And this is what we are commanded — to be holy *in the manner* that God is holy. The ideal placed before us is not the holiness of saints or angels, it is divine holiness.

Further: there is only one kind of holiness, and it is intended for all — for laypeople and religious alike, for housewives as well as for nuns, for the members of active religious communities quite as much as for contemplatives, for secular priests as well as for Trappists, for bus drivers and carpenters as well as for priests. Consider the multitudes of whom Jesus demanded perfection: farmers, shepherds, fishermen, housewives, publicans, children, hangers-on. The only group noticeable by their absence was the learned and professionally religious class, the scribes and Pharisees and doctors.

Over the ages Christ's words are still addressed "to the multitudes." He makes no distinction, not even the broad distinction between layperson and religious. Indeed, as St. John Chrysostom says in his *Apology for the Monastic Life*, if there will be any difference at all in God's attitude toward these two groups, laypeople shall have to stand the harder judgment, for they have the advantage of human supports not enjoyed by religious, and, accordingly, their lapses, especially in the matter of purity, will be the less excusable.

The saint illustrates this doctrine by making a list of the precepts given by Jesus, and he points out that the Divine Teacher, even in setting down His most exacting demands, like "Let your speech be, 'Yes, yes'; 'No, no'" does not in any case add, "But I mean this only for monks!"

To some this doctrine may sound strange; if so, this can be only because we have so far forgotten Christian fundamentals. After all, there is only one Christianity: "one Lord, one faith, one baptism; one God and Father of all" (Eph 4:6).

Why should we then make distinctions among ourselves, as though some Christians might exempt themselves from the Gospel law without suffering spiritual harm? Or as though the sublime ideal of the Christian life was meant only for a certain spiritual elite, while all the rest of mankind is doomed to wallow forever in sensuality and spiritual mediocrity!

This Is the Will of God

How to Be a Perfectionist

Can we know what perfection is? Can it be defined in the same precise way that "sin" or "grace" or "sacrament" is defined? Most attempts to explain the Scriptures, G.K. Chesterton said, seek in reality to explain them away. And a favorite method of evading the curt command of Jesus to be perfect is to say that He is telling us only "to do the best we can" or that He wishes us simply to "aim high" or to "hitch our wagons to a star." If His words were to be taken literally, it is alleged, most of us would be driven to despair.

As a matter of fact, the word "perfection" is a technical term in theology. A thing is perfect, says St. Thomas Aquinas, *when it achieves the end for which it was made.* For example, a knife is perfect when it cuts cleanly; a gun is perfect when it shoots accurately.

Now a person's end is to be united to God; accordingly, men and women will be made perfect by that which unites them to God. We will know what it is that perfects people, therefore, when we realize what unites them to God as to their last end. What can this be except charity?

It is charity, or love, that joins people to God, according to the words of the apostle, "He who abides in love, abides in God, and in him" (1 Jn 4:16). Therefore, Christian perfection consists essentially in charity — primarily in the love of God, secondarily in the love of neighbor.

To advance in perfection means above all else to advance in love. Day

25

by day, if we go forward in the love of God, we also make progress in perfection. And the day that we shall be able to say truly what many of us now say falsely or unthinkingly — that we love God with our whole hearts — on that day we shall be perfect.

Charity "is the bond of perfection," says St. Paul (Col 3:14). It is a *bond* because it unites us to our Creator. It is a bond of perfection because it satisfies our burning thirst for happiness, fulfills our deepest aspirations, unites us to our true last end, and thereby completes and perfects our nature.

There are two kinds of perfection — the one human and natural, the other divine and supernatural. We have the human kind in view when we speak of the perfection of a painter or musician, or of any human work or workman.

Many Christians, confusing the perfection spoken of by Jesus with this natural and human kind, fancy that they will attain the true and highest end in life by pursuing refinement and intellectual culture as their proper goal. But such objects, however excellent, are but goods of the natural order and therefore infinitely below what is least in the supernatural order.

This is why carpenters and fishermen can possess Christian perfection although having no intellectual culture, why men like St. Joseph Cupertino or St. John Vianney (the Curé of Ars), who seem by nature little if any better than dunces, can be raised to the altars of the Church. Those who devote themselves to the arts and sciences, or to the acquisition of culture as their solitary end in this life, do not live as Christians at all, but rather as good pagans.

It is the other, the *supernatural* perfection, that God demands of us. Nobody can love God as He deserves, nor can they love Him uninterruptedly with the totality of their powers, but they can *remove from their souls whatever opposes or hinders the upward movement of their affections to God.*

Our work in seeking perfection is simply the negative task of removing sin and imperfection from our souls, in order that God may pour into them His precious gifts of grace and charity. This does not mean that the work of perfection is itself negative. It means that the positive work of sanctification is the effect of the Holy Spirit's operations in souls. Our part is but to clear the way for the entrance of grace and free the soul from whatever would hamper the divine action.

Supernatural perfection is possible for us because, in the end, it is not our work at all — it is the work of God. And "with God all things are possible" (Mt 19:26), even to the making of saints from clods like ourselves!

This Is the Will of God

What We Have to Do

Granted that we are all called to perfection, are we *obliged* to heed this call? One of Christ's Vicars, Pope Pius XI, said in *Rerum Omnium,* his encyclical letter on St. Francis de Sales: "Christ has constituted the Church holy and the source of sanctity, and all those who take her for guide and teacher must, by the Divine Will, tend to holiness of life — 'This is the will of God, your sanctification,' says St. Paul. What kind of sanctity? The Lord Himself declared it when He said, 'Be ye perfect as your heavenly Father is perfect.' *Let no one think that this is addressed to a select few and that others are permitted to remain in an inferior degree of virtue. The law obliges, as is clear, absolutely everyone in the world without exception.*"

This Is the Will of God

No Spiritual Double-Standards

In these next two passages, Father Hugo looks at a basic error that has persisted in the Church since the earliest days — the notion that there is one set of spiritual expectations for clergy and religious and another, less rigorous set of standards for lay people. There is no "spiritual double-standard" in the Church, Father Hugo insisted. Each of us, by virtue of our baptism, is called to be a saint, a holy person.

We are *all* children of God. We are all "a chosen race, a royal priesthood, a holy nation, a purchased people" (1 Pt 2:9). No doubt there are different degrees of grace, "according to the measure of Christ's bestowal" (Eph 4:7). But the essential elements — divine sonship and participation in the divine nature — are possessed by all. Even the differences in grace depend on the mystery of God's love rather than on our position in the world. Thomas More, a layman, was a greater saint than the Carthusians who suffered martyrdom with him.

It is important to realize, also, that it is *because we are Christians* that we are "called to be saints" (1 Cor 1:2). It is baptism, not ordination or religious profession, which in the first instance implants in the soul the seed of holiness and imposes the obligation of cultivating this new life.

True indeed that a Carmelite must strive after sanctity, not because she is a Carmelite, but rather because she is a Christian. And her sister in the world, who is perhaps raising a family in a large city, has a similar duty. It is true that a priest should seek to be a saint. Again, however, not because he is a priest, but rather because he is a Christian. And his relatives in the world, as also his parishioners, are also bound to seek for perfection.

The foregoing truths are of fundamental importance. Errors in this matter — and they are only too common — work such havoc in the Church that they must be put down as diabolically inspired. One of the most common errors comes from thinking that the duty of pursuing sanctity derives primarily from ordination or religious profession. It is an error entertained by both religious and lay people, and it causes the gravest spiritual injury to both groups and of course to the whole Church.

For the laity conclude that they need not become holy, thinking that it is enough to fulfill the minimum requirements of natural law, and thinking that they can neglect the counsels and commands of the Gospel. Religious, on the other hand, seeing that laypeople live careless and worldly lives while still retaining the hope of supernatural life and happiness, are led to relax their own spiritual efforts. They defend their conduct by the sophism that the pursuit of perfection, however commendable, is not absolutely necessary. Thus both religious and laypeople fall into tepidity and — far worse — expose themselves to the very grave danger of damnation.

All Christians are bound, by the very fact that they are Christians, to seek after perfection. When one takes religious vows therefore, he or she does not then contract the obligation of becoming holy. They only acknowledge an obligation that exists already. Now they are doubly bound to seek perfection — in the first place because they are Christians, and in the second because they have entered a particular state of life which holds them permanently to the use of special means for obtaining this end of perfection, of holiness.

What is not to be forgotten, however, is that the primary and essential obligation comes from baptism. Because of the particular means that religious adopt, they have bound themselves to strive for the goal of Christian life in a more perfect way, the way of the counsels of the Gospel. They are like the daredevil who, accepting a challenge to perform some difficult feat, says: "Not only will I do it, but I will do it in the most dangerous and difficult manner."

This Is the Will of God

Two Ways to Be Religious

The way of the Christian religious, the Church holds, is the higher way — not because there is anything wrong with the way taken by the laity, but simply because the religious life enables those who enter upon it to put quickly aside the things that hinder our love from going wholly and at once to God. By his or her vows, the religious renounces the three great classes of human goods — those of fortune, of the body, and of the soul — goods which, by their attractiveness, tend to absorb people's attention and to alienate their affections from God.

Bound as we are to love God with our whole heart, we may love other things only in and through and because of God. By giving up all earthly goods in a heroic renunciation, there is a greater opportunity for religious to keep their affections from lighting upon the vain and fleeting pleasures of earth. They therefore abandon the things of the world, not because they fancy them evil (as Christians they even call them "goods"), but because they are able in this way to love and serve God with greater singleness of purpose.

If the way of the layperson is not so high or so difficult as that of the religious, when considered from a certain point of view, it offers an even greater challenge. "It is even a greater thing, it requires a clearer, steadier, nobler faith to be surrounded with worldly goods, yet to be self-denying, to consider ourselves but stewards of God's bounty and to be faithful in all things," as Cardinal John Henry Newman once observed.

Marriage and family life, which are the ordinary state of the layperson, are a means of perfection and a true vocation. Christ made marriage a sacrament, and in it He gives to the wedded pair special sacramental graces which will help them attain holiness in this new condition of life, as well as to sanctify the children who are born of their union. "Women will be saved by child bearing, if they continue in faith and love and holiness with modesty" (1 Tm 2:15).

Through Christian marriage and family life, new saints are brought into the world — converters of souls, lovers of the cross, citizens in the kingdom of God. Yet not only are parents to become holy by bringing children into the world, not only are they to cooperate with the Holy Spirit in sanctifying these children. Their own sacramental union is itself no mere human bond, but a partnership in holiness, a union transformed by charity and obliging husband and wife in special ways to support one another in charity.

Pope Pius XI summarizes this in *Casti connubii*, his encyclical on marriage: "This outward expression of love in the home demands not only mutual help but must go farther. It must have as its primary purpose that man and wife help each other day by day in forming and perfecting themselves in the interior life, so that through their partnership in life they may advance ever more and more in virtues, and above all that they may grow in true love toward God and their neighbor, on which indeed 'depend the whole Law and the Prophets' (Mt 22:40)."

The doctrine in this passage should be pondered deeply and at length.

29

Married couples are called to perfection, and even to the highest perfection. The effort to achieve holiness is the noblest expression of their mutual love. They are to lead an interior life. Such a life as is ordinarily thought of as belonging to convents and monasteries, but Christ's Vicar says that it belongs also to the home.

This is, after all, not remarkable: How else can there be saintly priests and religious, lovers of the interior life, unless as children they have been spiritually trained in deeply religious homes? Husband and wife are to cooperate in living a spiritual life just as two religious might assist each other in their efforts to reach God; the marriage union is in very truth a partnership in holiness.

All men and women must aspire to perfection; there is an obligation, a duty, a law from God; and no one may say, "This is not for me." Any honorable occupation is a fit means for acquiring perfection.

Some occupations are not honorable. Others are scarcely so. While in such walks of life, it is certain that people cannot become saints. But their duty then is to change their occupation, not to exempt themselves from their primary obligation as Christians. This holds for all conditions of life — for rich and poor, for learned and unlearned, for great and the small. All must aspire to the highest sanctity.

To the assertions that there are two *general* ways of striving for perfection, that of the Christian religious and that of the laity, we may now add that there are innumerable *particular* ways — as many as there are honorable occupations and various conditions of life.

This Is the Will of God

Pinocchio and the Mystery of God

Father Hugo here begins to enter deeper into the mystery of God, in particular, how each of our own lives is to be inserted into God's plan for the world. These next five selections ask us to reread the Scriptures in light of God's plan for all people to share in His holiness.

~·⊛·~

Geppeto, it will be recalled, was a lonely woodcarver, who, sad that he did not have a child, made a puppet to look like a boy and called him Pinocchio. Through a "lovely Maiden with Azure Hair" the puppet was changed into a boy — or almost into a boy. Before he could be a real boy, he would have to prove himself brave, truthful, and unselfish.

Everyone knows Pinocchio's story as he tried to prove himself, in order to become a real boy and the child of Geppeto. He did not always succeed, getting into various scrapes and at times even acting like a donkey rather than a boy. Yet in the end he did meet the test and become a real-life flesh-and-blood boy.

The story of Geppeto and Pinocchio may stand as a symbol of God's relationship with His human creatures. Indeed, this particular story, apart from all subsequent engrafted variations, was intended by its creator, Carlo Collodi, to do just that.

At first humans were only creatures made by God as a statue, or a puppet, is made by an artist. But God desired children, many children. He formed a loving plan — the mystery of God, St. Paul calls it — whereby His creatures would be adopted and expected to conduct themselves as children of God.

To accomplish this He planned that His own offspring, His Word, would take flesh in order that all humans in turn might, by a "holy exchange," share the divine life through the Son. They would be given a glorious destiny, but on condition that they would conform to the pattern of the Son's life. They would be told, "Once you were in darkness, but now you are the light in the Lord; walk as children of light" (Eph 5:8).

Accordingly, the Fathers of the Second Vatican Council stated in *Lumen Gentium,* "The basic source of human dignity lies in man's call to communion with God. From the very circumstances of his origin man is already invited to converse with God."

In other words, God's human creatures, even beyond their inherent excellence, by which they are already but "a little less than the angels" (Ps 8:6), were not to be left on the merely human plane of living, but were rather destined to a special intimacy with God, even to sharing the love-life of the Trinity.

If this calling was quickly shadowed by sin, it was not forgotten by God nor withdrawn. We watch the call to communion with God, beginning anew in Abraham, continue and develop, despite repeated temporary setbacks, throughout the history of Israel. This call reaches its climax in and through Christ. "Creation waits with eager longing for the revealing of the sons of God," as St. Paul said (Rom 8:19).

So is fulfilled the plan of God: "We love, because He first loved us" (1 Jn 4:19). And so are explained and enriched the Vatican Council's words about the source of human dignity lying in the call of God's human creatures to communion with Himself. Accordingly, "God so loved the world that He sent His only Son, that whoever believes in Him should not perish but have eternal life" (Jn 3:16).

The point here is that as Christians we enter eternal life *now* in sharing the divine life through grace and faith. The way of Jesus, the lifestyle He initiates, manifesting and extending the reign of God, is to be followed by us here and now. His followers are to rise above the way proper to humans while at the same time living as one among them.

The Christian is forced to continually make decisions in his or her daily life whether to follow the comfortable ordinary way of humankind or take the high road into the kingdom. St. Paul describes the two ways as living "according to the flesh" and living "according to the Spirit." He says: "Those who live according to the flesh set their minds on the things of the flesh, but those who live according to the Spirit set their minds on the things of the Spirit" (Rom 8:5).

It is important to note here that the flesh does not mean only the body, nor is the word deprecating. After all, the very Word of God "became flesh" (Jn 1:14). Nevertheless, there is something ominous in the apostle's words as he describes the actual workings of *the flesh*.

We cite here the translation of Msgr. Ronald Knox which, if departing from the Scriptural imagery, manifests its theological meaning — "Thus, brethren, nature has no longer any claim upon us, that we should live a life of nature. If you live a life of nature you are marked out for death. If you mortify the ways of nature through the powers of the Spirit, you will have life" (Rom 8:12).

Resistance to the divine turns us away from God and unless the direction is reversed will lead us to ruin. Hence Jesus, reproaching the Pharisees, said, "You judge according to the flesh" (Jn 8:15). *Flesh* is here used to describe the way of the self-sufficient person who does not respond to the Spirit. And "it is the Spirit that gives life — the flesh is of no avail" (Jn 6:63).

St. John describes the two ways as light and darkness, between which there is constant warfare. "I have come as light into the world that whoever believes in Me may not remain in darkness" (Jn 12:46).

Observe that the dwellers in darkness are not only those guilty of grave moral evil, but include all who do not live by faith in Jesus. Likewise, those who do not live by faith in Jesus are spiritually dead: "Truly, truly, I say to you, he who hears My word and believes Him who sent Me has eternal life; he does not come into judgment but has passed from death to life" (Jn 5:24).

Moreover, as St. Paul adds, nothing finally is of any avail except "faith working through love" (Gal 5:6). Therefore, love, issuing from faith, is the only conclusive evidence of the presence of the Christian life: "He who says he is in the light and hates his brother is in the darkness still" (1 Jn 2:9). Again, it is both those who violate basic morality, as well as those who do not live by faith and love, that move into the domain of darkness and death. They have not really found the Light (cf. Jn 3:18).

Jesus would also draw us beyond the merely human plane of goodness. "The seed is the word of God" (Lk 8:11) — a new principle of life, a divine spark, is given to those who have received God's word, and this new element is henceforth to quicken their lives.

In every Eucharist the celebrant, mixing a little water with wine, prays, "By the mystery of this water and wine may we come to share in the divinity of Christ, who humbled Himself to share in our humanity." The Incarnation becomes the pattern for all human existence.

The Christian's moral struggle is at the division between the human and the divine. Christians are expected to live, not simply as good human beings, but as children of God, leading godly lives in the manner of Jesus.

It is, then, not enough for Christians to take as the guide for their conduct the rule, "Avoid mortal sin." If this is our norm, we can never get beyond the merely natural standard of behavior, recognized also by good pagans or secular humanists. We will be led to believe that, provided we avoid serious sin, we may follow the slogan, "Eat, drink, and make good cheer!" But our vocation is so much higher — to conform to Christ and to conduct ourselves as children of God, seeking the divine good.

We fail, therefore, when, neglecting the call to divine intimacy, we seek happiness and fulfillment in our natural tastes and ambitions. St. Paul teaches: "Put off your old nature which belongs to your former manner of life and is corrupt through deceitful lusts, and be renewed in the spirit of your minds, and put on the new nature created after the likeness of God in true righteousness and holiness" (Eph 4:22-24).

Two ways open before us, the human and the divinized way of Jesus. At the crossroads He is there to direct us: "Enter by the narrow gate; for the gate is wide and the way is easy that leads to destruction, and those who enter by it are many. For the gate is narrow and the way is hard that leads to life, and those who find it are few" (Mt 7:13-14).

He also defines the two possible ways of life: "Do not lay up for yourselves treasures on earth where rust and moth consume and where thieves break in and steal, but lay up for yourselves treasures in heaven, where neither rust nor moth consumes and where thieves do not break in and steal. For where your treasure is, there will your heart be also" (Mt 6:19-21).

If Christianity does not consist in the avoidance of sin, it does involve unworldliness. In order to lay up treasures in heaven we must not lay up treasures on earth. The negative cannot be separated from the positive.

Inner freedom is requisite that love may reach fullness. St. John, who has told us that "God so loved the world that He gave His only Son," also states, "Do not love the world, or the things in the world. If anyone loves the world, love for the Father is not in him" (1 Jn 2:15).

St. James gives us a definition of holiness containing both its negative and its positive dimensions: "Religion pure and undefiled before God and the Father is this: To visit orphans in their afflictions, and to keep oneself unspotted by the world" (Jas 1:27).

So much is the negative element of detachment from earthly treasures required for attaining love that Cardinal John Henry Newman on one occasion simply described holiness as "inward separation from the world." This is what Jesus was saying when He told us that to gain the treasures of heaven, we should not lay up treasures on earth.

Every journey starts with the vision of a goal. Here two possible goals, one deceptive, one truly rewarding, are pointed out for the pilgrimage of life. Jesus starts us off by demanding a decision and a change.

Your Ways Are Not My Ways, vol. II

Adam's Choice and Our Lord's

Although originally sinless as they came from God's hands and destined to walk in the divine friendship, Adam and Eve had fallen. What was the nature of the fall? It could not have been moral failure such as a person now experiences, "attracted and seduced by his own wrong desire" (Jas 1:14). No, this kind of anguished moral struggle is the result of the first fall.

As St. Augustine observes in the *City of God*, the knowledge of good and evil, which the tree in Paradise stood for, is "the experience that results from disobedience to a command of God."

The original testing of humanity could only have been a choice, and this choice could only have been between the good of the human order, to be enjoyed in autonomy, and the destiny offered by God to partake in the divine nature and love. The fall of Adam and Eve was in the failure to make the choice which God desired for them — that all men and women might live in His love.

As St. Thomas Aquinas sees it, human beings originally chose the natural and human over the divine. Their sin was naturalism. This may be viewed either as the choice of their own natural excellence in refusing the divine intimacy held out to them, or as the desire to attain the exalted destiny freely offered to them by their own natural powers.

"You shall be as gods," was the deceptive promise made to them. They preferred their self-enclosed autonomy to the divine gift. "Man set himself against God and sought to attain his goal apart from God," as the

Second Vatican Council stated in its document on the Church in the modern world, *Lumen Gentium.*

The gift, the destiny offered to humanity, was love. The Council fathers continue in *Lumen Gentium,* that the Word of God Himself, "has revealed to us that 'God is love' and at the same time taught us that the new commandment of love is the basic law of human perfection and hence of the world's transformation."

This was the gift refused. Love is beautiful and pleasant: how can anyone refuse it? Yet love has its demands, and many recoil from these demands. They are alienated, divorced, lonely. Still, they prefer to endure this unhappy state rather than yield in self-surrender to the demands of love, which are severe and often call for heroism.

People, enclosed in their own excellence, resist all the more the invasion and invitation of divine love, which, in transforming them and enabling them to love as God loves, requires a self-stripping to the point of dying.

The refusal of love is still the original sin in all of us: original in the sense of primary and radical. No need to document or prove this refusal. Human history is the record of it. The scandal of Christian killing Christian is much of the story of "Christian" Europe. Among us, white and black find it impossible to love each other. The failure to love has resulted in a divisiveness that threatens the welfare of America, inheritor of the dreams of the ages.

The rejection of Jesus Christ is really a rejection of love — of love for all people as our brothers and sisters in Him, our brother and one mediator, rising thence to the love of God. At the same time, the rejection of love is in practice a rejection of Jesus Christ.

It was the mission of Jesus to reverse the choice of Adam. "I do nothing of Myself. What the Father has taught Me is what I preach. . . . I always do what pleases Him" (Jn 8:28, 29).

St. Paul says simply, Christ did not think of Himself, "did not please Himself" (Rom 15:3). The original rebellion of Adam's will is countered and repaired by the immolation of the will of the man Jesus within the divine. "As by one man's disobedience many were made sinners, so by one man's obedience many will be made righteous" (Rom 5:19).

In the new Head of the human race, Adam's choice is reversed. Mankind in its Head has now placed the divine over the human. In our name He has chosen the Father's will once and for all. He has brought our race back to the kingdom of God, which is the kingdom of love.

That Christ stood for sinful humanity should not obscure for us the nature of His personal struggle as a sinless man. His personal victory was not just over moral evil, which held no attraction for Him. It was a victory gained through dying, dying to the inclinations of His immaculate humanity. Indeed, while His death culminated on the cross, His whole life, as *The Imitation of Christ* says, was "a cross and a martyrdom."

He died to those goods which He, at least, could have sought and possessed without avarice and without fault. He renounced riches and whatever of pleasure or satisfaction they could procure. He renounced human learning: well-versed in the Scriptures, He did not undertake to visit the academies of Athens. He renounced marriage, although there was no inclination to disorder in His sexuality. He renounced eminent position, human success, honors — all of which He might have pursued without risk or fault. This lifelong renunciation of the *good,* rising in a crescendo to the cross, was the immolation of an unblemished humanity.

In His cumulative renunciations, Jesus reversed the first choice of man. In this reversal which was also an affirmation of what the first man had denied and an acceptance of what he had refused, Jesus became the new Head of mankind.

Love Strong As Death

Eve's Choice and Our Lady's

Associated with Jesus in His reversal of the primary sin was Mary, His mother and thereby our mother. She became the new Eve, as the Fathers liked to say, the mother of the eternally living, reversing the harm done by the first Eve.

As the Church sings in the ancient hymn, "Ave Maris Stella" ("Hail Star of the Sea"): *Sumens illud Ave/Gabriélis ore,/Funda nos in pace,/Mutans Hevae nome* ("You who received that 'Ave'/From the mouth of Gabriel,/Establish us in peace,/Reversing the name of 'Eve' ").

Mary's spirituality, like that of her Son, lay in her entire conformity to the divine will. The convictions of her life are epitomized in her reply to the angel: "Let it be to me according to your word" (Lk 1:38). The queen of martyrs, her immolation, like that of her Son, was the sowing of her own will within the divine: it was a dying which, joined to that of Jesus, shared also in His resurrection to new life and fruitfulness.

As with Jesus, so also with Mary: the cross shadowed her whole life, beginning with the prophecy of Simeon and extending to her vigil on Calvary. She did not seek the advantages of the world, not to mention the prerogatives of a queen. The poverty of Nazareth was hers also.

Deeper was the sorrow of gradual separation, breaking the visible bond which bound her to her Son. "Why were you looking for Me? Did you not know that I must be busy with My Father's affairs?" (Lk 2:49) These words, almost a reproach, marked the beginning of a separation that is painfully evident during the public life. Indeed, Jesus rejects with something like harshness the proffered tenderness of His mother. " 'Your mother and brother and sisters are outside asking for You.' He replied, 'Who are My mother and My brothers?' And looking round at those sitting in a circle about Him, He said, 'Here are My mother and My brothers. Anyone who does the will of God, that person is My brother and sister and mother' " (Mk 3:32-35).

The bonds of a natural relationship are set aside for a new relationship to God. To be sure, Mary in her devotion to the divine will, is preeminent in this new relationship also. As St. Augustine said in his book *On Holy Virginity*, "Mary was more blessed in accepting the faith of Christ than in conceiving the flesh of Christ." There can thus be no questions about priority. " 'Happy the womb that bore You and the breasts You sucked!' But He replied, 'Still happier are those who hear the word of God and keep it!' " (Lk 11:28).

Here again He seems to push aside Mary's maternal solicitude. Yet we know of no protest from her and no suggestion from Him, as in the case of Peter, that she is an "obstacle" because the way she thinks is "not God's way but man's" (Mt 16:23). Therefore also no "Get thee behind me, Satan!" On the contrary, He consummates her sacrifice with His on Calvary. "Woman, this is your son" (Jn 19:27). The human separation is now complete as, in leaving her, He bequeaths to her John, with the Church, in place of Himself.

Charles Journet writes of these renunciations in his *Our Lady of Sorrows:*

> The Virgin's sacrifice could only be the renunciation of things holy for the sake of things holier. A physical tenderness that was holy had to be denied in order that men might know how they must treat physical tenderness that was not holy.
>
> It was of necessity that what was sinless in the Virgin should bear affliction and that the rightful desire of her heart to bring visible consolation to her Son should be cast aside in order that she might perfectly resemble her Son and that she might suffer in the likeness of Him who was to suffer and die in desolation. Thus, like to her Son, and better than anyone who should come after her, she was to do the will of God.

In a word, Mary was also a grain of wheat that must die in order to live and be fruitful.

Love Strong As Death

The Christian Manifesto

The high point in the history of the entire human race came one day when Jesus, seeing the crowds, as St. Matthew says, went up the mountain and, seating Himself, uttered those beautiful and momentous words of instruction which we now call the Sermon on the Mount.

This was God's revelation to man of how He, the Creator, envisioned human life and had eternally decreed that it should be lived. Through His Son He was here outlining the pattern that human life and conduct was henceforth to follow. And we know also that the Son, during His earthly career, gave a living and perfect illustration of that pattern. From this time forward, all men are obliged to study the same pattern and reproduce it in their own lives.

You know the scene, which has so often been represented by Christian artists. Jesus seats Himself a little above a vast and varied crowd of men, women, and children. The disciples come close to Him. Then He opens His mouth to teach. And in this moment, as the music of the Beatitudes is poured forth on the air, human language and human thought reach the greatest sublimity they have ever attained or ever will attain.

Yet the quiet and simple beauty of that scene, and the lofty but still simple beauty of the Savior's thought and speech, seem at times so to enthrall people that they overlook or forget the fundamental importance and the austere practical demands of the message itself.

This is magnificent poetry, yes, but not only poetry — it is doctrine, divine truth, and also a very practical description of how Our Lord and His heavenly Father expect people to live and act. The Sermon on the Mount is the Manifesto of the Christian life; it outlines the practical program of Christianity; it sets forth the principles and ideals that are from now on to be the daily guide of Christians both in their individual lives and their social efforts and institutions.

In the first three Beatitudes, the three basic rules of Christian living, Jesus cuts diametrically across the philosophy of the world. The world considers wealth a blessing, the greatest of all blessings. The world considers bodily pleasure and comfort to be blessings, and pursues them every minute of every day. The world considers gaiety and present laughter a blessing, and shuns the company of the afflicted, the sorrowful, and the mourning. Jesus thinks exactly the opposite. The mind of Christ flatly contradicts the mind of the world. What the world considers a blessing, Jesus calls a curse. What the world considers a curse, Jesus calls a blessing.

Nowhere in the Gospel, better than in these first three Beatitudes, can we see the truly revolutionary character of Christianity and how completely it is opposed to the mind and the practice of the world. We are so accustomed to hearing the Beatitudes that we do not pause and ask their meaning.

And we never attempt to imagine what would happen if we really lived according to these truths — the sudden and sensational change would make us dizzy; our lives would certainly be transformed. And if people on a large scale would live according to the Sermon on the Mount, the world would be scarcely recognizable. Its whole economy would undergo a revolutionary change. Half or more of its cherished institutions would disappear, and new traditions, new customs, new institutions would arise.

Behold. All things would become new: Social life would no longer be organized around the possession of earthly goods. Poverty would be esteemed and sought as riches now possess the hearts of men. Wars would simply vanish, for there would be no occasion of war; the root and cause of war would have been dried up by Christian detachment. We would truly be living in the kingdom of God.

And bear in mind, this is not a fantastic dream. This is the way God wants and intends our lives to be. It is not wishful thinking, but divine law. From the moment in which these words are spoken, it becomes every person's strict duty to share in the work of carrying out this divine plan for the renewal of the earth. Here is the pattern of human life as designed by the Creator Himself. Henceforth, all people will be judged according to the perfection of their conformity to this pattern.

Jesus condemns not only the goods which the pagan mentality chooses as its end, but He condemns also the means which are employed to seek these ends. His teaching is found in the sixth chapter of St. Matthew's Gospel. First He lays down a general rule and then He gives three illustrations.

The general rule is this: "Take heed not to practice your good before men, in order to be seen by them; otherwise you shall have no reward with your Father in heaven." We are not to work from a natural motive, that is, not for a reward from our fellow men. And He tells us point-blank that if we do so, we shall have no reward in heaven.

Then come the three illustrations. First, "Therefore when thou givest alms, do not sound the trumpet before thee, as the hypocrites do in the synagogues and streets, in order that they may be honored by men. Amen I say to you, they have had their reward."

The second illustration is this: "When you pray, you shall not be like the hypocrites, who love to pray standing in the synagogues and at the street corners, in order that they may be seen by men. Amen I say to you, they have had their reward."

And the third: "When you fast, do not look gloomy like the hypocrites, who disfigure their faces in order to appear to men as fasting. Amen I say to you, they have had their reward."

Mark the repetition of the refrain — "Amen I say to you, they have had their reward." If we work from a mere natural motive, that is, to obtain the goods of this world, God will not give us a reward in heaven. There is no mistaking the matter; the Son of God tells us so. If we work for Smith, we would not seek our wages from Jones. If we work for the world, God will not have us seeking our reward from Him. If we desire the reward that God can give, then while we are here we must work for God.

Some persons might be inclined to shrug these examples aside, saying that people no longer have trumpets blown before them to advertise their good works. But nowadays there are other ways of gaining the same end. People now do their good deeds in order to get their picture in the paper or their names on a bronze plaque or have their generosity immortalized in stained glass or to obtain some other similar kind of recognition for their virtue.

In *Ascent of Mount Carmel,* St. John of the Cross observed that "the greater number of good works" which people "perform in public are either vicious or of no value to them or are imperfect in the sight of God since they are not detached from human intentions and interests."

How invariably we expect praise and thanks even for the least good we do; how prone we are to be disheartened when the desired commendation is not given. Often indeed we abandon well-doing simply because we have received no human reward. Such an attitude clearly, if we have it, reveals how imperfect and worldly are our customary motives.

Nor would we be correct in thinking that since the disappearance of the Scribes and Pharisees the unhappy attempt to live virtuously without grace is no longer made. It may be seen all about us today in that careful cultivation of an external respectability and righteousness that so often covers up, as of old, vainglory and sensuality and avarice. Often, too, as a consequence of the downward movement taken by unmortified human desires, this hypocritical respectability covers much darker crimes also — dishonesty, injustice, impurity, infanticide or abortion, and contraception.

After removing from men and women, as goals of effort, the various classes of natural goods, Jesus replaces them with a supernatural end and good which all are to seek. This end is proposed in the fourth Beatitude, "Blessed are they who hunger and thirst for justice, for they shall be satisfied." Justice is the end which all men henceforth shall strive after. Jesus is legislating for the entire human race, and this is the goal that He fixed for human life.

Now *justice* in the Scriptures means *holiness* or *sanctity*. Consequently sanctity or holiness is the supreme good which all people shall seek in their lives. Men and women are now directed to lay aside the feverish race for riches, for the pleasures of the body and for merely human satisfaction in order to strive henceforth at the imitation of a divine attribute, namely the very sanctity of God.

Elsewhere in the Sermon on the Mount Jesus says the same thing when He exhorts us to "seek first the kingdom of God and His justice." Jesus has just taught us to renounce human goods in order that we may now live divine lives.

The fact that the fourth Beatitude tells us to seek for a share in a divine attribute opens the way to the correct understanding of the following Beatitudes. Each of these, in fact, mentions a divine attribute which Jesus would have us imitate and introduce into our own lives.

Thus Jesus says, "Blessed are the merciful, for they shall obtain mercy." Now mercy, in its plenitude, is one of the divine attributes. By becoming merciful, we become godlike. And this is precisely what Jesus wants us to do — to reproduce the divine mercy in our lives and actions.

Next we are told, "Blessed are the pure of heart, for they shall see God." Here we are enjoined to imitate the perfect purity of God, which is contrasted with the mere external righteousness of the Pharisees. Jesus wants us to observe complete purity, clear to the roots of our actions. He wishes us to emulate the divine purity which is without blemish whatsoever.

Again He tells us "Blessed are the peacemakers, for they shall be called the children of God." The Scriptures speak of God as the God of peace, and the gift which Jesus said that He came to bring us was the gift of peace. Those who live in charity with others, keeping peace with their neighbor as well as in their own hearts, have then a special relationship to God and are in a particular sense called the children of God.

Finally, Jesus recognizes beforehand and clearly foretells that living a divine life will bring persecution upon those who do it, and He blesses those who bear this persecution. Jesus is perfectly well aware that He is condemning the world and going counter to the philosophy of the world. He is well aware of the ruin that His doctrine will bring on Himself.

The Son of God became flesh and the brethren of His flesh rose up against Him, the Light came into the world but the darkness did not receive it. And He warns His followers that they will be engaged in a similar conflict and will have to endure like difficulties.

In all this it is evident what Our Lord is driving at. He wants us to live not human lives, but divine lives. That is why He has told us to give up human and natural goods, and now places before our eyes as the object of our lifelong endeavors a divine good, the divine ideal of holiness. This is what it means to be children of God, elevated to a share in the divine nature.

He says, "You therefore are to be perfect, even as your heavenly Father is perfect." Here in the clearest possible terms He repeats His demand for divine holiness and describes what He means by it. We are not just to be holy, but we are to be holy as God is holy. Clearly we cannot attain to the infinite degree of holiness which is God's alone. But we can imitate and share in God's holiness, that is to say, we can possess the same kind of holiness.

What we have given is a skeleton outline of the Sermon on the Mount. This Sermon contains, of course, many other words of our Lord, all deserving of devout meditation. Still, you will find in studying it that all its other teachings may be placed within the framework of this general outline, added to it as flesh to the bones of a skeleton.

I leave to your own study and meditation and prayer the other teachings of Jesus in the Sermon on the Mount. We will go at once to the conclusion of the Sermon. Let me first read it to you:

> Everyone therefore who hears these My words and acts upon them, shall be likened to a wise man who built his house on rock. And the rain fell, and floods came, and the winds blew and beat against that house. But it did not fall, because it was founded on rock. And everyone who hears these My words and does not act upon them, shall be likened to a foolish man who builds his house on sand. And the rain fell, and the floods came, and the winds blew and beat against that house, and it fell, and was utterly ruined.

Observe what Jesus is teaching here. Why is it that in one case the house falls and is destroyed, and in the other case it stands? Clearly the house does not fall because the rains and the floods and the storms come — a house must be built strongly enough to withstand such assaults of the elements. The reason that the one house falls is because it is built on sand.

And the reason the other house remains is because it is built on rock and is therefore able to withstand the shock of storms and floods.

We may ask, similarly, why it is that some souls collapse, fall into sin, and are ruined? This is precisely the question that Jesus is here answering for us. We may ourselves have asked it many times: Why does weakness overcome us? Why do we fall, perhaps repeatedly, into these offenses? It is because we build on sand. Often we blame our falls on the violence of temptation, but this is not the explanation. Just as a house must be built strong enough to shelter men against storms, so our souls must be strong enough, with the help of God's grace, to repel temptation.

The reason why we fall into sin, therefore, is not because temptation is too strong, but because we have built our spiritual edifice on sand. What is this sand? It is the natural mentality.

Jesus says, "Everyone who hears these My words and acts upon them shall be likened to a wise man who built his house on rock." In other words, anyone who lives a supernatural life, becomes as a god, rejecting the goods of nature and acting habitually from supernatural motives — this is the person who builds on rock, and his house will stand.

"But if anyone does not hear My word" — that is if anyone still retains his attachments for the goods of the natural order, seeks after the pleasures and the comforts and riches of this world, and acts from natural motives — he is the person who builds on sand, and his house shall fall.

Jesus gives us here His analysis of the cause of sin. And the cause is the attempt, always ultimately unsuccessful, to live on the merely natural plane. Natural actions, natural motives, natural attachments for the creatures of this world dispose the soul toward sin, lead it in the direction of sin, and, therefore, although appearing innocent in themselves, are the cause of spiritual ruin. The wise man therefore, will heed this warning and build his house on the rock of the supernatural.

You Are Gods

Born in God

In this last of a series of Scripture interpretations begun above in the selection, "Pinocchio and the Mystery of God," Father Hugo shows how these biblical truths become real for us, how we are made children of God.

᪒᪒᪒

Early in St. John's Gospel, Jesus uses a vivid image to reveal and explain the divine inflow into our lives by comparing it to the greatest miracle of nature, the birth of a human child. To Nicodemus He said, "Truly, truly,

I say to you, unless one is born anew, he cannot see the kingdom of God" (Jn 3:3).

These words, which we may hurry over thoughtlessly through routine, are puzzling, even startling. Once a person is born, he is born: How can he be born again? "How can a man be born when he is old? Can he enter a second time into his mother's womb and be born?" So, at least, asked Nicodemus, blinded by the corrupt "wisdom" of the Pharisees (Mt 5:20). Although "a teacher of Israel," his incomprehension was so complete that he could find no other way to greet the divine wisdom. It seemed like a weak joke.

Jesus answered insistently, "Truly, truly I say to you, unless one is born of water and the Spirit, he cannot enter the kingdom of God."

By His *unless,* Jesus reveals the absolute necessity of this rebirth. In so doing He likewise explains the meaning and purpose of baptism. He also indicates why this birth in the Spirit is so necessary to raise us to the Way of Jesus: "That which is born of the flesh is flesh, and that which is born of the Spirit is Spirit."

Born once as humans, we need to be born again of the Spirit if we are to be in truth children of God and enter into His kingdom. The higher way of life, elevating us to share the divine, the way of Jesus, as distinguished from the way of mere humans, is thereby made possible for us.

In his letters John throws further light on this divine filiation, whereby humans become the sons and daughters of God. It is given to those who turn to God in faith: "Everyone that believes that Jesus is the Christ is a child of God" (1 Jn 5:1). And of course, since "God is love," the one who loves is "born of God and knows God" (4:7).

Describing a believer as born of God is no mere metaphor, but a reality: "See what love the Father has given us that we should be called children of God; *and so we are*" (3:1). If, then, we are called adopted children of God, this does not mean that we bear this name only by legal arrangement, but rather to distinguish our sonship from that of Jesus, who is the only-begotten Son of God.

Sonship implies identity of nature. Fish and animals and humans all reproduce their own kin; between parents and offspring there is an identity of nature. If we are to be in any real sense children of God, as St. John says, then we must also in some way share in the nature of God. This is implied in the text.

St. Peter makes this explicit: "He has granted to us His precious and very great promises that through these you may become *partakers of the divine nature*" (2 Pt 1:4). Although most of the New Testament is phrased in the concrete and graphic, but therefore limited, language of the Old, the sacred writer here bursts through these bonds and reaches for a word from Greek philosophy to express the reality of sharing in the eternal life of God of which the Gospels, especially St. John's, so frequently speak.

Therefore, what we mean by grace, that special favor given by God to His already rational creatures, can only be this partaking, this sharing of the divine nature. God's overflowing love is creative, as He then made the love of man and woman in marriage procreative. And in loving us, He brings us in some mysterious way to share in His own nature, which is the ultimately real life, eternal life.

Pinocchio the puppet becomes a boy, the human creature becomes a child of God. "The followers of Christ are justified in the Lord Jesus, and through baptism sought in faith they truly become sons of God and sharers in the divine nature," as the fathers of the Second Vatican Council wrote in *Lumen Gentium*.

We mark here the difference between being a creature of God and being His child. Although in popular usage these terms are often used interchangeably, their meaning is very different. All men and women are God's creatures, but when Scripture speaks of Christians as God's children, it obviously means something special. A sculptor may carve a statue that looks like himself or his wife, or both. It is his creation, we say, but is different from the child they brought into the world.

On Holy Saturday the paschal candle, representing Christ, is plunged into the baptismal font, which symbolizes the womb of the Church, to fertilize and make her the mother of many children. Grace is thus an implantation of the divine nature in human beings, an impregnation of the creature, man, with God's own life. The best description of grace, indicated by Sacred Scripture itself, is a "sharing in the divine nature."

Your Ways Are Not My Ways, vol. II

Repentance, the Other Face of Love

Here Father Hugo unfolds the biblical meaning of repentance or metanoia — *the only way for us to enter into the life of Christ.*

The mission of the precursor, the Baptizer, was to "prepare the way of the Lord" by a "baptism of repentance" (Mt 3:3, Mk 1:4). John's message was, "Repent, for the kingdom of heaven is at hand" (Mt 3:2).

Jesus, in His own preaching, took up where John left off: "Repent, and believe in the Gospel" (Mk 1:15). Later on, at the beginning of the Church, there would be the same demand: "And Peter said to them, 'Repent, and be baptized every one of you in the name of Jesus Christ for the forgiveness of your sins; and you shall receive the gift of the Holy Spirit' " (Acts 2:38).

To us, who like to think in terms of positive action, this may seem an uninspiring start. Repentance looks backwards, to mistakes and failures. Of course both John and Jesus also told us to look forward when they spoke of entering the kingdom and believing in the Gospel: Jesus would fully delineate the kingdom to which John but pointed.

Actually, the word *repent* is an unhappy compromise in translating the Greek word *metanoia,* which has no fully satisfactory English equivalent. It means, "Change! Be converted." Or, *turn away* from one thing and *toward* something else.

Jesus turns us by His Good News, by which He makes it clear that He wants us to abandon the desires and ways of our old unregenerate nature to enter the kingdom of His Father.

We must turn away from whatever hinders us from entering: this is *metanoia* in its negative phase, repentance. But as Pope Paul VI said in a golden sentence that has been enshrined in the Rite of Reconciliation, "The ultimate purpose of penance is that we should love God deeply and commit ourselves completely to Him."

The one entrance into the way of Christ is *metanoia.* Through *metanoia* we at once look backwards with the Baptizer and forward with Jesus. The word describes as one movement a backward rejection of whatever hinders entrance into God's kingdom and forward seeking of that kingdom through acceptance of the Gospel.

Metanoia is a complete change of mind, of thinking; it is a turning around, a turnabout, a somersault; in the most literal and deepest sense, a revolution. When we join this evangelic revolution by turning around — a complete 180 degrees — we turn away from something and toward something, a *Someone!* In *metanoia,* we look back to that from which we have turned and forward to Him toward whom we are now turning.

In *metanoia* we are like oarsmen who look and pull backwards in order to move forward. In penance, by struggling against the currents that have carried us away, we go back to God. Repentance is the other face of love.

Your Ways Are Not My Ways, vol. II

The Gospel and the Grain of Wheat

In this spiritually rich passage, Father Hugo preaches on the meaning of the cross and the resurrection, the significance of baptism and the basic pattern of Christian living.

While theologians today strain language and credibility in speaking of God, Jesus Himself, the Master Teacher, needed to go no farther for pedagogical assistance than to a neighboring farmyard. For Him, the God allegedly "way out there" was in fact no farther than the barn. He speaks of Divine Providence, about which philosophers have such grave doubts, by pointing to the birds of the air, the lilies of the field, yes, the grass of the fields, and even to a clucking hen with her chickens under her wings.

We propose to consider two of His sayings, with analogies drawn from the farmyard, which, despite their homely setting, provide as penetrating a look into divine wisdom as the human mind can essay.

Both readings were given in the most solemn circumstances, on the very eve of Our Lord's death and resurrection. They were intended, for His disciples and all subsequent generations, to be at once an explanation of these events and a disclosure of the deepest meaning of the Christian life. If we had nothing else from Jesus, they would still be a profound revelation of His thought and teaching on those events so important to man, namely life and love and death.

The first of the sayings is spoken after the raising of Lazarus from the dead. The raising of Lazarus was at once an illustration and a prophecy of the yet more wonderful instance that was to come.

As yet even the Apostles could not understand or foresee what would come, despite the fact that Jesus had repeatedly forecast His passion. "Heaven preserve You, Lord; this must not happen to You." So had Peter spoken, voicing the human response to this dread possibility (Mt 16:22). Now on the eve of the passion, the disciples had no idea that within a few hours their beloved Master would die in a manner most painful and humiliating, had no thought that it would be in this way that He would attain His glory, which they anticipated in an all too human way.

Jesus began: "The hour has come for the Son of Man to be glorified." Not *crucified,* but *glorified.* He continued: "I tell you, most solemnly, unless a grain of wheat falls into the ground and dies, it remains only a single grain; but if it dies, it yields a rich harvest. Anyone who loves his life loses it; anyone who hates his life in this world will keep it for eternal life" (Jn 12:24-25).

What does this mean? Obviously and in the first place, it refers to Christ Himself. He is the grain of wheat who, in dying, will rise to a life of glory. His death, which the disciples were so soon to witness, will not be an end — it will be a beginning, a germinating, the start of growth and transformation, a movement toward resurrection.

Moreover, Jesus will not rise alone. There will be a *harvest.* His death will fructify into eternal life for mankind. Were He not to die, His glory would not be attained and the harvest would not be gathered.

This is not the logic of reason, nor of human achievement, which goes from victory to greater victory: not like Alexander's conquest of Greece, which led to the conquest of the world and left him still unsatisfied. But it is the law of life.

If a man from another planet were to see a farmer sowing seed, he would think that the farmer was discarding something he did not want. He would be surprised to learn that the farmer was throwing it away, and even burying it, because he wanted it very much, and a great deal more of it. It took our ancestors, *homo sapiens,* we do not know how many aeons to discover this law of life-through-death, so simple and yet so disconcerting. St. Paul would call this law, as exemplified in Jesus and set forth as His teaching, "the folly" of the cross — "We are preaching a crucified Christ, to the Jews an obstacle, and to the pagans madness" (1 Cor 1:23).

Throughout nature we see an annual death and resurrection: and the resurrection could not take place except through death. Plants mature and die. In dying they cast forth the seeds of future life. In the dissolution of death they provide the fiber and substance for a new flowering. Meanwhile, the seed itself, as Jesus says, "died." It is buried and ceases to exist as a seed, but precisely in its disintegration it rises marvelously to life. Its disintegration is a germination.

It is only among men and women that we do not see that death is in process of resurrection. When they die, they simply disappear from our vision.

Jesus applies the law of life-through-death, universally exemplified in nature, to human life, beginning with His own. His Church will afterwards be able to exult, "For those who have been faithful, O Lord, life is not ended but merely changed." The change is a transformation, through death, into glorified life.

Any hope that we have of future life, of transformation and resurrection, rests on the promise of Jesus and on His own resurrection, "the firstfruits of all who have fallen asleep" (1 Cor 15:20). All depends on that first grain of wheat.

This is the message, so concrete, so rich in meaning, so fruitful of hope, that Jesus leaves with His disciples as He approaches the climax of His life, His "glorification." They will be able to think of it during the dark days ahead. Under the action of the Holy Spirit they will later meditate on it fruitfully, dissolving their bewilderment and incomprehension, and ready to become grains of wheat themselves in dying for their Master. They will understand that it was "ordained that Christ should suffer and so enter into His glory" (Lk 24:26). They will realize why it was written that Christ would suffer and on the third day rise from the dead (cf. Acts 26:23).

They would also have the courage and conviction to preach the risen Christ: "God raised this man Jesus to life, and all of us are witnesses to that" (Acts 2:32). St. Paul would soon affirm, "If Christ has not been raised then our preaching is useless and your believing is useless." He would add, "If our hope in Christ has been for this life only, we are the most unfortunate of all people" (1 Cor 15:14, 19).

Apart from the hope of resurrection in Christ, we might as well be followers of Aristotle or Confucius or Sartre or any other human teacher. Apart from this hope, life would have no real lasting significance. It would indeed be absurd. All that we would need would be some reasonably acceptable norms — "authenticity" would be enough — to help us move with dignity across the stage of this world into oblivion. Nevertheless, it does in truth require a great leap into the dark to make this act of faith in the resurrection. That so many Christians make it routinely should not obscure the fact that, for reason alone, it is truly an act of folly. Yet only in view of this faith does the rest of Christ's life have any real significance for us.

Jesus explicitly speaks of others and extends the law in a general way to apply to them: "Anyone who loves his life loses it; anyone who hates his life in this world will keep it for eternal life."

St. Paul understood this teaching: "We believe that Jesus died and rose again, and that it will be the same for those who have died in Jesus: God will bring them with Him" (1 Thes 4:14).

The Apostle, though he does not cite the words of Jesus, is aware of the analogy of the sowing. He invokes it to explain the resurrection of the body: "Whatever you sow in the ground has to die before it is given new life, and the thing that you sow is now what is going to come; you sow a bare grain, say of wheat or something like that, and then God gives it the sort of body He has chosen; each sort of seed gets its own sort of body" (1 Cor 15:36-38).

Resurrection is not mere resuscitation but complete transformation, like the seed that grows, flowers and bears fruit. If the final flowering of this change takes place only through physical death, the beginning has taken place long before in baptism, through an impregnation of men and women with divine life.

They begin then to "share the divine nature" (2 Pt 1:4). Here the divine seed is sown, the divine life implanted: "they are born through water and the Spirit" (Jn 3:5). This involves an interior renewal: "For anyone who is in Christ, there is a new creation; the old creation is gone, and now the new one is here. It is all God's work" (2 Cor 5:17).

Renewal, however, can take place only through the *death* of the old man — "You have been taught that when we were baptized in Christ we were baptized in His death; in other words, when we were baptized, we went into the tomb with Him and joined Him in death, so that as Christ was raised from the dead by the Father's glory, we too might live a new life. If in union with Christ we have imitated His death, we shall also imitate Him in His resurrection" (Rom 6:3-5).

Water is a symbol of death as well as of life. The water which saved the Israelites destroyed the Egyptians. The catechumen's descent into the waters of baptism signifies the death and burial of the "old man," while his ascent from the water as a Christian signifies his sharing through grace in Christ's risen life. Thus the seed of new life, from its implantation in baptism to its final flowering from death to glory, is governed by the law of life-from-death.

Between the terms of implantation of the divine life and its final flowering through death into glory, there is the whole course of the Christian life. Here, this law enters the practical and moral sphere — the interior region of personal response, the outer world of responsible action. Here it governs the Christian's conduct as he directs it under the impulse of the Spirit.

Anyone who loves his life loses it; anyone who hates his life in this world will keep it for eternal life. These words reported by John have a universal, hence also a practical, application. In a word, the law of life-through-death shows how those living in Christ are to understand the whole element of renunciation in their lives and therefore how they are to meet daily duties, sacrifices, challenges, vicissitudes, and sufferings — they are to *die,* like the grain of wheat, in order to reap a harvest.

The analogy of the grain of wheat does not appear in any of the synoptic gospels, the Gospels of Matthew, Mark and Luke. Yet the principle it discloses and its applications are found in all of them.

In St. Luke we read, "Anyone who tries to preserve his life will lose it; and anyone who loses it will keep it safe" (17:33). The passage appears within a description of the judgment and it makes clear the readiness in which we must live, a frequent theme in St. Luke, and the attitude we should take toward our earthly existence because of the judgment. It not only refers to our eventual death — and judgment — but shows us how to evaluate and conduct our present lives in relation to these climactic and decisive events.

The context in St. Matthew is immediately practical. There is no direct reference to physical death and resurrection. "Anyone who prefers father or mother to Me is not worthy of Me. Anyone who prefers son or daughter to Me is not worthy of Me. Anyone who does not take up his cross and follow in My footsteps is not worthy of Me. Anyone who finds his life will lose it; anyone who loses his life for My sake will find it" (10:37-39).

Physical death is here implicit, while the explicit reference is to moral and mystical death. We are united to Christ in practice by a life spent in carrying the cross. We must carry the cross to follow Jesus. We live a "dying life," as *The Imitation of Christ* puts it, that the divine seed may grow into eternal life.

In St. Mark the context is also moral and mystical. By mystical, I mean the union of the believer with Jesus in practical faith, hope and love, hence in the whole conduct of his life. "If anyone wants to be a follower of Mine, let him renounce himself and take up his cross and follow Me. For anyone who wants to save his life will lose it; but anyone who loses his life for My sake, and for the sake of the Gospel, will save it. What gain, then, is it for a man to win the whole world and ruin his life?" (8:34-37)

How does one *hate* or lose one's life in order to *love* and *save* it? One thinks of an Albert Schweitzer "sowing" his great gifts in an African jungle "for the sake of the Gospel." Or of Dr. Dooley "sowing" his medical skill — which might have been so lucrative at home — among the lame, the halt, and the blind.

By the same token all who serve others in the spirit of love without asking remuneration — that is, by "dying" to human rewards — are "sowing." Certainly, according to the forecast and promise in St. Matthew they will reap abundantly. "Come, you blessed of My Father. . .I was sick and you visited Me. . ." (Mt 25:31-40)

"Losing one's life" can be summed up most briefly and graphically, perhaps, in the context supplied by St. Matthew — in which Jesus enjoins His followers to "carry the cross."

This is the way to follow Him now, to share in His eternal glory. It may involve nothing dramatic or sensational; only day-in, day-out duties and trials — although at times also great and even supreme sacrifices — carried out in union with Jesus. But out of these daily partial deaths, joined to His immolation, we will rise to share the harvest of His glory. "I die daily, I face death every day," says St. Paul (1 Cor 15:31).

St. Paul brings the matter to specifics, and he does so by citing the analogy of the sowing. In appealing for alms to help the faithful in Jerusalem, he writes: "Do not forget, thin sowing means thin reaping; the more you sow, the more you reap" (2 Cor 9:6).

The giving of alms, he is telling us, is not merely to be understood as a negative renunciation, not only as a loss, but as a "sowing." For a Christian it stems from the conviction that life comes from death, that by sowing money and thus letting it "die" to our personal use, we reap a crop in the kingdom of heaven.

The Apostle's example obviously has a much wider application. Money stands not only for itself, but for what it can procure, including all material goods. All of these may be "sown" through helping others to reap the goods of eternity. Even time can be "sown." The time "wasted" in serving others, or in prayer, is harvested in eternity.

Not that *all* goods *must* be thus sown, or even can be. The farmer is a good guide here also. He holds back whatever grain he needs for himself and his family, sowing the rest. He may be generous, but will not be careless in estimating his needs, for he knows that the more he sows the greater will be his crop.

The more you sow, the more you reap. The rule of sowing thus contains its own guide, to encourage generosity indeed, or rather, prudence, but at the same time to discourage excess or fanaticism. To gain an abundant crop we should sow as much as we can, but personal and family needs prevent us from actually sowing all possessions.

While we are with the farmer, we can also learn from him that sowing goods and satisfactions is not opposed to the spirit of joy that should mark the Christian. When he sows, it is not gloomily, but cheerfully and in hope. He undertakes hard work and exposes himself to inclement weather, and he does all this gladly, whistling while he works, because of the abundant harvest he anticipates.

The Christian is similarly joyful. Not in the spirit of the pagan slogan, "Eat, drink, and make good cheer," but rather by a readiness to sow the good things of earth in order to join the Savior in reaping for the Church an abundant harvest of eternal life and blessedness. "Add a smiling face to all your gifts" (Sir 35:8). St. Paul transposes this text, as he encourages sowing money for the needy: "God loves a cheerful giver" (2 Cor 9:7).

The message of life-through-death is found everywhere in the Gospel. I said above that, if we had from Jesus only the analogy of the grain of wheat, we would have the kernel and quintessence of His most important teaching. The teaching appears in His simplest sayings.

The Sermon on the Mount, for example, is usually taken as a summary of His moral teaching, so beautiful, idealistic, poetic in its bucolic setting. Yet the message of the grain of wheat, at once grim and glorious, is already implicit here.

The Sermon begins in the account of St. Matthew by promising blessing and beatitude to the poor in spirit, those that mourn, and the meek — that is, to those free of the love of riches, deprived of this world's comforts, pleasures, goods, and joys, those enabled by faith to persevere with equanimity in the face of the slings and arrows of outrageous fortune. In a word, those ready to sow this world's goods in the hope of eternal harvest.

The contrast is even more direct in St. Luke's report of these sayings: "How happy are you who are poor: yours is the kingdom of God. Alas for you who are rich: you are having your consolation now. Happy you who are hungry now: you shall be satisfied. Alas for you who have your fill now: you shall go hungry. Happy you who weep now: you shall laugh. Alas for you who laugh now: you shall mourn and weep" (6:20-26).

To the extent that we *die* — morally, spiritually, mystically — to wealth, to the fullness of earth's goods, and to merely human joy, to this extent will we rise to new blessedness and beatitude.

Clearly, therefore, the analogy of the grain of wheat provides also the fullest explanation, indeed the only explanation, of the Gospel counsels and their expression in vows of poverty, chastity and obedience. To the human mind there is no reason for a renunciation of goods which can contribute so much to human welfare and happiness.

Why give up material goods? Not money itself but "the *love* of money is the root of all evils" (1 Tm 6:10). Why renounce the unique good of marriage, conjugal love, and family life? The Scripture itself says that it is "not good for man to be alone." Why relinquish that most intimate personal good — the will — and with that the right to direct one's own life? The will is, after all, the key to the innermost regions of the soul as well as to the control of all one's outward activity. No satisfactory or acceptable explanation can be provided as reason for such renunciations. They can be explained only by the folly of the cross. "None of you can be My disciples unless he gives up all his possessions" (Lk 14:33). Jesus Himself led the way by sowing material goods, marriage, family, and His own human will.

Especially in the sowing of the will, it will be seen more and more clearly as we study the personal spirituality of Jesus, we come to the most profound meaning of Christian spirituality.

Laypeople and religious, married and celibate, start from the Mount of the Sermon to follow their different paths that will inevitably converge at the Mount of Calvary on their way to resurrection. The passage from Ephesians that exalts conjugal love as the sign of the love of Christ for His Spouse reveals also that this love is sacrificial: ". . .as Christ loved the Church and sacrificed Himself for her to make her holy" (5:25).

The married and the religious make their pilgrimage within hailing distance of each other, encouraging each other. The married are a living example of the love which, metamorphosed through grace, leads to union with the Spouse. The celibates remind the married that human love, however noble, is but a fragment of the divine and a stair to that ultimate reality of love in which alone is the final beatitude and fulfillment.

If the married illustrate love possessed yet looking beyond itself, the celibate symbolize love desired and wholly fulfilled. The celibate in their vocation point to the resurrection where "they will neither marry nor be given in marriage, but are as the angels of God in heaven" (Mt 22:30). Yet it is here in the final kingdom that love finds its home, since "God is love." And John's statement that "he who abides in love abides in God" is equally true the other way round: *He who abides in God abides in love.*

This evangelic dualism arises simply from the hierarchial order of the goods that come from God — a distinction of goods that demands a choice and an ordering on our part. Neither the Sermon on the Mount nor the gospels in general are comprehensible without this dualism between goods temporal and goods eternal: "So do not store up treasures for yourselves on earth, where moths and woodworms destroy them and thieves can break in and steal" (Mt 6:19). "None of you can be My disciple unless he gives up all his possessions" (Lk 14:33).

Again, Jesus says that our present life will be changed into another: "Whoever drinks this water will get thirsty again; but anyone who drinks the water that I shall give will never be thirsty again" (Jn 4:13).

On our part, we sow temporal goods to reap the eternal good. We sow transitory pleasures to reap unending joy. We sow time to reap eternity. A merely human life to reap divinized life. Creatures to gain the Creator. He who hates his life in this world keeps it unto life everlasting.

Sowing, like the Christian life generally, has an active and passive phase. That is to say, we may take the initiative ourselves, always presupposing divine grace, or we may second the action of the divine Husbandman.

Sickness, failures, disappointments, trials of whatever kind — above all, the slow, painful, and humiliating process of growing old and slipping toward death — these are all losses of our most prized possessions. They may be called diminishments, a term that relates them to the secret life of grace developing, in virtue of the law of life-through-death, into holiness.

Yet this term is negative; while in thinking of trials rather as opportunities for sowing, the scriptural word, the pain of loss dissolves in the hope of harvest. Tribulations are an occasion for sowing, and the more precious the good sown, the more glorious the harvest to be hoped for.

Moreover, while possessions, inward or outward, may be regarded as grains that may be sown, we ourselves, in the end, are the wheat that must die in order to live. Every renunciation or loss along the way is a partial death that leads, climactically, to the final sowing — and harvest. "We all have to experience many hardships before we enter the kingdom of God" (Acts 14:22).

To the natural man there is no explaining renunciation, suffering, and death. Ivan in *The Brothers Karamazov* made his devastating criticism — How can a God that is merciful and loving allow evil to stalk abroad freely in the world? How can He permit such suffering as we can see everywhere, especially the suffering of the innocent and children?

The devout Alyosha listened, disturbed but unconvinced. For an answer he went to Father Zossima, who spoke to him inevitably about the grain of wheat dying in the ground. As for Ivan, he ended in madness, which is perhaps Dostoevsky's way of answering those who seek to explain by reason what in the end can be understood only in faith. "For God's foolishness is wiser than human wisdom" (1 Cor 1:25).

Further than this — beyond the truth contained in the analogy of the wheat grain — the mind cannot go. If this is not the explanation, there is no explanation. If it is not true, then life is certainly absurd, without purpose and finally without meaning.

Yet the explanation, given so concretely and so clearly in the grain of wheat, cannot be proved. It rests absolutely on faith in the risen Christ. What we sow — and therefore lose — are the goods of this life and finally this life itself. But what we hope to reap is infinitely more precious — "the things that no eye has seen and no ear has heard, things beyond the mind of man, all that God has prepared for those who love Him" (1 Cor 2:9). But to obtain what the eye has not seen nor ear heard, and what surpasses the mind of man, we must wisely make the leap of faith into the apparently absurd.

Love Strong As Death

II
Bread of the Strong:
The Christian Life as Call to Heroism

Avoidance of Sin Is Not Enough

Father Hugo often preached against a "pious minimalism" that too often passes for Catholic life. This view reduces our divine vocation to a mere duty , an obligation to fulfill a handful of precepts while we avoid serious sin. He contrasted such half-hearted and grudging commitment with the spontaneous, generous devotion of the true lover of God.

❧

Those who aim only at the avoidance of mortal sin do have some love, sufficient for their salvation — provided that, being so lukewarm, they are able to retain it. Yet in proving their love by the fact that they have not committed grave sin, they resemble a man who proves his love for his wife by the fact that he does not murder her.

Remember, we are talking here of apostles, of those who are ambitious to serve Christ in a special way. "It is to be noted," says St. Gregory, "that the commandment stipulates a certain measure in the love of neighbor: 'Love your neighbor as yourself.' But the love of God is not restricted by any measure: 'Love the Lord thy God with thy whole heart, with thy whole soul, and with thy whole strength.' We are commanded here, not merely to love God as much as we can, but to love Him wholly, from our whole heart. . . . For he loves God truly who leaves nothing of himself for himself."

Homily for the Feast of St. Joseph Cupertino

Three Steps on the Way

The way to God, for Father Hugo, is a way of gradual renunciation of earthly attachments. The first thing to go is sin. Eventually, though, the Christian should live detached even from good things, thus remaining free to love God and God alone. Father Hugo insisted that the best path to righteousness is the one proven by the saints and ratified by the Church in canonizing the saints. Again and again, he cited the great doctors of the mystical and ascetical life: St. Thomas Aquinas, St. Francis de Sales, St. John of the Cross, St. Teresa of Ávila.

If you wish to be a typist, you must follow some method. If you desire to draw or to paint, you must seek out a master who will show you what to do. Without some kind of a definite program, we can scarcely know how to begin, much less how to go on.

St. Francis de Sales, in the first part of his *Introduction to the Devout Life*, outlines the steps that are to be taken first by one desirous of advancing in virtue. Altogether there are three steps, or, as he calls them, purgations. The first purgation is that from mortal sin. The second goes deeper and seeks to get at and destroy the "affection for sin," in addition to all the "affections, connections, and occasions which lead toward it." Finally, the purpose of the third purgation is to find and destroy, not sin, but the hidden roots of sin. This is the one that will chiefly occupy souls, who, while not living in serious sin, have not yet reached perfection. It consists in eliminating, first, affections for venial sin, secondly, evil inclinations, and thirdly, affections for creature-pleasures, or, as the saint puts it, for "unprofitable amusements."

This Is the Will of God

Worldliness Makes Us Lukewarm

Married love is Father Hugo's favorite metaphor for the interior life. The soul of the Christian is in love with God. Like spousal love, the Christian's love for God must be faithful, exclusive, and lifelong. Such a love is consuming, demanding. It tolerates no rivals for the heart's affection. But we humans are fickle lovers, dallying with worldly trifles, preferring the delights of God's creation to the delights of the Creator. Our attachment to creature comforts keeps our souls earthbound, unable to rise to God — and ultimately ineffective even in our "good works" on earth.

In one word, the cause of lack of fervor — and the reason accordingly, why Catholic organizations are ineffective in their fight against paganism — is *worldliness*, which inwardly and secretly destroys the life of Christians and nullifies the spiritual effect of their work. We lack life because we lack the love of God, and we lack the love of God because we are filled with the love of creatures. That is what worldliness is — a merely natural love for the creatures of the world.

This earthly love, innocent as it may seem, has an immediate and disastrous effect on our spiritual lives. For we have but one heart, with a finite capacity of love, and the love that we give to creatures weakens and reduces the love that we have for God. Not that there is any opposition between creatures and Creator, but there is rivalry for man's love. A woman must love her husband exclusively — she may not share her love among several men. Similarly, the soul, which is the spouse of Jesus Christ, if she is true to her Spouse, must relinquish mere earthly loves, and the measure in which she does this is the measure of the perfection of her love for God. The soul who persists in loving earthly things is called by the Scriptures an adulteress.

Every Christian talks vaguely against worldliness and the love of earthly things. Cardinal John Henry Newman makes the accusation definite and shows us exactly what we must be aware of — of the comforts of life, good food, soft raiment, the pleasures of sense, the consciousness of wealth. These are precisely the things that we are most naturally prone to enjoy, and which our particular civilization supplies in profusion. Yet they are undermining our spiritual strength, and we must learn to dispense with them in good measure if we would recover that strength. To increase our fervor and fill our societies with new life, we must deprive ourselves as far as possible of these earthly goods. When this is impossible, we must at least detach our affections from them inwardly, thereby fulfilling the scriptural injunction to use the things of the world as though we used them not (1 Cor 7:31).

To condemn worldliness is not for a moment to teach or to imply that the creatures of the world are evil. They are God's creatures and therefore they are good. The point is that we are not for this reason to become attached to them and consume our energies in a purely natural enjoyment of them. Almighty God desires that we love with our *whole hearts.*

Detachment from creatures, moreover, is an elementary condition of the Christian life. "I say, then, Philothea," wrote St. Francis de Sales, "that although it be lawful to play, to dance, to dress, or to be present at innocent comedies, yet to have an affection to such things is not only contrary to devotion, but also extremely hurtful and dangerous. The evil does not consist in doing such things, but in a fond attachment to them."

When, starting from the fact that creatures are good and created by God, we go on to conclude that they are here just to be enjoyed in a purely natural way, as the pagans enjoy them, then we have jumped from an unassailable Christian doctrine to a frankly pagan principle of conduct.

What a pleasant way to interpret the doctrine of One whose central teaching was, "If anyone wishes to come after Me, let him deny himself, and take up his cross daily and follow Me!" (cf. Mk 8:34). Desire is truly father to the thought. The concupiscence of the flesh, by an almost imperceptible twist in logic, produces from Christian teaching a maxim of conduct that is diametrically opposed to the scriptural "Do not love the world or the things that are in the world" (1 Jn 2:15).

I do not hold that these things are wrong in themselves — they are indifferent. But once we allow our affections to become wrapped up in them — and it is almost impossible for our weakened human nature to avoid it — then we begin to suffer spiritual harm. For they lessen our love for God, and this is the very life of the soul. There is not here a question of right or wrong, of sin or the absence of sin, it is entirely a matter of love, that is, whether our hearts are attached to creatures or to God. When apostles allow their affections to rest on merely worldly trifles, the good that they started out to do for souls will remain undone, the glory that they had vowed to win for Christ will never be gained.

Detachment, not only from sin and attection to sin, but also from what St. Francis de Sales calls "unprofitable amusements" is necessary for one who wishes to live a devout Christian life. And can anyone who is not leading such a life pretend to be an apostle? As examples of "unprofitable amusements" the saint names "play, dancing, feasting, dress, and theatrical shows." What would he think of Catholic action that is centered in elaborate programs of such "unprofitable amusements" or that uses them as the starting point for what in all simplicity is called a spiritual program, on the assumption that they are "the bait" by which men can be won to Christ? As though worldliness could be used to intensify the practice of a religion whose very heart is unworldliness!

In the Vineyard

Detachment Is Not Optional

The goods of the earth are not evil. The saints renounce worldly riches and pleasures precisely because these things are good. As Christians turn away from earthly goods, they turn toward something better.

❧

Unworldliness is not an added touch to the Christian life — acceptable in the saints, who have passed from this earth, but really superfluous, and of course wholly impossible in our modern environment. It is an essential condition for realizing the Christian life. St. Thomas Aquinas wrote: "Man is placed midway between the things of this world and spiritual goods, in which eternal happiness consists, so that the more he clings to one set of goods, the further he gets away from the other, and vice versa."

We cannot grow in the love of God unless we first further detach ourselves from creatures. There is, indeed, an inverse proportion between the love of creatures and the love of the Creator, so that the latter increases as the former decreases.

By showing why these two loves are opposed, St. Francis de Sales carries the matter a little further. Since we are finite beings, he says, our capacity for love is limited. Hence, before our hearts can contain a greater love for God, they must be further drained of attachments for creatures. "To love many things equally," he says, means "to love each in a less strong and less perfect way, for our capacity for love is limited . . . hence we ought not to divide our love but concentrate it on one thing as much as possible." For this reason, he ceaselessly praises "holy indifference," which, he teaches, should extend to all created goods.

But what need is there to labor the point? Are not Our Lord's own words sufficiently clear? "No man can serve two masters; for either he will hate the one and love the other, or else he will stand by the one and despise the other. You cannot serve God and mammon" (cf. Lk 16:13).

For all desirous of advancing in the love of God, for all who wish to extend God's kingdom on earth, this is a most illuminating principle. It offers a definite procedure for effecting those ends, and makes eventual success a certainty for those willing to be generous with God. Piety that ignores this principle is weak and will end by becoming mere sentiment. Piety that proceeds on its basis will certainly grow substantially in charity and supernatural life.

What Christians must do if they would work for God is to grow in love. And every growth in love presupposes a further detachment from creatures. Of course the love of God is a supernatural gift which comes with grace and is not the result of activity on our part. Nevertheless, if we wish our hearts to grow in this love, the necessary condition is that we set to work and clear them of earthly affections. If we love God with our whole hearts, then our hearts must be wholly emptied of affection for the vanities and the riches and pleasures of this world.

This is a basic law of Christian life, a fundamental truth of Christian asceticism.

The saints, it is to be observed, are aware that creatures are good and come from God. But, unlike worldlings, they do not draw from this fact the conclusion that creatures are to be enjoyed by men in a merely natural way. On the contrary, saints practice detachment and mortification in a heroic degree. Blessed Angela de Foligno says that the lover of God will use creatures only as required by the "straightest necessity."

Yet the saints do not imply by their conduct that God's creatures are evil, or that the pleasures of the world are in themselves sinful. With them mortification is not a matter of obligation, nor does it proceed merely from a fear of evil — it is a matter of love. They wish to detach their hearts from the things of earth, no matter how good these might be, that they might be better able to keep the first commandment and give their whole hearts to God, who is infinitely more lovable than any created good.

The Church herself, in demanding that we fast during Lent does not intend to take the view that food is bad or that the act of eating is sinful. She wants us to deny ourselves food because it is good, as an act of love and reparation toward God.

Mortification, then, does not involve the belief that creatures are evil, but it does definitely imply that I should not be *attached* to them, and it moreover helps me to achieve and to practice detachment. By fasting and giving up pleasures we at once perform an act of reparation for sin and make an act of pure love, independently of sin, by preferring God over the consolation and pleasure that is attached to creatures. In each sacrifice we say in effect to God: "It is You that I love and not creatures; to show this I am giving up these creature pleasures that You may know that I am seeking my happiness, not in their enjoyment, but in the possession of Your divine love." The Christian gives up creatures *because they are good*, because he thereby shows a preference for God over other attractive objects. For love, as we see also in human love, requires a preference and a choice.

The saints understand the paradox well enough. Knowing that the creatures come from God, they know too that there is a higher use for God's creatures than mere sensual enjoyment. Three higher uses have been indicated by St. Alphonsus Liguori: creatures are a means of thanking God — they are a means of loving Him by voluntary renunciation. They are a means, likewise through renunciation, of glorifying Him. Indeed the highest of all use for creatures is to renounce them. So Father Reginald Garrigou-Lagrange, O.P., writes: "It can aptly be said: 'The best thing that one can do with the best of things is to sacrifice it.' "

In the Vineyard

Seeing God in Creation

Beginning with creation, we can come to know the Creator. From the artwork, we learn of the Artist.

⁂

Seeing created goods as samples (of God's glory) thus clearly reveals the Christian's double attitude toward these goods. On the one hand we value them as images of the divine. On the other, because they are but samples, and not the Reality, we need to relinquish them in order to obtain the pearl of great price. If we fail in this, the love for the sample can become so great as to rival and even exclude the love of God.

We may compare a sinner to a man, who on a mission to a distant country, has a huge mural of his wife painted in his home or office, so that he may gaze on it continually. Then, when he is relieved of his charge and permitted to return home, he refuses to go because he finds himself unable to separate from the portrait to rejoin the original.

Your Ways Are Not My Ways, vol. I

From Attachment to Addiction

Our earthly desires rarely stay small. Our appetites seem to grow the more we try to satisfy them. If we do not control our desires, they begin to control us. Think of the addictions consuming entire classes of people to-day—alcoholism, overeating, tobacco, sex, drugs. "Trifling" attachments can be just as deadly to the soul: gossip, white lies, boasting. These earthly "needs" become gods, demanding a greater and greater share of our attention, turning us away from God.

❧❀◉❀☙

Freedom to love involves, not only avoidance of evil, therefore, but also the relinquishment of attachments to created goods. An attachment may be thought of as clinging to some object for its attractiveness, apart from need, and apart from God. Thus holding to any created good marks a beginning of that flirtation with God's rival, the world, in all its allurements, which can draw us away from Him. An attachment for athletics, as well as for money, or any other creation or pleasure or good can absorb our minds and affection, and, as we commonly see, turn upside down our whole system of values.

St. John of the Cross, showing the way to the perfection of love, indicates three ways that even the smallest attachments can be a hindrance and also injure us. He observes that, in the first place, such attachments, "however slight," prevent "divine union," that is to say, reaching the perfection of love. Moreover, they prevent any "progress" in this perfection. His examples of such minute obstacles, if they need updating — and extending — are in our time still illuminating and suggestive: "These habitual imperfections are, for example, a common custom of much speaking, or some attachment which we never quite wish to conquer — such as that to a person, a garment, a book or a cell, a particular kind of good, tittle-tattle, fancies for tasting, knowing, or hearing certain things, and such like."

To illustrate the idea the saint offers the image of a bird prevented from flying by a single thread. It comes to the same thing, he says, if the bird is held by a slender cord or a stout one, so long as it does not break away. St. Francis de Sales, despite his reputation for urbanity, goes just as far when he remarks: "Whoever desires something which he desires not for God, that much less desires God."

The Carmelite saint uses another image, the "sucking fish" or *remora*, to illustrate the unhappy condition of many Christians who hold on to a single attachment. Although very small, the remora was commonly thought in prescientific days to be capable of holding back a ship. Some people, he says, are like rich vessels laden with good works and virtues and the gifts of God. "And yet, because they have not the resolution to break with some whim or attachment or affection (which all come to the same thing), they never make progress or reach the port of perfection."

There is also a third reason why these voluntary attachments are hurtful. In bringing an end to forward progress they at the same time initiate a reversal of direction. Here we meet the law of life and growth which applies to life according to the Spirit as well as to all forms of natural life: not to grow is to decline, not to progress is to retrogress, not to move forward is to move backward. If attachments are not sinful, they nevertheless mark the beginning of the movement away from God. This momentum, unless reversed, will end in sin and ruin.

It has been said sneeringly of St. John of the Cross that, if followed, he would turn the world into a monastery. He may indeed seem to be a fanatic when he holds that total detachment, complete singleness and purity of heart, is needed to make progress in holiness, and it might seem more extreme to hold that small attachments might hinder brotherhood among men.

Yet in *The Brothers Karamazov* Father Zossima, a man of wide experience before becoming a monk, observed: "Interpreting freedom as the multiplication and rapid satisfaction of desires, men distort their own nature, for many senseless and foolish desires and habits and ridiculous fancies are fostered in them. . . . I know one 'champion of freedom' who told himself that, when he was deprived of tobacco in prison, he was so wretched at the privation that he almost went and betrayed his cause for the sake of getting tobacco again! And, such a man says, 'I am fighting for the cause of humanity. . . .' "

We may be tempted to smile when a spiritual master, a mere friar, so remote from the world, rebukes Christians for indulging "fancies for tasting." Yet we live in a society in which even overeaters, imitating the alcoholics, must organize to protect themselves from a damaging attachment to food. And this attachment, too, grows into a public health problem, attracting government concern when children, but also adults, become addicted to "junk foods."

Smoking is also widely seen in our day as a cause of disease and death, a public health hazard. What appears at first as an innocent pleasure becomes an attachment, then an addiction, next a compulsion, and finally a ruinous obsession. So it is with alcohol, eating, gambling, sex, and drugs. At this point organized crime appears on the scene, wraps its countless slippery tentacles around these "goods" with their addicts and brings immeasurable corruption and ruin.

Oh, the pity of it! And all from trifling attachments! As a "champion of freedom" may be diverted from his high purpose by such an apparently trifling thing as tobacco, so may attachments for any goods, grown into addictions, derail the noblest seekers for justice and betray even those dedicated to establishing the kingdom of God.

Your Ways Are Not My Ways, vol. I

No Christianity Without the Cross

Preaching against comfort-seeking, Father Hugo inspired some converts and more than a few critics.

⁂

"Your outlook is too one-sided and negative."

With modern people, especially with modern youth, it is a bad policy to emphasize the renunciations and restraints demanded by religion.

The modern person, accustomed to more comforts than a medieval sultan, is disturbed by what he deems an overemphasis of self-denial, and to him any emphasis is an overemphasis. He believes that there is a more pleasant way to holiness.

Those who speak in this way generally have inaccurate ideas as to what is meant by negative and positive Christianity. If men will have the life of Christ — His love, His joy, His peace — then they must accept Calvary and the cross. There is no Christianity without the cross, and those who accept Cana but reject Calvary separate themselves from the divine Master at the very outset of the way.

The warning that St. John of the Cross gave in his day is just as necessary for our age: "He who seeks not the cross of Christ seeks not the glory of Christ."

In the Vineyard

The Price and Measure of Love

Those who wish to live by the rule of love must live by renunciations. Jesus proved His own love for us by His death on the cross. "Greater love than this no one has, that one lay down his life for his friends" (Jn 15:13). He expects the same of us: "Walk in love, as Christ also loved us and delivered Himself up for us an offering and a sacrifice. . ." (Eph 5:2). No one who refuses to prefer Jesus above all things, by complete detachment from the goods of the world, can claim to love Him fully. There are some who say that they desire to love God, although they will not hear of renunciation. Let them not be deceived: the price and the measure of love is sacrifice. The Christianity without the cross, so popular in our day, is also a Christianity without love. It is not really Christianity.

In the Vineyard

A Cautionary Tale from History

Father Hugo believed that the Church's failure to demand holiness from its members — especially the young — had dire consequences. He wrote the following passage as the pagan forces of Nazi Germany waged war on the rest of the world. The Church's offering of a relaxed, "positive Christianity" had proven to be poor competition for Hitler's challenging, ascetic ideal.

When Germany, after World War I, was engaged in the work of reconstruction, the leaders of its several parties and interests, recognizing that the future of the country was largely in the hands of its youth, inaugurated a number of youth movements through which they hoped to realize in the coming generation the ideals in which they placed their hopes of national greatness. Knowing that true greatness and prosperity can be obtained only through Christianity, German Catholics did not fail to grasp the importance of the situation. And they, like the others, started a movement in which they sought to embody the noblest ideas of Christianity in a form that would exert the greatest influence over youth.

The method they considered best for obtaining this end was to emphasize the positive aspects of Christianity while not making its negative side too prominent. By the positive side they meant the privileges and dignity of the Christian vocation, the nobility of the Christian ideal of life, the transformation that Christ's teaching can effect in the lives of individuals and societies. One of the chief means by which it was planned that this positive Christianity should spread its beneficial influence was through the liturgy and liturgical participation.

The purpose of the Catholics, thus carefully planned, was also ably carried out, as was evidenced by the books inspired by the German Catholic youth movement. There was only one defect in the program, yet so important was this that in the end it caused the whole effort to fail.

The defect was the attitude of the Catholic leaders toward negative Christianity. This, the shadowed side of the Master's teaching, was to be kept in the background, or at least not pushed too prominently into the foreground, because, since it comprises the avoidances entailed by moral living, together with the sacrifices and denials that Christ demands of us, too much attention to it (so the Catholics thought) would tend to repel young people marked by lightheartedness and love of life.

Here a profound mistake was made. Sometimes indeed negative Christianity is falsely understood to embrace only the "Thou shalt nots" of the Ten Commandments. And there is no doubt that insistence only on these "don'ts" would fail to inspire youth (or anyone else for that matter). But then, too, if our instruction were not to go beyond that, we would not be teaching Christianity at all, either positive or negative. For these "Thou shalt nots" are the negative, not of the Gospel teaching, but of Natural Law.

The negative practice of Christianity is the elimination from the soul of that selfish, possessive, merely natural love of creatures which retards the work of grace and prevents the soul from advancing in divine love. It includes, of course, the avoidance of sin, but goes much deeper and requires a renunciation, at least interiorly, of all the goods of earth. It is a demand for sacrifice, for a kind of heroism, from those who would reach what is high and holy. And to gloss over this aspect of Christianity, we say, is a fatal mistake.

In the first place it is a psychological mistake. For the young love heroism, high loyalty, and sacrifice in the name of noble ideals. Cutting out these elements takes from Christianity precisely that which would most appeal to them. When dignified Churchmen, aging theorists, tired intellectuals, or comfort-loving bourgeois formulate youth programs they should keep this in mind. Warm-blooded youth is not much attracted by such dull ideals as comfort, security, regularity, respectability. They want adventure, surprise, novelty, insecurity, strenuous effort, heroism.

Moreover, an underemphasis of negative religious practices gives a false and distorted view of Christianity itself. For the negative is but the reverse of the positive, and the latter is impossible without the former, just as it is impossible to have the sun without shadows — indeed, it is the very brightness of the sun that causes the shadows. You must take them together, as a unit — both, or neither. As light appears, darkness must disappear, and you cannot imagine the coming of light without the disappearance of darkness. So also divine life (the positive) cannot come into our souls except with the disappearance of that spiritual darkness which St. John of the Cross teaches consists in a love for the vanities of this world, a love which must be expelled through the negative practices of renunciation, self-denial, penance.

The final and deepest reason for the *inevitable* failure of the policy we have been describing comes of the fact that the neglect of negative Christianity means disregard of the indispensable means for realizing the positive values of supernatural living.

Only on condition of removing darkness can the sun flood the earth with its light. Only on condition of removing darkness from our souls can divine grace flood them with its light. But if men love darkness rather than the light, and accordingly cling to darkness, then certainly they cannot possess the light.

No doubt there is need to make speeches and write books about the positive aspects of Christianity, about grace, the splendor of the sacramental system, the liturgy, the love of God. But men cannot realize in their own lives these positive values simply by listening to the speeches or reading the books. For this they must be *purified*. And only in proportion as purification is accomplished in them will God's grace have freedom to work its marvels in their souls. This purification is the work of negative Christian practice — of denial, of renunciation, of penance. Without these the positive in Christianity, although it may be known abstractly, cannot be experienced.

The German youth leaders failed to insist on the heavy demand for sacrifice that our Lord makes of us all. In doing this they lost the very essence of Christianity and the source of its life. For what is called negative Christianity is best symbolized by the cross. Can you take the cross from Christianity? If you do, you take away its center and essence and the secret of its divine vitality. Christianity is the cross.

At the same time that the Catholics were making their supreme effort to gain the young, another movement, dominated by an outstanding leader, was working for the same end. The methods of this leader, however, were quite different from those of the Catholics. He had his own positive ideal of a greater Germany. This was certainly inferior to the Christian conception, nevertheless, that it might be realized, he did not hesitate to call upon all Germans, and especially the young, to make heavy sacrifices.

He put them in uniforms, housed them in barracks — in short, he demanded that they live a hard and laborious life, far different from the softness that they had enjoyed before. He even required that they should sacrifice their private careers in the interest of their country. Finally, at a time when the world was still sickened from the slaughter of World War I, these young people were taught that they must be prepared to give their lives for their Fatherland. The leader of this movement, you know, was Adolph Hitler.

There is no need to say who won the youth of Germany. It was not the Church. Catholic leaders were afraid to ask heroism of youth lest they lose them altogether. Hitler won the youth of Germany or a very large section of it, precisely by demanding the heroic.

Are not Catholic leaders all over the world making the same mistake that was made by the German Catholics? When will we come to the realization that youth wants heroism? That the way to win youth is to demand the most, not the least?

Of course to teach heroism to others, Catholic leaders, both lay and clerical, must themselves have a heroic devotion to their cause. They cannot, amid ease and security and the comforts of life, outline an abstractly admirable (or highly respectable and dull) program that will be capable of winning the loyalty of the young. The leaders must themselves be on fire with the love of Jesus Christ. They must have the glorious inward vision of the Christian way of life as described in the Sermon on the Mount. They must know *from personal experience* (not simply from books) the sublimity of the Christian ideal, and they should be able to *lead* others to it, and not merely direct them, as from a map, over territory with which they themselves are not personally familiar.

If Catholic youth leaders fail to do this, then in our generation also they will hand over the world to Christ's enemies.

This Is the Will of God

We Want to Be Heroes

We tend toward a soft life, but such a life never satisfies. What our hearts really desire is adventure, heroism, sacrifice — and these are precisely the demands of love, especially divine love.

Why do people like novels? Is it not because they are carried away by the imaginary exploits of the heroes and heroines of whom they read? Would you say, then, that average men are repelled by heroism? On the contrary, they have the greatest admiration for it. Nor are they content with contemplating as from afar the actions of the hero in the tale. They must fancy themselves in his (or her) place that they too may enjoy these marvelous adventures, at least vicariously. It is their own dull and drab lives — not the heroic and strenuous life — that they find distasteful. Moving picture theaters testify to the same truth — crowded as they are with seekers for adventure, even if only at second hand.

The heroes of fiction can also reveal to us why it is that ordinary men love heroism and are capable of it themselves. What makes a hero heroic? It is love. Love demands sacrifice. Indeed, sacrifice is the measure of love, and heroism is nothing but great sacrifice inspired by love. Because all men and women are capable of love, so are all capable of sacrifice and heroism, for these are love's best and truest — nay, inevitable — expressions. The hero performs his deeds for love of country, or love of family, or love of her whom he desires to make his wife, and his heroism consists precisely in overcoming the obstacles that hinder his love's fulfillment.

Sacrifice is usually difficult and irksome. Only love can make it a joy. We are willing to give in proportion as we love. And when love is perfect the sacrifice is complete. "God so loved the world that He gave His only begotten Son; and the Son so loved us that He gave Himself for our salvation. Greater love than this no man hath, that man lay down his life for his friends." These are the words of no less than the Church herself. She addresses them to couples standing before her altars seeking to be married. That on so happy an occasion as this our heavenly Mother should thus already speak of sacrifice, and complete sacrifice at that, shows how inseparable it is from love. Whether the love is that between humans, or between God and humans, it is a giving of self, a surrender, therefore a sacrifice.

This Is the Will of God

Positively Penitential

Christian life is rich in paradox. While some truths defy ordinary reason, our experience proves them true. Happy are those who mourn, Jesus said. Father Hugo insisted that true riches come only when we choose to be "poor," through penance and self-denial.

⚜

The Christian who slights the duty of penance to obtain joy will one day see his joy turned into sorrow. But he who generously accepts the burden of penance will one day see the much more marvelous transformation of "sorrow turned into joy." "For he who sows in tears will reap in joyfulness."

Would you have positive Christianity? Would you have supernatural life and joy and riches and love? The way to get them is clear. You get eternal life by death to your life here on earth. You get joy through sorrow and mourning. You get riches by renouncing all things. You obtain love by renouncing the love of earthly things.

If you desire to advance in the love of God, if you wish to promote the work of Christ by spreading the divine life and love in the world, you see here how it is to be done in this law fixed by God. It is not done by your speeches or articles or books, not by your charming personality or your cleverness in organization. These can no more bring about spiritual effects in the souls of men than a wire can cause the electricity that lights a house, or than a brush can cause the genius that is evident in the painting of an artist.

What alone can give supernatural value to your work is fidelity to self-denial and penance, the minute self-sacrifice of a life that is wholly consecrated to God, detachment from the world and its vanities, meekness in bearing injury, patience and humility in trials. When you make your speech or write your article or plan some project, you do not thereby create the living water that alone gives life to souls. You but release it and allow it to flow forth upon souls — the real source is a reservoir of prayer and sacrifice hidden in the distance.

How foolish it is to say, as so many do: "Let us hear nothing of this odious duty of detachment and self-denial. There are more pleasant things to think of. The saints were not gloomy, but joyous. Let us be more positive in our outlook. Let us speak more of divine life and love and joy. Then filled with the desire for these things, the renunciation will take care of itself."

That is like saying that, if only we are anxious enough to have flowers, the digging and planting will take care of themselves. Like the lies of political propagandists, this error seems to go unquestioned because it is so bold. If heeded, it would release us from the only spiritual effort that it is possible for us to make. Divine life and love are God's gifts, the fruits of His grace, and they are supplied in profusion the divine Goodness to those disposed to receive them.

The part assigned to us by God is simply to *empty ourselves* that we may be able to receive His gifts. In other words, mortification and renunciation are *man's part* in the work of sanctification. And much grace is necessary for us even to accomplish that. *Precisely the thing that we must never take for granted is the practice of negative Christianity.* It is all very well to dream of the treasures of heaven. But they are in God's possession, not in ours. To get them, we must stop dreaming and set to work. And our work is to cast out of our hearts the treasures of earth.

In the Vineyard

Infinitely Better than Chocolate and Mozart

Father Hugo had a keen appreciation for the wonders of God's creation. In the following poetic passage, he shows how easy it is for us to be dazzled by the beauty of the world — so dazzled that we stop there, with the created goods, and do not proceed beyond them to their Creator. Yet all creation, dazzling as it is, ultimately disappoints, because we are made for God, and our hearts are restless until they rest in Him.

⁂

We wander through the cosmic picture gallery for a lifetime, and one who lives by faith, indeed every person of good will, is able to follow these likenesses back to the Divine Artist. Suppose that you were to become deeply absorbed in a collection of snapshots — mementos of pleasant excursions with your friends — but meanwhile you neglect these friends when they call on you.

Or consider those people who become so enthralled by stage and film dramas and stories that they fail to recognize the true artist as seer helping them to decipher the meaning of life. They rather seek in novels and drama escape into a world of dreams and fantasy, oblivious of the profound truths that the writer or painter or sculptor is inviting them to contemplate.

This is what happens when the pagan, or the Christian with a pagan mentality (and *a fortiori*, the sinner) so admires created goods that he neglects and forgets the Creator. Here we see the ambivalent attitude of the Christian to creatures and why it is really no paradox but a simple fact that while handling and admiring and in a sense even loving them (only persons can really be loved), he must not allow them to draw his affections away from the Creator whom he is to love with his whole heart. Created goods should draw us rather to God: "He who planted the ear, does He not hear? He who formed the eye, does He not see?" (Ps 94:9).

Other images similarly help us to realize what our attitude should be toward created goods. Every creature is a crumb, a ray, a fragment of the divine goodness and tells us something of God who gave it being. We might therefore say, while contemplating created goods, "If a tiny ray of God's beauty brings such delight, what a boundless joy it will be to possess the Light itself! If but a fragment or crumb of His goodness affords such pleasure now, what happiness will there be in partaking of 'the bread of the children' (Mk 7:27), the whole loaf, at the banquet table of the Father!"

Our comparison of the creature-sample to the Reality of which it gives us a taste may be made in a threefold way. First, the pleasure received from the sample — say, a piece of chocolate or a glass of wine — lasts but a minute, but the joy of possessing the Real is eternal.

Transitoriness is a characteristic of all created pleasures. They may of course be repeated, but this leads in time to satiety and even revulsion. The pleasures of earthly joys are indeed found largely in our anticipation whereas possessing them often proves disappointing as well as poignantly brief. The delights of the Spirit, however, although at times painful in anticipation, because of the price we must pay for them, never pall but rather increase in their capacity to rejoice the heart.

> *Come to Me, you who desire Me,*
> *and eat your fill of My produce.*
> *For the remembrance of Me is sweeter than honey,*
> *and My inheritance sweeter than the honeycomb.*
> *Those who eat Me will hunger for more,*
> *and those who drink Me will thirst for more.*

(Sir 24:19-21)

Secondly, the created good is only a sample in respect to quality. Here we purify the comparison. The wine rejoices the bodily appetites but does not touch the spirit. God also satisfies the spirit. To be sure, certain created goods — music, literature, indeed all the arts — provide satisfaction also to the human spirit, but not at the deepest personal level, not completely or finally. Even so, such satisfactions of the human spirit surpass sensual pleasures in quality and thus suggest how the joys of the divine Spirit can be more absorbing still. Yet all human joys can pall. The poet Keats wrote:

> *Where's the cheek that doth not fade,*
> *Too much gazed at? Where's the maid*
> *Whose lip mature is ever new?*
> *Where's the eye, however blue,*
> *Doth not weary? Where's the face*
> *One would see in every place?*
> *Where's the voice, however soft,*
> *One would hear so very oft?*
> *At a touch sweet pleasure melteth*
> *Like to bubbles which rain pelteth . . .*
> *Everything is spoilt by use.*

Here we are brought to the third manner of comparison. In point of intensity also, created goods, even the most exalted are but samples of the ecstatic joys of the kingdom of heaven. And so St. Paul, citing Isaiah (religious people have always appreciated this fact), cries out: "No eye has seen, nor ear heard, nor the heart of man conceived, what God has prepared for those who love Him!" (1 Cor 2:9).

Every beauty of place of person, not to mention art, can but feebly suggest the beauties of heaven and the joy of possessing God. The paradisiac music of Mozart but faintly hints at "the new song" played by the harpists before the throne of the Lamb: "No one could learn that song except the hundred and forty-four thousand who had been redeemed from the earth" (Rev 14:3).

In a word, to update the sayings of Paul and Isaiah, our wildest dreams of castles in Spain fall infinitely short of the Reality awaiting those who love God.

Your Ways Are Not My Ways, vol. I

Falling Away

To speak of hell is unfashionable these days — and it was in the 1940s, when the following passage first appeared. Yet Father Hugo insisted that hell is a real danger, and it is a real danger for every Christian. Seemingly "good" people do fall into complacency, then venial sin, then mortal sin. Without God's grace, no one is immune to the disease. Father Hugo upheld the traditional ascetical means of care for the soul.

⚜

Suppose that, in spite of all the considerations we have put down in these pages, one would still refuse to strive for high sanctity and limit himself to the lowest degree, asserting that this is enough for him! What would be the effect of that decision? What would happen to such a person?

Here is St. Augustine's answer to our question: "If you say, 'It is enough,' you have already perished." St. Alphonsus Liguori adds: "Do you say that for you it is sufficient? If you do, *you are lost.*"

These strong words from men who are saints and doctors of the Church cannot be airily dismissed as hyperbole. They are sober, doctrinal fact. It is completely and literally true that those who say they have done enough, have already taken the road which will at length bear them to perdition.

Spiritual blindness is the first step in the downward movement. This is commonly spoken of in the Scriptures. "Go, and thou shalt say to this people: Hearing, hear, and understand not: and see the vision, and know it not. Blind the heart of this people, and make their eyes heavy, and shut their eyes: lest they see with their eyes, and hear with ears, and understand with their heart, and be converted and I heal them" (Is 6:9-10).

The same effect is indicated by St. Paul when he says, in the text quoted, that those so punished are delivered to a reprobate sense, a dullness and deficiency of spiritual perception, which allows souls to fall into every manner of sin, as a blind person might fall into a pit.

73

Carnal persons, those without spiritual perceptions, cannot understand the things of God. They have no sense to guide them in the spiritual world. They are like ground moles that can feel their way about in the darkness of the earth, but stumble and cannot see in broad daylight.

Accordingly they have no knowledge of their own position in relation to God, no appreciation of the malice of sin, no sensitiveness to the presence of temptation, no awareness of their own danger. And though they were not at once, as a result of this, to fall into gross sin, yet they would be unable to perform those supernatural acts of virtue so necessary to spiritual life and growth. Thus their souls would slowly wither and finally die, as does the body when it is given no nourishment or opportunity for exercise and movement.

In the spiritual life, there is no standing still. The fact that development ceases is already evidence that disease has set to work. The person may be aware of no change. They may be regular in their devotions. They are, they feel sure, in the state of grace, and this is, after all, sufficient for salvation. They are resolved not to commit serious sin, and so long as they hold to this purpose, surely they cannot be lost.

But the masters of the spiritual life tell us in one of their axioms that "Imperfections dispose the soul to venial sins, and venial sins dispose it to mortal sin." That is the process of decay, once deliberate imperfection has begun, that is, once a soul has ceased striving for perfection. Yet the lukewarm soul fancies himself healthy and has a great contempt for imperfections and venial sins, refusing to bother about them. He is like a person who is contemptuous of his ailment because it has not yet killed him.

Those who fall into sin through weakness can confidently hope for the grace of repentance and the forgiveness of their offenses. And as their souls are filled with unmortified passions, disordered affections, and worldly desires, they are scarcely in a condition to correspond with the grace God would grant them.

This Is the Will of God

Mary in Action

Father Hugo believed, as the Church teaches, that Mary plays a key role in salvation history, and in the story of each individual Christian.

It was only through Mary that divine life came to our humanity. She was, by God's will, the instrument through which life came into the world. And, since God does not change, it is still through Mary that life must come into the souls of men.

So it must be the work of the apostolate. This can be done only through a right devotion to Mary. Men cannot afford to neglect the instruments designated by God for His work.

You and I have a supernatural life through Mary and all our future growth in that life shall likewise be through her. It is a cold doctrinal fact that, if Christ is to reign in the world, He shall do so through Mary. Father Faber goes so far as to call the age in which Christ shall be everywhere known and loved, "the Marian age."

In the Vineyard

III

Prayer and Practice:
The Life of the Saint

The Prayer of the Busy

To Father Hugo, the active and contemplative ways of life were not separate, mutually exclusive categories. Since all people are called to the fullness of Christian perfection, all are called to live rich lives of prayer — even those who live busily in the middle of the world. In this retreat conference, delivered just weeks before his death, Father Hugo sketched out what he considered the "best life of all" — a "mixed life of prayer and activity." Along the way, he treats many of the peculiar spiritual ills of our day: workaholism, burnout, boredom.

Jesus entered a village where a woman named Martha welcomed Him to her home. She had a sister Mary who sat at the Lord's feet and listened to His words. Martha, busy with the details of hospitality, came to Him and protested, "Lord, are You not concerned that my sister has left me to do all the household tasks alone? Tell her to help me!"

The Lord replied to her, "Martha, Martha, you are anxious and upset about many things. One thing only is necessary. Mary has chosen the better portion and she shall not be deprived of it."

That's the story that has been taken from ancient times as a commentary on the Christian way of life. Martha stands for the active life and Mary stands for the prayerful, contemplative way of life.

For Martha, we have fellow feeling, we moderns with our society and our fuss. We can sympathize with her and think she had a bad deal, but we are here to learn from the Savior, not to tell Him what He should have said. No doubt Martha learned from this passage herself. We honor her as a saint in the Church.

But she made a mistake. It was an understandable mistake because among the Jews hospitality was a very important virtue. Abraham had entertained God once under the form of strangers until he discovered it was the Divine Presence, and so the Jews never forgot that. They gave hospitality a very high ranking in their list of virtues. Martha was dutifully kind, but she was doing something else, she was neglecting her guest, the Teacher, the One who brought us the divine wisdom. She evidently forgot that temporarily and Jesus chided her about it. That was her temperament.

She appears once again in the Gospels and we have the same thing. She didn't learn altogether. She jumps up at the very end of His life and runs forward and Mary stays. Our forefathers, theologians, and teachers, in taking Martha and Mary as standing for two ways of living the Christian life — the active and the contemplative, the active and the prayerful — were concerned with which way is the better way. They lighted on the answer: the contemplative life is better than the active because Jesus praised it to Mary. Martha's life, representing the active life, is secondary.

That idea took hold in the Church. That is why for centuries the only religious communities were contemplative rather than active. Only in modern times have *active* religious communities come into existence: the Jesuits for men, and for women the Sisters of Charity of St. Vincent de Paul and St. Louise de Marillac.

St. Thomas agreed that the contemplative way is more perfect. But they had the wrong idea of active life, too, in those times. We know from experience that the active life is sterile. Everyone here probably has in his family a workaholic. They work under compulsion. They take no joy in their work. They get no satisfaction, no enrichment from their work. They are drained by their work, and they just can't stop working. We have them in the priesthood, have them in religious life, and in your homes. I see them in Ann Landers and Dear Abby. A common complaint of wives is: "My husband takes care of us beautifully. We have everything we need. We have cars, a beautiful home, and everything to eat, but we don't have a husband or a father. He is always on the go, always moving, always active."

Workaholics are unhappy people. They are all busy. They keep talking about it. But they get no joy. A person's first joy should come from his work. We think of work as a burden, the punishment of Adam. It is not a punishment at all. It is an extension of God's creative activity. Often when a man or woman retires, you see that. They wilt, they die. They lose that which they know best if they are fortunate to have a true vocation.

There is much work today that is not a true vocation. It is just mechanical work. There is a difference between a job and a vocation. People are bored by jobs and hate them, but are never bored by a work which they have chosen, which they love. The point is: work is sterile of itself. It is spiritually draining. It does not make for happiness.

But prayer is something that fills us, something we can enjoy.

Now, it is important to note what Mary was doing when she received these words of praise from Jesus. What was she praying? Mary was listening to the word of God through Jesus. She was not busy about many things and not even busy about prayers. She was not reading them out of a book, not reciting them — she was listening to the words of Jesus Christ.

"My words," Jesus said on one occasion, "are spirit and life." Mary was listening to words that are spirit and life. This is what prayer is. This is why it is filling, fulfilling, and satisfying if we really learn the secret. Many of our contemporaries are rediscovering this, even in our very busy society.

St. Thomas Aquinas, when he discussed this problem, ended up by saying that the best life of all is the mixed life of prayer and activity. He had only one reason for saying that: That was the kind of life Jesus lived.

You might say, "That is the kind of life I'm living already." Not so fast. As St. Thomas understood it, a mixed life is one in which the prayer is not incidental to the activity, squeezed in here and there as best you may, but in which activity proceeds from prayer. Prayer flows into activity. It makes you more energetic. It doesn't drain your spiritual energy. It gives you more energy. It multiplies itself.

It is sad today to read in magazines complaints from priests, religious, and lay people who complain of being burned out. Burned out! I sat on the other side of the table not long ago from a young priest who had everything going for him. He is the head of a youth movement in a great archdiocese, and he was telling me how burned out he is.

That is sad. He should be increasing in energy if he were playing the game right, if he were living a life of prayer. St. Thomas put it this way: "Our activity should then proceed from us not by way of subtraction but by way of addition." We reinforce, we increase our inner resources by means of prayer instead of exhausting them. That is what the mixed life is.

St. Bernard will explain it this way. You must be a cistern before you become a channel.

Gandhi worked fifteen hours a day. He got a couple of hours of sleep at night. He had the most difficult work with people, all kinds. He was asked one day, "Mr. Gandhi, don't you think you should take a vacation?" His reply was evidence of a contemplative life. He said, "I don't need a vacation. I'm always on vacation." That is a supreme accomplishment. When your work does not drain you, when it does not exhaust you, but it inspires you and fills you with more. This is what St. Thomas meant by the mixed life. Ceaseless activity, but endless prayer, and prayer becomes a source. We are never to become burned out, but should grow until we die.

This is the kind of life that I recommend to you, a mixed life in which prayer is the source, not an addendum, not something incidental but right at the center, right at the heart. I mean the kind of prayer that Mary indulged in, the kind that Jesus said is the one thing necessary: the love of God, interior prayer, mental prayer: meditation or contemplation.

Prayer must be the center of our active lives. For, as St. Teresa said, this is the only way to God. There is no use justifying substitutes. You must take the time to pray.

Retreat Conference, September 1985

Lack of Prayer Is Lack of Love

The spiritual life, for Father Hugo, was a love affair. And lovers by nature want to spend time — spend a lifetime, in fact — with their beloved. Christians who do not make time for prayer are placing their love, their very life, at risk.

The want of love for God shows up in a distaste for prayer and the exercises of devotion. Prayer is looked upon as pietism, idleness indulged in by those who have not the stomach for more strenuous activity.

Prayer — mental prayer or meditation — is our most direct way of expressing love for God. It is a union of our minds and hearts with Him, the beginning of that union with Him that will be consummated in heaven. "Prayer is true happiness in this life," said St. Jane Frances de Chantal. And of course she meant to be taken quite literally. To find prayer tedious and distasteful is to find God tedious and distasteful.

The insufficiency of prayer points to an even deeper trouble. It shows that such workers regard God's part in their projects as of less importance than their own activity. Almighty God is considered a sort of spectator along the sidelines, whom, by our prayers, we can perhaps change into an enthusiastic rooter for our private projects.

Prayer and a fervent interior life are not just graceful ornaments for the life of the apostle — they are the instruments necessary for making his work spiritually fruitful. Failure to recognize this explains why the most frantic activity of Catholic organizations produces no spiritual results. A St. Anthony, who spent whole nights in prayer, was more effective in his work for souls than the greatest of the modern go-getters, who are equipped with all the latest methods of doing things but have "no time to pray."

The person who has no time to pray is not doing God's work. We do not stint our time with those we love. The apostle who has no time to pray has no ardent love for God. Yet since all human activity is finally motivated by some kind of love, apostolic activity, if it does not come from love of God, can only come from love of self.

In the Vineyard

Conditions for Prayer

"Teach us to pray," the disciples begged Jesus. And the question echoes down to our own age. "But how should I pray?" is probably the question most asked of spiritual directors today, especially by those just setting out on the path to God. Father Hugo offered very practical suggestions in the following conference, preached on the last retreat of his life.

We are told it takes forty minutes every day — or sixty minutes, a holy hour. It doesn't have to be all at once — twenty-minute periods will do. But it can't be fragmented any more than that and still be effective. You must find time to do it. Don't tell me, as one priest did, that you don't have time to pray. He spent forty minutes telling me that, justifying himself. He could have put that time into prayer.

We have to organize our day, and some of us especially have to learn a wrist motion: turning off the switch of the television. Prayer is the one thing necessary. Martha learned from Mary, and we must, too.

Here are four rules or conditions of prayer. They are very simple.

1. Find a quiet place. It can be a church if you have access to one. Bishop Fulton Sheen used to urge everyone to make a holy hour in front of the Blessed Sacrament every day. No doubt the Blessed Sacrament is the preferred place if there is a church nearby, and it is quiet. But not everyone is a bishop with a private chapel next door. So there might be some difficulties.

Sometimes churches are in use, groups are using them, sometimes janitors, painters, and electricians are using them. So you can't always go to a church for quiet.

But we don't need a church to pray. All we need is a quiet corner. Catherine de Hueck Doherty has been advocating that every house should have a *poustinia,* Russian for "prayer room," a little closet or corner of the house where you can pray, where you can retire in silence. If you do it at home, you should have a place you can make your own certain times during the day and pray alone.

The quiet should be uninterrupted, at least twenty minutes. Nothing less can be efficacious.

Eliminate certain noises. Sometimes there are background noises, such as children playing in a schoolyard, but noises like telephones are death to this type of prayer. Radios have to be turned off, as does the television. Conversation should cease. We have to set ourselves off from all that.

This is apart from liturgical prayer. Liturgical prayer depends on interior prayer. Otherwise our liturgies become a mere externalism, a routine, a shell. In which case, though it may be a valid Mass, it holds little personal value. In order to give the soul to our participation in the liturgy, we need this interior prayer.

2. The second condition is a prayer word, some word that will direct your prayer. The prayer word can be any word that would help orient yourself to God, just the name of God, a word like "love" or "joy," or the name of Jesus. Perhaps you will take a scripture passage for your prayer word or a scripture passage to meditate on. Perhaps there is some aspect of religion, a virtue, an insight that you would like to use.

3. The next rule is a passive or receptive attitude, a completely relaxed attitude. One doctor calls this attitude the "relaxation response." Some of the masters of prayer will give you an exercise on how to relax your body, starting at your left toe, right toe, relax your muscles, then the ankle, the leg, up the body to the hip and torso, the left side, the left shoulder, the head, and the other side. You go down the other side until your body is completely relaxed. Now you are ready to pray.

Those who teach this type of prayer say that the most important of the four conditions is a relaxed, receptive attitude. That is not surprising. When you go to the theater, you are relaxed and thus receptive. But at the same time, you are very active. Your mind is enthralled with the music, the drama. To be receptive is to be active and passive at the same time. At the Mass, we sit during the reading and the homily because we are to be *passively* participating, not actively participating. Like Mary the sister of Lazarus, we are being receptive to God's word. It is the same during this type of interior prayer.

4. The last condition is a comfortable position, a position that can be maintained for twenty or thirty minutes without moving nervously. You might sit upright in a comfortable chair. We are told that we are most relaxed when our back is upright. This may be hard for us because we tend to be very lazy. But we have to learn to do this because in the end we will find it rewarding.

Retreat Conference, September 1985

An Eastern Remedy for Western Activism

Father Hugo took advantage of a 1970s fad (Eastern mantras) to reacquaint Christians with the ancient practice of praying or chanting a prayer word, such as the name of Jesus or a phrase from the psalms. As always, he met people where they were, then led them along the way of the fullness of Christian mystical and ascetical life, to which he believed every believer was called.

With the coming of the Oriental gurus to teach prayer (Transcendental Meditation) to the sorry pragmatists of the West, the mantra, or prayer word, has become increasingly familiar. J.D. Salinger even features it in one of his popular stories. The repetition of the mantra is urged as a way of developing concentration, especially in prayer.

The word mantra derives from a root that means "instrument of the mind." It has also been thought of as a craft that enables one to cross the sea of the mind, like those frail catamarans, with two canoe-like hulls joined, that enabled the oriental islanders to ride and explore the vast and tumultuous Pacific Ocean.

The mantra again has been aptly compared to a bamboo baton used by mahouts to control their elephants, which otherwise would be enormously and destructively mischievous passing through towns and bazaars. So also the hungry mind that seeks God finds itself diverted by a universe of seductions.

The mantra has even been advocated as a means of personal transformation. Although no mechanical means or technique can really transform anyone, the mantra used by a religious person can be an efficacious way of developing prayerful attention and concentration.

"There is only one way that leads to God," said St. Teresa of Ávila, "and that is prayer. If anyone shows you another way, he is deceiving you." Even prayer is only a part, but the prow, of the total effort to attain that holiness, to be "like God," which is the goal of the spiritual and Christic life. "One thing I ask of the Lord, this alone do I seek; that I may dwell in the house of the Lord all the days of my life, to behold the beauty of the Lord" (Ps 27:4). Here we may compare the mantra to an archer as he takes aim for his target.

While interior prayer has been widely neglected in our activist Western culture, in favor of getting things done, there is nonetheless a wide and strong current of Christian prayer, which — beginning with Jesus, then absorbing the Old Testament as well as other traditions — still flows tranquilly alongside the modern Babylon, offering serenity and peace to all who allow themselves to be drawn into its living water.

Even the mantra (if by another name) has come down to us, for example, in *The Cloud of Unknowing*, a Christian classic dating from the fourteenth century, written by an unknown Englishman, at once theologian and servant of God. Although he first states, "A naked intent toward God, the desire for God alone, is enough," he goes on: "If you want to gather all your desire into one simple word that the mind can easily retain, choose a short word rather than a long one. A one-syllable word such as 'God' or

'Love' is enough. But choose one that is meaningful to you. Then fix it in your mind that it will remain there."

Then the author adds two images that help to explain: "This word will be your shield and your spear, whether you ride in peace or in conflict." As a shield it will defend you against both seductive and disturbing distractions, as a spear and sword it will enable you to cut through the most absorbing preoccupations. The author also explains the title of his book: "Use it [i.e., the word] to beat on *the cloud of unknowing* [the darkness to reason] above you and to subdue all distractions, consigning them to the *cloud of forgetting* beneath you. If some thought should go on annoying you, answer with this one word alone."

The simplicity of the prayer word becomes a way of fulfilling the Lord's injunction: "Blessed are the single-hearted, for they shall see God."

The images of spear and shield recall preparations urged by St. Paul for spiritual struggle: "In all circumstances hold up faith before you as a shield. Take the helmet of salvation, and the sword of the Spirit, the Word of God" (Eph 6:10-18).

Although the author of *The Cloud of Unknowing* recommends a one-syllable word, because of its simplicity, our Eastern Catholic brethren have adopted the name of Jesus, making it the focus of what they call the "Jesus Prayer."

While there are many frames in which the name of Jesus may be placed, an Eastern monk writes: "The Name of Jesus only is the most ancient mold of the invocation of the Name. It is the shortest, the simplest, and, as we think, the easiest. Therefore, without depreciating the other formulas, we suggest that the word 'Jesus' alone should be used."

We might also add that this Name, while it has two syllables, stresses only one, the other being like a "weak" syllable in poetry. The classic work on this Jesus Prayer is *The Way of a Pilgrim*.

The use of the Holy Name as a prayer is certainly supported by Scripture. "God highly exalted Him and bestowed on Him the name above every other name" (Phil 2:9). Jesus Himself said, "Anything you ask in My Name I will do" (Jn 14:14). "And Jesus also told them a parable, to the effect that they ought always to pray and not lose heart" (Lk 18:1).

There is an even deeper propriety and value in the prayer word — its use is rooted in the Incarnation.

"In the beginning was the Word, and the Word was with God, and the Word was God. . ." (Jn 1:1). "And the Word was made flesh and dwelt among us, full of grace and truth: we have beheld His glory as of the only Son from the Father" (Jn 1:14).

In the Mass we hear, "By the mystery of this water and wine may we come to share in the divinity of Christ who humbled Himself to share in our humanity."

The Word thus made flesh, also comes to us as the revealed Word of Scripture. In the Letter to the Hebrews we watch, as it were, this transition of the spoken Word into the living Word, learning also its power for us: "Indeed, God's word is living and effective, sharper than any two-edged sword. *It* penetrates and divides soul and spirit, joints and marrow, *it* judges the reflections and thoughts of the heart. Nothing is concealed from *Him*; all lies bare and exposed to the eyes of *Him* to whom we must render an account" (Heb 4:12).

In the Word made flesh a fundamental difficulty, even a seeming contradiction, of Christianity is resolved, explaining how human creatures, in bodies of flesh, can nevertheless, in spirit, approach the all-holy and uncreated Spirit of God.

"Jesus is honey on the tongue, melody on the lips, a song of exultation in the heart" (St. Bernard).

The Prayer Word, or Mantra

Distractions in Prayer: A Ladder to God

Distractions need not be an impediment to prayer. They need not even distract. Father Hugo saw even distractions as a way to deeper union with God.

━━━◈━━━

Theology sees in every created good and excellence an analogy or likeness or sample of God Himself. This is the one positive or affirmative way of approaching God and seeing Him as He is. It becomes a means of contemplating God in His boundless perfections, as St. Paul has enjoined us to do (Rom 1:20), and as we ourselves seek to do in prayer. The beauty, the goodness, the truth, every excellence contained in creatures is to be seen infinitely multiplied in the boundless goodness of God. From this point of view, even what otherwise appear to be distractions in prayer may in fact serve our devotion.

For distractions come from preoccupation with some earthly pleasure or delight that absorbs us and draws us away from God. What we can do, instead of fighting such distractions, which often seems useless anyway, is to see them rather as a ladder to God. "If this created pleasure is so absorbing, what would it be like to embrace the Creator and Source of all joy?"

Your Ways Are Not My Ways, vol. II

Resisting Temptations

St. Augustine defined sin as a turning away from God and a turning toward created goods. To resist temptation, Father Hugo showed, is often to reject something good (one of God's creations) for the sake of something even greater (God Himself). To resist temptation is an act of love.

❧❦❧

When we are tempted, a creature, in all its attractiveness, is placed before us, inviting us to choose between itself and the Creator. If we choose God over the creature, we demonstrate and celebrate the triumph of love. Giving in to temptation, on the other hand, means surrendering to the allurements of the creature — the allurements that we have promised in baptism to renounce. And it is at this point that the temptation becomes seduction — not through God but because one is "lured and enticed by his own desire."

In each temptation, God is in effect saying to us, "Which do you prefer — Me or this sample?" By choosing God over the creatures, one makes an act of love, precious even to God.

Your Ways Are Not My Ways, vol. II

How to Discern God's Will

While Father Hugo emphasized the necessity of dedicating time for mental prayer and liturgical prayer, he also outlined a way to discern the will of God in everyday events — to see God's providence in "the sacrament of the present moment."

❧❦❧

Discovering and embracing the will of God are necessary and inevitable steps in loving God. They are at the same time steps in the larger drama of translating into personal action "Thy kingdom come."

"The just shall live by faith" (Gal 3:11). Now it is possible by means of faith to discover God's will, in manifold explicit indications and, further, in all the events of life. Thus we recognize His will and supreme dominion everywhere. Each moment is, as it were, a sacrament — "the sacrament of the present moment" — opening up a vision of the divine will, just as a sacrament contains, under humble material appearances, the power and presence of God.

Complementing our quest for God in prayer, we can attain to continual union with Him by looking to His supreme dominion in all actions and events, seeking His will in whatever occurs. As a child waits eagerly for his father to return home, then runs to welcome him with a kiss, so the child of God seeks in faith the Father's will and joyously embraces it in all that he does.

Jesus Himself gives this lesson in Divine Providence. If God cares for the lilies of the field and the birds of the sky, even for "the grass of the field which today is alive and tomorrow is thrown into the oven," how much more will He watch over those who have faith in Him, even those of "little faith." His concern is like that of a hen "that gathers her brood under her wings" (Mt 23:37). The promise of concern goes to almost ridiculous lengths: "Not a hair of your head will perish!" (Lk 21:18).

However, it is not to be expected that, because God's will is invariably benign, it is always humanly agreeable. If it were so, we would not need His will to be expressed: Our own will and inclination would be sufficiently divine. (Some seem to think that this is actually the way it is.) But doing God's will means "sowing," a dying to self-will, a confidence that God's will alone leads to wisdom and love.

Love is indeed the very heart of Christianity and the center of holiness. All the other virtues are its satellites. Yet we have also seen how obedience is the core of the life and spirituality of Jesus. How is this? Can love and obedience be reconciled? To say the least, obedience is a less gracious virtue than love — in Jesus it was harsh and crucifying. Yet precisely through obedience Jesus brought His will into union with the Father's in supreme love.

"Obedient unto death": He "learned obedience through what He suffered" (Phi 2:8).

"If anyone loves Me, he will keep My word and My Father will love him and We will come to him and make Our home with him" (Jn 14:22-23).

Your Ways Are Not My Ways, vol. II

Make Frequent Confession

Father Hugo believed that Christians should go often to the sacrament of penance — even when they were not required to go, even when they were not in a state of mortal sin. Even those who commit venial sins are sinning against love. Confession, then, becomes a way of growing toward a more healthy love, a genuine spiritual renewal.

≈⚬❀⚬≈

Penance, through which Christ acts upon us to forgive sins committed after baptism, is thus a kind of second baptism, an abiding means of renewing baptismal innocence. While its reception is necessary, strictly speaking, only when the grace of baptism has been lost, it can be received also to renew baptismal innocence continually and fully. So the Church has encouraged frequent confession even among the just. As long as "the just man falls seven times" (Prv 24:16), there is sufficient basis even for *his* reception of the sacrament.

Apart from our sinfulness, there is no need for a Savior and Redeemer. His grace therefore, in the present economy, not only raises us to friendship with God, although this is first and the reason for His coming, but also cures the evil of sin that such intimacy might be possible. "Those who are well have no need of a physician, but those who are sick; I came not to call the righteous, but sinners" (Mk 2:17). The sacrament of penance gives effectiveness to interior repentance and *metanoia* by grafting it into the propitiatory sacrifice of Christ.

If we recognize our sinful state, there is also reason to approach the sacrament of penance as an anticipatory strengthening in our warfare against evil. We speak of preventative medicine for physical ailments. Here, in the sacrament of penance, with its healing grace, is preventative medicine for us as we seek to live according to the Spirit. In the life of the spirit it may also be said that an ounce of prevention is worth a pound of cure. "He who despises trifles will sink down little by little" (Sir 19:1).

Health and Spiritual Renewal

Three Reasons to Go to Confession

Here then are three reasons why even the just may avail themselves profitably of the sacrament of penance: to assist in the struggle against minor or venial falls, to strengthen themselves in advance against temptation, to reduce constantly the residue of past failures and firm up the positive inclinations of virtue.

Of the inspired theologians, St. Paul stressed the healing power of grace: "In Him we have redemption through His blood, the forgiveness of our trespasses, according to the richness of His grace which He has lavished upon us" (Eph 1:7). Yet St. John, while seeing grace as the source of life, also does not neglect this healing power: "Truly, I say to you, he who hears My word and believes Him who sent Me, has eternal life; he does not come into judgment, but has passed from death to life" (Jn 5:24).

Health and Spiritual Renewal

The Place of Spiritual Direction

Father Hugo insisted on the "necessity" of spiritual direction—apart from religious instruction, and apart from any psychological counsel a priest might give. Since everyone is called to perfect holiness, everyone needs an experienced guide to show the way in paths of prayer. Often, this guide will be the individual's confessor.

The sacrament of penance provides us priests an appropriate locale for spiritual direction to those who recognize that the struggle against evil is the underside and reverse of the positive quest for holiness. Indeed, as soon as one accepts one's vocation even to "the summit of perfection" (in Pius XI's phrase), the benefit, not to say the necessity, of spiritual direction becomes evident. No doubt some direction is already given in the confessional, but usually of a rather rudimentary kind, limited largely to counsels for avoiding sin. The pursuit of holiness requires more positive counsel.

While a spiritual director endowed with psychological knowledge is of special value, his real task is not to bring about psychological adjustment or fulfillment, but rather to relate the aspirations of the seeker to God, in whom alone is found fulfillment at the deepest level.

Spiritual direction is likewise not the same as instruction, which is rather related, wherever it is given, to what we have called the theology of the pulpit. Nor need direction be confined to the confessional — lay people and religious may be wise and holy counselors. Nevertheless, the confessional is the natural, and all but inevitable, locale for the intimate self-revelation which effective spiritual direction calls for. Here, too, Christ the Physician extends, through the priest, His healing sacramental hands. And the detached position of the priest is an asset for spiritual direction. Even Teresa sought the collaboration of Friar John.

Still, as we do not consult a physician every week, every confession need not be an occasion for spiritual direction. Instructed Christians, no doubt with counsel, should be able to map out their own daily regimen. At the same time, even advanced theological learning is not sufficient for making practical judgments in one's own case, especially where strong feelings are involved. Physicians, at least in critical cases, do not treat themselves or their own families.

Thomas Merton says that spiritual direction is "a continuous process of formation and guidance, in which a Christian is led and encouraged *in his special vocation,* so that by faithful correspondence to the graces of the Holy Spirit he may attain to the particular end of his vocation and to union with God."

Perhaps a spiritual director can best be described by analogy with a navigator who steers his ship over the vast and trackless and threatening ocean by reference to the pole star. The director's task is to help his penitent discover the will of God, or pole star for guiding us through the varied circumstances, duties (at times conflicting), trials, choices, blinding afflictions, and frequent confusions of daily living.

Such spiritual direction is not restricted to some secret or purely inner and spiritual sphere. It encompasses the whole of Christian life. Although the Christian should live, as Paul says, "according to the Spirit," it is the whole man, the whole person, and the whole of human life, including its most mundane activities, that is to come under the rule of the Spirit: "Whether you eat or drink, or whatever you do, do all to the glory of God" (1 Cor 10:31).

Obviously, therefore, the name "director" is to be understood relatively. The Holy Spirit is Himself the Supreme Director. Any human counselor is of an altogether secondary and instrumental order. Yet even the human guide can be of help to his fellow pilgrim in discerning the ways of God in human surroundings. God's will, although strong and wise, may seem to be elusive amid the contingencies of life.

The human director may thus not impose his own will. It is his task to help the penitent discover God's will guiding in his own unique personal vocation. St. John of the Cross describes as "blacksmiths" those confessors and directors who, contemptuous alike for the ways of God and the interior freedom of men, seek to impose their own narrow formulas of sanctity, like straitjackets, on those who come to them seeking guidance. On the other hand, while spiritual freedom must be respected, it may be on occasion necessary for a director to nerve the penitent to a great effort or supreme sacrifice.

Karl Rahner writes that if we were really to recognize the hazards and obstacles to the Christian vocation, and the possible demand for heroic choices, "then there would be fewer confessors and spiritual advisers who, for fear of telling their penitents how strict is God's law, fail in their duty and tell him instead to follow his conscience, as if he had not asked, and done right to ask, which among all the many voices clamoring within him was the true voice of God."

Health and Spiritual Renewal

What to Look for in a Spiritual Director

Since most moderns are unfamiliar with the practice of spiritual direction, and so wouldn't know where to look for a director, Father Hugo drew up a job description, based on the teachings of St. Teresa of Ávila.

According to St. Teresa, who wrote much on the subject, the two most desirable qualities in a director are learning and experience. Of these she places theological learning first, although evidently experience is necessary for a director who is really to guide rather than merely point.

Perhaps the greatest contribution that a spiritual director can make to his penitents is negative. Since sanctity in practice means discovering God's will through every camouflage of appearances, the great hazard of the Christian life is the constant and irrepressible temptation to do one's own will, to follow one's own natural and personal inclinations, and indeed to mistake and honor these as the will of God. Here precisely is where a spiritual director is most valuable and, perhaps, most necessary: detached, without personal interest in the problem or situation, yet deeply concerned, and (if St. Teresa's standards are met) enlightened and experienced, he will be able to warn the penitent against the vagaries and blind alleys of self-will. Such vital if negative direction is especially necessary at a time when so many people speak glibly of the Holy Spirit, claim to seek His guidance, and invoke His authority for their decisions. Here certainly there is need for the gift which St. Paul calls "the ability to distinguish between spirits" (1 Cor 12:10). The penitent faces in a critically important personal matter the truth enunciated by the prophet, "For My thoughts are not your thoughts, nor are your ways My ways, says the Lord" (Is 55:8). There is also the axiom, "He who judges his own case is judged by a fool."

Health and Spiritual Renewal

How to Find the Best Books

Which spiritual books are reliable? Father Hugo offered some simple criteria, in his last retreat.

❧

Lectio divina can be translated as spiritual reading. But *lectio divina* says more than that. *Lectio divina* recognizes that the direction of prayer is toward God, so it is *divine* reading, *godly* reading, *Godward* reading. Above all, it is the reading of Scripture. It is essential to be familiar with the Word of God, to read it, to ponder it, and to study it. It will be assimilated into our mind and become part of us.

The next step is study — the study of theology, the study of spiritual books. There are many spiritual books. We have, today, almost too many. They are not all equally good. Some of them are not good at all. It is too difficult to make distinctions, we have to be selective and make what distinctions we can.

When I was younger, I received the best advice: that the best spiritual writers are the ones whose names begin with a capital "S."

The saints have made it, and the rest are guessing or talking from the tops of their heads. The most capable are the ones who have taken the road and have arrived.

90

When you read, start at the beginning of the journey, the bottom of the climb.

St. John of the Cross writes about the bottom and the top stages. Many who read him want to start at the top. That would save all the trouble of the climb. But we should start with the first book of St. John of the Cross, *The Ascent of Mount Carmel*.

A very practical book to start with is St. Francis de Sales' *Introduction to the Devout Life*. This is *must* reading for one who is trying to live a spiritual life.

There are different methods of meditation. You will find one in the *Introduction to the Devout Life*. St. Ignatius developed a system of meditation as well. Another comes from what is called the "French School" of spiritual writers.

Retreat Conference, September 1985

What Is Meditation?

When I explain to people what meditation is, I tell about a little incident that happened to me.

I went into a second-grade classroom and talked to the children. They told me who God is and that God made the heavens and the earth. And I asked, "What is the earth?"

One little fellow said with scorn in his eyes, "You're standing on it."

You ask me what meditation is. Well, we've been doing it together here on this retreat. We have been taking God's word and masticating on it. I have been trying to help you assimilate His word so that it will become a part of your spiritual substance and you will live with Him always.

This is meditation.

Retreat Conference, September 1985

Breath of Prayer, Touch of God

There comes a time when meditation as such ends. It tends to become simplified.

We talked about Mary (the sister of Martha). What was she listening to? She was listening to God's word. She was not laboring in any way with her mind, but simply drinking it in. So we can speak of a prayer of listening.

Prayer should become more and more affective. Our affections come from our desire. Through knowing God and His goodness, we desire God. These affections express our desires for God. We can speak of a prayer of desire. When our desires are set on God, when they reach out for God, they are eager for God, we are praying already.

"One thing I ask. This alone I seek: to dwell in the house of the Lord all the days of my life."

Or we can think of prayer as a simple gaze. Some writers call this the "prayer of simple regard." The Curé of Ars, St. John Vianney, used to go to his parish church and he would always see there an old peasant man rapt in prayer. So one day he said to him, "What do you do? How do you pray?"

Well," said the peasant, "I look at Him and He looks at me."

Those of you who went to parochial school were taught by the sisters to use aspirations as prayers. They were affective prayers — more emotion than thought. Maybe at that stage they were too much emotion. You hadn't been converted to prayer yet. You really hadn't deepened your religious knowledge. But they help.

Now we need to fall back on those affective prayers. The psalms give us that: "Out of the depths I cry to You, O Lord, Lord, hear my voice." Isn't that affective? When you can realize you are in the depths and cry out to God like the psalmist, then that is really the touch of God, and He is there.

Retreat Conference, September 1985

IV
Believing in the Church:
Discipleship in Time of Division

The Spiritual Condition of Our People

Father Hugo did not write or speak much on the internal workings of the Catholic Church. His writings on ecclesiastical matters focus more on prayer and conversion than they do on intramural debates over Church teachings or discipline. When he did address Church affairs, it was usually to criticize individual Catholics — clergy and laity — for failing to live up to their Christian obligations to strive for holiness and to preach conversion and salvation through Jesus Christ.

These texts show Father Hugo's concern for the spiritual flabbiness that had developed in the American Church around the middle years of this century. Although he raises issues that are still contested, his criticism is free from the various species of nostalgia, apocalypticism, and progressive triumphalism that mar many of today's debates: Father Hugo does not wish to harken back to some supposed golden age of discipline and devotion in the Church. Neither does he feel that the age of the anti-Christ is drawing near. Nor does he believe that the Church is a medieval and antiquated institution in need of reforms that will make her more acceptable to current trends and prejudices.

As Father Hugo sees it, faith in God and the supernatural has been eclipsed in the Church by an overemphasis on material matters, a merely practical and utilitarian approach to the faith. He decries the widespread religious illiteracy among American Catholics, and castigates Church leaders for not having taught people about their faith or their heritage. The end result, he complains, is a Catholic faithful — clergy, lay, and religious — that is ill-equipped to combat the powerful forces of secularism and materialism that hold sway in the modern world.

⁂

The need of genuine supernatural teaching and authentic spirituality is clear from the Scriptures. But its need is also shown by the actual spiritual condition of our people. It is customary for some to take a rosy view of that condition, basing their optimism on tables of statistics concerning the growth of the Catholic population, the income and resources of the Church,

93

the number of communions, etc. But such a method of computation is very unreliable where spiritual realities are concerned: were it of any value, we could compute the degree of religious fervor from the quantities of grease burnt in votive stands, and our optimism would soar to the very skies.

It is quite by other standards that we must judge the spiritual condition of our people — by their pursuit of holiness, their spirit of poverty and detachment, their practice of mortification, their love of prayer, their generosity to the poor, their readiness of outlook, deliberate simplicity of life in imitation of Nazareth, their steadfastness in meditating on the Scriptures — in a word, by their devotion to an interior life.

The measure of the success of a priest is his ability to convert souls to such a life. The spiritual health of a parish is to be judged by the number of people who lead it, as also by the ardor and perseverance with which they continue in it. No other standard is of any value. The purpose of Christianity is to unite souls to God; and the success with which it is preached and accomplished can therefore be judged by one norm alone, that is, conformity to evangelic standards of conduct.

Rarely do we find souls in our parishes devoted to an interior, supernatural life. A few *devotuli* in each parish, a mere handful. Nor can it be said that even all of these are living a real interior life. They are perhaps sincere enough. But want of instruction and spiritual direction leave many of them ever at the beginning, permanently retarded by the most elementary attachments. How truly did Pope Pius XI write in *Ubi arcano Dei consilio* that "the habit of life which can be called really Christian has in great measure disappeared."

Indeed, even optimists are not without a secret uneasiness. They talk constantly about "Catholic leakage," as though our spiritual failure were to be hidden by giving it a technical name and treating it as the subject of a mere sociological survey. Now the reason for "Catholic leakage" is not far to seek. Statistical charts are unnecessary. St. Paul explained the matter long ago: "Their end is ruin, their God is the belly, their glory is in their shame, they mind the things of the earth" (Phil 3:19).

Our people are simply sunk in naturalism — in paganism, to give the modern trend its more concrete and popular name. This is why there can be so much external devotion to religious practice, but so little fervor.

Even in the case of those who are wholly faithful to the external obligations of religion, there is often little evidence, aside from their devotions, that they are living Christian lives. Large areas of their lives are wholly unilluminated by their faith. Their ideas, their attitudes, their views on current affairs, their pleasure and recreations, their tastes in reading and entertainment, their love of luxury, comfort, and bodily ease, their devotion to success, their desire of money, their social snobbishness, racial consciousness, nationalistic narrowness and prejudice, their bourgeois complacency and contempt of the poor. In all these things they are indistinguishable from the huge sickly mass of paganism which surrounds them.

Why is it that so many Catholics abandon their faith upon marriage? Certainly it is worldliness: their love of the world overcomes whatever love they have for God. They weigh in the balance, on the one hand, the advantages of serving God, and on the other, the worldly advantages to be gained by the marriage — leisure, companionship, satisfied vanity, worldly position, wealth, advantageous connections — and they abandon God.

Or again, it is obvious that the sin of birth control is making headway among Catholics. Not only do the statistics published by birth control clinics show this, but also the fact that a large number are loud and perfectly candid in their defense of birth control, contemptuous and disbelieving in regard to the laws of the Church on this matter, saying that it is none of the Church's business.

And what is the reason for such an attitude? Economic pressure is alleged. This may be at least the occasion for sin among poor families, hence the just indignation of men against those priests who thunder against birth control while being themselves very comfortable in the social conditions that make birth control appear to many as a necessity.

Economic pressure however does not explain the prevalence of this sin among the prosperous — worldliness does. Those who commit it balance the law of God over against the advantages to be gained through birth control — unrestrained pleasure, physical beauty, leisure, freedom from the responsibility of a family, the opportunity to use all one's income on luxuries, and the satisfaction of earthly ambitions.

For the vast majority of our Catholic people it is possible to combine with a blameless *notional* or speculative assent to the chief mysteries of the faith a multitude of diminutions and evasions in the practical mind. And the *practical* attitudes and maxims of action of most Catholics today can scarcely be thought to originate in Christianity at all. They come rather from the sub-pagan mentality of the popular press, the moving pictures, radio and stage entertainers, the hedonism and hypersexuality of the whole modern outlook.

A Sign of Contradiction

Practical Priests

Father Hugo loved his vocation of serving "in the person of Christ"
in the solemn offering of Mass and in guiding people in the ways of holi-

95

ness and salvation. *If there is irony or bitterness in the following commentaries, it is because he mourned the loss of apostolic zeal in so many of his priestly brothers.*

⚜

The chief concern of the priesthood, of the *practical* priesthood, is to "keep things going." The "things" here referred to are the material elements of the Church. For this, money is necessary. And so the young priest is taught to raise money, and he soon learns that his value to a parish and his status among his fellow priests, as also among the better fed section of his parishioners, rests on his ability to learn this great art.

And now he learns: the "envelope system," card parties, dances, bazaars, bingos, prizefights, raffles and in short every variety of easy-money device. These activities are promoted from the pulpit, originally intended for teaching the word of God; while the word of God is shortened or omitted, so that adequate attention can be given to the *one thing necessary* — money.

Here he is, the artificer of souls, the craftsman who alone can fashion the most precious of all works — here he is among his account books, his index cards, his money boxes, his raffle wheels, his gambling supplies. This mixture of penury, charlantry, and cunning is now euphemized as "pastoral theology." And in it many priests spend their whole lives. Meanwhile what happens to the souls?

A Sign of Contradiction

Bad Homilies

The clergy's preoccupation with the material interests of the Church is only one side of the picture. There is another, less pleasing still. As a man in giving his affections to the world withdraws them from God, so also a priest, in giving his attention preponderantly to material affairs, withdraws his attention from his spiritual duties. A priest's concern for temporal matters is simply the accompaniment and reverse side of his neglect of the positive duties of the priesthood.

And of the various duties of the priest which are neglected, I wish to draw attention here especially to the duty of preaching. It is through neglect of this duty especially that so much harm comes to our people.

I do not wish to argue here which of a priest's duties is the most important. There will be some to say perhaps that his liturgical functions as mediator, as one charged to offer sacrifice, or as minister of the sacraments, is most important. Let those who wish, argue which of these duties, all of them lofty beyond description, is more important metaphysically or absolutely speaking.

It is at least apparent that they are not opposed to one another, that they in fact complement one another, and consequently all are neglected when priests are concerned with secular affairs. Priests who have no taste for preaching are not likely to have much zeal for administering the sacraments or much love for the liturgy. Accordingly, our people today, besides being denied the benefit of preaching, also live an impoverished liturgical life.

It would indeed be one of the functions of preaching to teach them of the liturgical life. As it is, they know but few of the Church's ceremonies; they often see these carried out in a hurried or slovenly fashion by men whose chief anxiety seems to be to get finished, and they do not understand, or understand but imperfectly, what they do see. Priests nowadays have no time for such matters: they are occupied with "more important" affairs.

Mark too that bringing a rich liturgical life to our people would mean far more than technical precision in observing rubrics. It would call for thought, study, care, patient instruction. And it would require a genuine spiritual life on the part of the priest and, in some measure, on the part of the people. For the liturgy is the expression of the Church's deep spiritual life and her means of communicating it to the faithful. We can enter into it and understand it only in the degree in which we ourselves are living such a life.

But whatever the respective importance of these several duties, there is a sense in which preaching is first: it is first in time and first psychologically. This is brought home to us even in the sacrifice of the Mass. Instruction forms part of the Mass — the first part, the preparatory part, before the coming of Jesus. St. Gregory explains this as follows:

> And with good reason it is said (Lk 10:1) that He sent them two and two before His face into every city whither He Himself was to come. The Lord follows His preachers; for preaching comes first, and when the words of exhortation have preceded, and the intellect has been enlightened by the truth, Our Lord comes to take up His abode in our minds. For this reason Isaiah says to preachers: "Prepare ye the way of the Lord, make straight His paths."

St. Paul *preached* wherever he went. In his epistles he shows how he had everywhere preached the Gospel. That was his special work. He reminds the Corinthians how he had not even baptized them (1 Cor 1:14). And he presses on those who were to continue his work the need of doing as he had done: "I charge thee, in the sight of God and Christ Jesus, who will judge the living and the dead by His coming and His kingdom, preach the word, be instant in season, out of season" (2 Tm 4:1).

In another forceful passage he drives home the absolute necessity of preaching, and at the same time explains why so many Catholics are in the frightful spiritual condition that I have been describing: "How then are they to call upon Him in whom they have not believed? But how are they to believe Him of whom they have not heard? And how are they to hear, if no one preaches? And how are they to preach unless they be sent?" (Rom 10:14-15)

As to how a priest may most profitably spend his time, St. Paul gives his thought beautifully, revealing both the mind of Christ and the mind of the Church: "Reading, preaching, instruction, let these be thy constant care" (cf. 1 Tm 4:13-16).

Some will simply deny this neglect of preaching. There are few churches, they will say, in which there are not at least short sermons or homilies every Sunday. And short sermons, they will go on, are, after all, the best: witness the excellent saying that, after the first ten minutes, a sermon is of profit to none except the devil.

For my part, I believe that the devil may himself be responsible for that saying; at least he would be vitally interested in its spread. The supreme value we put upon the short sermon is an utter absurdity. What teacher would be satisfied with one ten-minute class each week? Or, supposing he were forced to accept such a limitation of time, what progress would he make in imparting his subject matter? Or his pupils in mastering it? Not much, certainly. Yet that is the amount of instruction we give our people. Is it any wonder they are religiously illiterate? That they know scarcely anything about even the externals of their religion?

Remember the words of the Apostles. They withdrew themselves from secular affairs not only to give themselves up to the ministry of the word, but first to prayer and then to the ministry of the word. These two things go together — prayer and the ministry of the word, and the latter must proceed from the former as from a source: *aliis tradere contemplata (to pass on the fruits of contemplation)* is the formula given by St. Thomas for preaching.

Furthermore, under prayer we must include all that the ancients meant by *lectio divina: lectio, oratio, meditatio, contemplatio (reading, prayer, meditation, and contemplation).* The life of a priest should be a life filled with such prayer, which is the pursuit of sacred science, meditation, contemplation.

But a priest who would give himself to such matters today would be considered a misfit, not adapted to parish life. He must, according to contemporary standards, be a good fellow, a money-getter, a kind of ring-master for all the social and recreational activities in the parish or the town. But a priest's house should be a house of silence and prayer, not a noisy business office filled with all sorts of odds and ends.

The Scriptures tell us what preaching should be for us when it calls the Word of God the "sword of the Spirit" (Eph 6:17). Preaching is our sword; it is to us what the sword was to soldiers of old: our offensive weapon, our way of forging ahead, of gaining new ground, of cutting down opposition.

In preaching, we are John the Baptists — forerunners, pushing ahead in order to make straight the path of the Lord, opening a way for the coming of Jesus into hearts. Our other duties are largely conservative. But with the sword of the Spirit, we can destroy error, misunderstanding, heresy, the maxims and mentality of the world, the paganism of the natural man, which so strenuously opposes step by step the advance of the New Man (Eph 4:24, 2 Cor 5:17). But without preaching the word of God, we are helpless; like a soldier who has thrown away his sword.

And since we have thrown it away, we do not realize its power. We do not understand, we scarcely believe in the power we might wield. We are not accustomed to see any results come of our preaching — we have not seen any souls converted, any lives transformed, any worldlings changed into pursuers of holiness as a result of our words. We regard preaching as a sort of routine, a mere form, a part of the liturgical ceremony, a devout practice, but having no real effect.

These evils are self-perpetuating. As in times of war, one generation goes off to do the fighting while the younger generation is mentally conditioned for the next war, so here the conditions created or accepted by one generation of priests are gradually imposed upon the next generation. That is why these abuses go on unchallenged, uncorrected, uncriticized, and even unsuspected, so that at length they are taken for normal and proper, while anyone who protests against them is an eccentric or a fool, a fanatic or a madman.

A Sign of Contradiction

The Scandal of Bingo

This selection, an edited transcription from a 1979 radio talk show in Pittsburgh, is a rare example of Father Hugo "doing" theology in the marketplace. Fielding skeptical questions from a provocative host and listeners in the radio audience, Father Hugo demonstrates a methodical and engaging debating style, and makes a compelling case against gaming in the Church and in American society.

KDKA-AM Host, John Cigna: Why are you opposed to bingo as a means of getting money for the workings of the Church?

Father Hugo: Now, like you, I'm opposed to them because they're illegal. But that is not the paramount reason why I am opposed. Although I believe it is a good thing for the civil law to protect moral values, and in fact that is part of the art of government — to promote good, to help people do good. And I don't think that in any way promoting gambling does this. So I'm for that and I'm glad that the civil law protects the moral values involved in nongambling. But my reasons are rather spiritual or theological. I just think it is an unworthy way for the Church to raise money. It is contrary to our faith.

Cigna: Contrary in what way?

Father Hugo: The first reason is a standard ethical one — that gambling is opposed to human reason because it rewards chance, not merit or labor. Therefore it is unreasonable. Reasonable beings wouldn't do that. We're placing our hopes on chance.

Cigna: You say it's unreasonable, but I'm wondering about the legalized operation of the Pennsylvania Lottery. It's certainly unreasonable, as you say, to try to get money from chance, which the lottery is. But the money going into that lottery certainly helps a lot of elderly in the state of Pennsylvania. . . .

Father Hugo: But I don't think that having a good purpose makes it good. I'm opposed to the lottery, too. It is an unworthy way for the state to raise money for the elderly, although I think we should find some other way to raise money for the elderly.

The state is working counter-productively against its own citizens when it promotes lotteries. This increases the selfishness of people and increases this gambling passion and all that goes with it. Gambling is a corrupting influence — it causes addiction, it ruins character, it ruins families, it destroys marriages, and therefore it is an evil influence in society. It causes a compulsion. We have an institution now in this country called "Gamblers Anonymous," which is a public confession of the harm that gambling is doing everywhere. It's got ahold of people and they can't control it anymore.

Also, it kills Christians' motivation. Our churches and our schools should be built out of faith and out of love. . . .

Cigna: In other words, the parishioners should be supporting that church through their contributions to that church.

Father Hugo: Through their contributions and through their faith and through their love. And if we don't have faith and we don't have love of

God and love of our fellows, then we don't really deserve the churches. This should be the compelling reason to do it. And this is why they were built, I think, before there were ever bingos.

For us as Catholics and as Christians, bingo is a loss of nerve. We don't have the faith that moves mountains. In other words, if we have faith in God and faith in our fellows, too, why, I think that we would be able to take care of our needs. St. Paul tells us that we are to live by faith, faith that works by love. And if we have faith in God's generosity, His abundance and in our people to give, then we would be able to support it.

There is a story in the Bible where Christ was walking on the water and St. Peter asked the Lord if he could walk to Him. And the Lord said, "Yes. Come." And St. Peter stepped out on this wave, you know, just like they were on dry land — firm and strong and deliberate. Then, all of a sudden, he lost his nerve. He saw the waves batting up around him, you see, and he sank. Now that's what I mean by a loss of nerve. I know that there are great practical difficulties. But as Christians we ought to be operating in the area of faith, faith in God.

Cigna: As you mentioned before, I'm against bingo because it happens to be illegal. I don't know if it is a bad thing spiritually. But parishioners have stopped giving to the churches and the churches had to find another way to get money to keep the schools open and they had to find another way to keep their parish afloat. And bingo is the way they've gone. Now is it better to go that way or just let the parish go downhill?

Father Hugo: Oh no, I wouldn't let the parish go downhill. I think we ought to evangelize, to teach the Gospel — to teach these spiritual values and the priority of spiritual values. If I spend time talking about bingo on Sunday, I'm not teaching them the truths of the Gospel. And if I run bingos, I am killing Christian motivation, and if I teach people to do good because there's some material gain possible in it, this isn't Christianity.

Listener Call-in: All the other churches tithe. Look at the Mormons, they pay so much of their salary to the church. And the Roman Catholics don't do that. So the churches are forced to go the way of the bingos and the bazaars and everything else to raise the money.

Cigna: That's a good point, Father. If you ask somebody to give one percent or ten percent of their salary to the church and they refuse to, you can't excommunicate them, or say you can't come to my church any more. So the church has run into that problem and the way to solve it , they figure, is bingo. Now, I know you're going to come back with the spirituality of it and the moralistic approach. But still, what other way is there to go for the church?

Father Hugo: Well, you don't need another way. My own experience tells me that that works. But you have to work at it. You do have to give the spirituality, to give the motivation to people. There are many priests who do this in their parishes and they believe in it and it works. This is where I say we have to walk on the water, we have to believe that it works. That if we appeal to people on high motives, motives of love and the glory of God, they will respond. My people love this way of giving money to the church, but I think it's up to the priest to lead them.

Listener Call-in: Let the bingo players have their bingo! A lot of those people really enjoy it. . .

Father Hugo: Well, I'm sure people enjoy it. But we don't bring them to church for their enjoyment, we bring them to church to worship God and to help others, to serve others. We're not entertainers in church.

Anyway, bingo is a failure as a social means in parishes. Any kind of gambling is unsocial. I would like to read a little thing that I brought here in preparation. It was written by a saint, who was also a bishop, who was attacking gambling for Christians. And he speaks on this very point, on the social aspect of it.

He says, "Can there be any attention more painful, more gloomy, more melancholy than that of gamblers?" Did you ever go to a bingo game as I have as a priest, and walk into a parish hall and try to socialize with people? You get turned off, they don't want to talk to you. . . .

Cigna: They don't want to talk to you, they're watching 25 cards. . .

Father Hugo: That's right, they're watching 25 cards and jumping from one to another. They're not there to socialize with anybody — the pope, as much as a pastor.

This saint continues, saying, "You can neither speak, nor laugh, nor cough for fear of giving offense. In fact, there is no joy at play but when you win." That's the only joy they're going to get. And then he adds, like a good Christian and as a saint, "And is that joy not iniquitous that cannot be felt but by the loss or the displeasure of a friend or a companion?" The only joy you have comes at a cost to somebody else.

And this saint and bishop of the Church, St. Francis de Sales, says, "Surely, such satisfaction is infamous." And that's what I believe — there is no joy in it, there is no satisfaction in it.

Cigna: I wonder how many would come if you said, "Let's have a tea." You would have four times as many, Father, if you have a bingo.

Father Hugo: But you wouldn't have the same results. Spiritually, I wouldn't have the same satisfaction of people who were giving for the love of God and the same benefit as these people who were giving for the love of God. And I think that's what we in the Church should be thinking of — the benefit to the people, as well as the buildings and the money.

Listener Call-in: Father, you say you've been a pastor, could you please tell me, how you raised money and how much you raised without gambling?

Father Hugo: My first pastorate, I was appointed to found a new parish. We didn't have anything. We started from scratch. We had 500, 600 families. We spent about $2.5 million in the 10 years I was there. Now, I didn't pay off all of that debt. I had to leave my successor with part of that debt. But we paid our part and we ran a school at the same time and we paid our bills. And the people were happy with that way of raising money. So it does work, it works in practice.

You know the first sermon ever preached on money-raising was in St. Paul's second letter to the Corinthians. Paul was the first one. St. Paul was sent out on his mission with the instruction from Jerusalem that he was to raise money for the poor of the church of Jerusalem. And wherever he went he took up a collection and he raised money.

Cigna: Father, are you being realistic about today? Now you can talk about the Scriptures and how they raised money the first time, but are you really being realistic about today's world, with the inflation, with how tough it is to raise a family, with payments of automobile and everything else? People really can't afford what they would like to give to the church and they welcome a bingo because it helps them get out of that bind. Even the state lottery, how could the elderly get what they need aside from raising taxes — here again putting another burden on the people — were it not for the lottery? I'm just wondering, Father, would it be accomplished without the gambling and the bingos?

Father Hugo: I think it could be. You see, we sell short the generosity of people and their concern, if we don't appeal to the motive of love. Listen, was Christ practical? I think He was super-practical. I think Christianity is practical, yes. But you have to live it. You have to believe in it.

Cigna: Well, then my next question would be: How many live it? How many true Christians are in this world?

Father Hugo: Well I don't know. I wouldn't even attempt to answer that. I think it's the duty of those of us who are Christians to try to be good Christians and to try to be constantly better. . . .

Cigna: I know that, and it's great theory, but. . . .

Father Hugo: That's not theory! That's the purpose of the Church! You didn't let me finish telling you about the fundraising plan of St. Paul. Well, St. Paul gives this sermon and he never uses the word money, he was very diplomatic, he uses words like "offering" and he gives us that little saying, "God loves a cheerful giver." He talks about the superabundant generosity of God. Then he appeals to the generosity of his hearers. And here's the way he does it: He tells them what I guess even city folk know, about sowing seed — that the farmer sows seeds, in order to reap. St. Paul was a city man himself. But he knew this. He says, "If you sow sparingly you will reap sparingly. If you sow abundantly you will reap abundantly."

In other words, we should deal with money as a farmer deals with seed — you sow it, you give it away. And the more you sow, the more you reap. The less you sow, the less you reap. If the farmer wants a big crop, he sows a lot of seed.

Cigna: Yes, Father, but how do we do that? How do we get back to that kind of thinking, that kind of giving?

Father Hugo: Through the Gospel. Through teaching and living the Gospel of Jesus Christ, that's how we get back to that kind of living. That's where we priests have to find it, that's where we have to get the source of it to teach it and that's where Christians and Catholics have it. It would really change the world. . . .

Listener Call-in: If the people won't support a church, they don't deserve a church, the faith isn't alive. Why don't we just close it down if they won't support it freely. It's a weeding out. . . .

Father Hugo: Well perhaps this is what's happening to some extent today. I don't favor closing the churches. We ought to keep the churches open and preach the Gospel in the churches. If they accept it, if they have the faith, then they'll want to build their churches.

If you go up to a place like French Canada, up along the St. Lawrence River, in these little towns, the biggest building in every town is the church. They're poor farmers but they built their churches and it's the center of their lives. I don't think they knew about bingo up there. I don't think they had been taught that by the Americans yet.

KDKA-AM Pittsburgh, date uncertain, 1979

Pharisees — Cause of All Conflict in the Church

The next several selections show Father Hugo parsing the internal problems of teaching, discipline, and authority in the Church today. At their root he finds, following Cardinal John Henry Newman, a "pharisaism," a tendency on the part of many Catholics, including people in Church leadership positions, to diminish Christ, to reduce the demands of His Gospel to their own limitations and the weaknesses of the human condition.

Why is there so much controversy and conflict among Christian people and within the clergy? Why so much quarreling about piety? Why these divisions in the Church? Shouldn't agitators quit rocking the boat? Or accept correction? Can the "experts" and those in authority go wrong?

Conflict, alas, is an inevitable part of life in this vale of tears. Even the Christian religion, which alone can ultimately resolve divisions and bring about genuine reconciliation, begins by introducing conflict. Said Jesus, "Do not think that I have come to bring peace on earth; I have not come to bring peace, but a sword!" (Mt 10:34).

Resistance to God is the original sin, the source of all other sins, and the beginning of that conflict between the godly and the ungodly, between what the Scriptures call light and darkness, between what St. Augustine will call the city of God, pivoting around the love of God, and the human city, which centers in the self-love of humans. The conflict existed among the Jews in Christ's time, and He entered the world to resolve it. "He came to His own, His own home, and His own people received Him not" (Jn 1:11).

What was particularly scandalous here, and yet typical of all peoples, and within the Church, is that the religious leaders themselves, with few exceptions, entered the struggle against God and His Son. His enemies were the *Pharisees,* paragons of the currently accepted human virtues and the *Sadducees*, that is, the priests — worldly, comfortable, and corrupt. His enemies included also the *scribes* or scholars and *the lawyers*, experts in divine law reduced to externals and human proportion.

All these reduced God to puny human stature to make Him available to satisfy human needs, rather than stretching humans to reach up and meet the demands of the all-holy God. All these Jesus condemned. For example, "Woe to you lawyers! for you have taken away the key of knowledge; you did not enter yourselves, and you hindered those who were entering" (Lk 11:52).

Cardinal John Henry Newman, one of the great religious spirits of modern times, sees the stricture as generally applicable to all humans. This he does in a sermon on the parable of the Pharisee and the publican praying in the temple, a sermon whose very title, "The Religion of the Pharisee, the Religion of Mankind," reveals its gist and universal application:

> I am well aware that the theology of this age is very different from what it was two thousand years ago. I know men profess a great deal, and boast that they are Christians, and speak of Christianity as being a religion of the heart.
>
> But, when we put aside words and professions, and try to discover what their religion is, we shall find, I fear, that the great

mass of men in fact get rid of all religion that is inward; that they lay no stress on acts of faith, hope and charity, on simplicity of intention, purity of motive, or mortification of the thoughts; that they confine themselves to two or three virtues, superficially practiced; that they know not the words contrition, penance, and pardon; and that they think and argue that, after all, if a man does his duty in the world, according to his vocation, he cannot fail to go to heaven, however little he may do besides, nay, however much, in other matters, he may do that is undeniably unlawful.

Thus a soldier's duty is loyalty, obedience, and valor, and he may let other matters take their chance; a trader's duty is honesty; an artisan's duty is industry and contentment; of a gentleman are required veracity, courteousness, and self-respect; of a public man, high-principled ambition; of a woman, the domestic virtues; of a minister of religion, decorum, benevolence, and some activity.

Now, all these are *instances of mere pharisaical excellence;* because there is no apprehension of Almighty God, no insight into His claims on us, no sense of the creature's shortcomings, no self-condemnation, confession, and deprecation, nothing of these deep and sacred feelings which ever characterize the religion of a Christian, and more and more, not less and less, as he mounts up from mere ordinary obedience to the perfection of a saint.

And such, I say, is *the religion of the natural man* in every age and place — often very beautiful on the surface, but worthless in God's sight; good as far it goes, but worthless and hopeless, because it does not go further, because it is based on self-sufficiency, and results in self-satisfaction. I grant, it may be beautiful to look at, as in the instance of the young ruler whom our Lord looked at and loved, yet sent away sad. It may have all the delicacy, the amiableness, the tenderness, the religious sentiment, the kindness, which is actually seen in many a father of a family, many a mother, many a daughter, in the length and breadth of these kingdoms, in a refined and polished age like this.

But still it is rejected by the heart-searching God, because all such persons walk by their own light, not by the True Light of men, because self is their supreme teacher, and because they pace round and round in the small circle of their own thoughts and their own judgments, careless to know what God says to them, and fearless of being condemned by Him, if only they stand approved in their own sight.

And thus they incur the force of those terrible words, spoken not to a Jewish ruler nor to a heathen philosopher, but to a fallen Christian community, to the *Christian Pharisees* of Laodicea — "Because thou sayest I am rich, and made wealthy and have need of nothing; and knowest not that thou art wretched, and miserable, and poor, and blind, and naked; I counsel thee to buy of Me gold fire-tried, that thou mayest be made rich, and clothed in white garments, that thy shame may not appear, and anoint thine eyes with eye-salve, that thou mayest see. Such as I love, I rebuke and chastise; be zealous, therefore, and do penance" (Rev 3:17-19).

Accordingly, although "pharisaism" has its varieties of place and time, of which the Pharisees of Scripture exhibit but one, it can always be broken down into the same components — externalism; rationalism; hence reductionism, that is, accommodation of the divine perfection to a shrunken human stature; a human imposture of divine holiness, the supposed "justice of the Pharisees"; and finally and simply, a regression to paganism.

In giving us the phrase "Christian pharisaism," Newman unveils pharisaism as "the religion of the natural man in every age and place." Moreover, his description of the pharisaic "ministers of religion" brings us to the very center of the present discussion, the responsibility of the clergy.

Omne malum a clero, "all evil comes from the clergy," which Jacques Maritain transposed, "a fish rots from the head." The virtues of clergy, ironically enumerated by Newman, a mere counterfeit of holiness — "decorum, benevolence, and some activity," does indeed seem less than adequate for those who like to think of themselves as sharing the priesthood of Christ, committed to loving God with the whole heart, and commissioned to bring the Gospel to every creature.

What is described here, indeed, to cite Newman's phrase again, is not true Christianity but "the religion of the natural man" or "pious naturalism," which Father Frederick William Faber, a disciple of Newman, described unforgettably as "a supernatural formalism outside, perfectly natural principles of action inside, and a quackery of spiritual direction to keep everything safe and comfortable."

Saint Paul speaking of some Jewish converts to Christianity, and thus covering both milieus, writes: "For many, of whom I have told you often, and now tell you even with tears, live as enemies of the cross of Christ. Their end is destruction, their god is their belly and they glory in their shame, with minds set on earthly things" (Phil 3:18).

Jesus Himself reveals the two contrasting varieties of holiness when, admitting some kind of justice in the Pharisees, He nevertheless reveals its inadequacy for the kingdom of heaven: "For I tell you unless your righteousness exceeds that of the scribes and Pharisees, you will never enter the kingdom of heaven" (Mt 5:20).

Your Ways Are Not My Ways, vol. I

'Why Does the Truth Call Forth Hatred?'

Some cannot understand why it is that preaching Christ and His Gospel should cause division, conflict, or contradiction. From the very beginning He was marked to be a sign of contradiction, and in fact we find that He was followed by two kinds of people — those who loved Him and those who hated Him. They could not remain merely indifferent to Him.

You recall how His very first appearance in the world as an infant was an occasion for slaughter; how later, the first time that He announced His mission, His fellow Nazarenes tried to kill Him: not merely to ridicule Him, not merely to walk no more with Him, but to kill Him. And finally, those whom He came to save, did kill Him.

Here is something about Jesus that we find hard to understand: that many hated Him, pursued Him constantly with objections and calumnies, were tireless in their efforts to trip Him up in His speech, plotted against Him, and finally, could not satisfy their fury until they had destroyed Him.

We regard Christ as a purely benevolent figure; and how could one of such benevolence excite hatred? Accordingly, a great many people today, even among Christians, are indifferent to Jesus. The reason for this is that we have substituted a false picture, a caricature, for the real Jesus.

You have seen this falsified picture of Jesus often: pale, eyes perpetually raised to heaven, soft, even girlish in beauty, a very incarnation of impotence. It is the picture that is found in almost all popular religious art. It looks at you from holy cards, in particular from so many representations of the Sacred Heart; it is the image that the moving pictures delight in and are only too willing to feature.

It is a falsification and doubtless it has been perpetuated by His enemies and pretended friends. And they have been able to achieve it by misunderstanding His meekness and gentleness, concentrating on His benignity, which they misinterpret as being that of the world — a mere soft, flabby kindness — and simply cutting out or refusing to acknowledge certain other traits of His character that do not fit into this picture.

Jesus did not hesitate to condemn the rich, to warn the powerful, to denounce in vehement language the very leaders of the people. His love and goodness were chiefly for the poor, the simple, the needy. And His love for them was not a limp, indulgent love, like that of a silly, frivolous mother. To His friends He preached poverty of spirit, detachment, the carrying of the cross. No more did the kindness of Jesus spare His followers than the kindness of God the Father spared His own Son. We are to drink of the chalice that He drank of.

The false portrayal of Jesus is not merely a defective convention of art. Out of the heart the mouth speaketh. Such a picture, both in the creator and the admirer, comes from a false conception of Christ Himself, a false idea of His teaching, a false view of the Christian life. It expresses and fosters a type of devotion that is flaccid, sentimental, and worthless.

If in actual life we should come into contact with men resembling the ordinary popular portraits of Jesus, we would treat them with contempt or pity. Even in popular actors a virile appearance and the suggestion of strength is expected. Yet most portraits of Jesus lack these qualities, even these natural virtues.

How then can we have a true admiration for such a portrait of Him? Devotion to the Sacred Heart, for example, is an invitation to total love of Jesus, to consecration and reparation. True love is no easy thing: and the love that Jesus wants is *love strong as death*. Are our popular representations of the Sacred Heart, which every one pronounces "nice" or "pretty" — a feeble, languid figure with a pretty girlish face to which the attached beard is scarcely appropriate — are these representations capable of suggesting such thoughts?

It was inherent in the very nature of the world and the mission of Jesus, sent to raise reluctant human nature to the level of the divine, that a deadly endless conflict should exist between Him and the world. The world He regarded as His enemy, and its prince, He said, is the devil. He did not even include the world in his prayer to His Father: "Not for the world do I pray" (Jn 17:9).

This conflict, and its culmination in the crucifixion, was so rooted in the nature of things as they are, that Simeon had predicted it at the Presentation: "Behold, this Child is destined for the fall and for the rise of many in Israel, and for a sign that shall be contradicted" (Lk 2:34).

And as this conflict and contradiction was foreseen and predicted in the case of Jesus Himself, so He in turn foretold that His disciples would be caught up in the same dread warfare with "the spirit of evil in the high places" (Eph 6:12).

To them, therefore, He said: "If the world hates you, know that it has hated Me before you. If you were of the world, the world would love its own. But because you are not of the world, but I have chosen you out of the

109

world, therefore the world hates you. Remember the word that I have spoken unto you: No servant is greater than his master. If they have persecuted Me, they will persecute you also" (Jn 15: 18-20).

These words, if specially applicable to the Apostles — and their successors — refer also to all Christians, as St. Paul in his turn affirms: "All who live godly in Christ Jesus shall suffer persecution" (2 Tm 3:12).

Wherever Jesus is truly presented and rightly known, no one will be indifferent to Him: men will either love Him or hate Him: whether in Himself or borne about by His Apostles. He is forever a sign of contradiction, set for the fall of some and for the rise of others, the object either of ardent love or furious hatred. Wherever preaching does not produce this twofold result, it cannot be Jesus Christ crucified Who is being preached. For Jesus Christ and His doctrine are a stumbling block and foolishness, bringing all kinds of afflictions on His ministers.

The invariable pattern of divine activity shown in the works of all true disciples of Jesus, is that they shall be signs of contradiction, wielding the two-edged sword of the Word of God to reveal the thoughts of many hearts, that is, to find out at once the friends and foes of God.

If then persecution and contradiction suffered by priests in the course of their ministry is a scandal to certain Catholics, this is because they are living in ignorance of the nature of the Gospel message, the relation of this message to the world, and the *foreseen* effect of its impact upon the world. Who, indeed, were the men who rejected Christ's teaching and crucified Him? They were the scribes and Pharisees, the leaders and teachers of the people, the men, divinely appointed, who sat in the chair of Moses and wielded his authority.

So it happened to Jesus. We take that fact for granted. That is our mistake — taking it for granted. So doing, we treat as only an historical fact, now long since past and gone, what was intended by God to be typical of what would happen to all who would follow Christ's teaching and example. Hence the persecution of the Church; hence also, *within* the Church, the persecution of the saints by their fellow Catholics, and the similar persecution, also by fellow Catholics, of all who seriously try to conform their words or conduct to Christ's.

Of course I do not mean that men in high position, men of learning or authority in the Church, invariably or necessarily oppose the truth and persecute its followers. Even among the Pharisees were to be found men who accepted Jesus.

And in the Church there have been not a few but multitudes of holy men occupying the places of honor: priests, bishops, popes, scholars, apostles, administrators — men of the stature of St. Ignatius of Antioch, St. Augustine, St. Ambrose, St. Athanasius, St. Gregory the Great, St. Bonaventure, St. Charles Borromeo, St. Francis de Sales, Pope St. Pius V.

Nevertheless, there have also been in the Church large groups of articulate, noisy, and fierce opponents of those who have striven to preach or live "*Christ and Him crucified*" (1 Cor 2:2). Let us consider some examples.

It was the mission of St. John of the Cross, together with St. Teresa of Ávila, to reform the great Order of Mount Carmel. There were, however, a number of friars who viewed these plans for their reform without enthusiasm, and, when the saint obstinately continued his project, they kidnapped and imprisoned him.

The cell where they kept him was a vile hole where he had no air, and it was only by standing high at a tiny opening that he could get a little light for reading his Divine Office. They gave him food that revolted even his heroically mortified appetite. They would not permit him to offer Mass. Daily they beat him to blood for the spectacle for the community, while they were at dinner indeed — though the novices at any rate had the humanity to weep — so that he was never afterwards able to wear clothing without pain.

And who was it that did this? The Moors, who afflicted Spain for so long a time? By no means. It was Spaniards, Christians, religious, priests. Yet St. Teresa said that she would rather St. John were in the hands of the Moors! To the king of Spain, seeking for his protection for her reform, she wrote: "These friars seem to fear neither justice nor God. As they have long desired, our confessors have fallen into their hands — I am deeply grieved, for I would rather have seen our fathers in the power of the Moors who might be more merciful. This friar, who serves God very fervently, is so weak from all he has suffered that I fear for his life."

Nor did she see in this persecution of Friar John of the Cross decisive evidence against the principles for which he stood. She drew, in fact, quite an opposite inference: "But I am much distressed about Friar John, lest they should bring some fresh charge against him. *God treats his friends terribly*: though, to tell the truth, He does them no wrong, for He served His Son in the same way."

The imprisonment of St. John lasted for nine months; he then escaped, through a miracle, but the fierce opposition from brother religious and priests continued until he was on the very edge of the grave. Such is the repugnance of the Old Adam to the putting on of the New.

Another example is that of St. Louis Grignon de Montfort, a French priest of the eighteenth century. Hounded all over France by bishops and their officers, frequently condemned publicly even in the midst of preaching missions (whose fruit nevertheless lasted for more than a century wherever he had spoken), forbidden finally to preach in all the dioceses of France except two, rejected by the very superiors whom he sought only to serve. Such was his life.

What shall be thought of it? Nearly all the priests and ecclesiastics of his day condemned him, and they thought they spoke for the Church. In our day the Church has raised him to its altars as a saint. Many such instances could be given. But these are sufficient to illustrate that it is far from unusual for priests and ecclesiastics to attack doctrines whose purpose is to lead souls to holiness. In fact, they will be the *first* to attack such doctrines and will attack them most violently, although it is their clear duty both to live by such principles and to teach them to others.

Even fathers and doctors of the Church have been charged with heresy. For example, St. John Chrysostom, Archbishop of Constantinople, was deposed by Theophilus, Archbishop of Alexandria, on a charge of Origenism — a charge to which the saint had apparently given some foundation by protecting some Origenist monks from the tyranny of Theophilus.

The saint, who had also condemned the misconduct of an empress and denounced the corruption of court and nobility, was exiled, and he died from the hardships of his exile. It is of interest to note that assisting Theophilus in this unjust trial was a young man whom the Church today honors as St. Cyril of Alexandria.

St. Athanasius, also, was accused in his day of Apollinarism and Sabellianism. We regard him as one of the greatest champions of orthodoxy, one of the most heroic defenders of truth of all time. In his own day he did not receive such appreciation. Hunted down like a criminal, forced to live for a time in his father's tomb, fleeing to the desert, exiled five times — he spent his whole life in a struggle for a victory that came only after his death. He lived in a day in which, as St. Jerome said, the world awoke to find itself Arian. Practically every bishop in Christendom was a heretic.

The pope himself, St. Liberius, was exiled and mistreated for resisting the heretical emperor. And at Athanasius, model and epitome of orthodoxy, formulator of the Christian creed, standing almost solitary for the truth at that time, while most of its other professed defenders had deserted — at him the same tyrannical emperor could fling the taunt "Athanasius against the world!"

When the Spanish Inquisition was in its heyday, under the inspiration of Melchior Cano, a renowned theologian, it condemned together with many heretics, a number of quite orthodox writers, subsequently recognized as such. Among these were Ven. Luis de Granada, St. John of Ávila, and St. Francis Borgia.

Another famous and orthodox writer, Luis de León, was imprisoned for five years by the Inquisition. No one was safe: Cardinal Carranza, Archbishop of Toledo, and author of a perfectly orthodox book on the spiritual life, was also held in the prisons of the Inquisition and was only released after several years of insistence by Pope Pius IV.

St. Teresa herself barely escaped the attentions of the same high tribunal. St. John of the Cross was likewise held in suspicion by some, and his works were "expurgated" and "improved" even by admirers, so that they could escape condemnation along with the works of false mystics. The cloud of suspicion was not finally lifted from this saint until a few years ago, when he was made a doctor of the Church. In spite of this recognition, however, his works are commonly prohibited as "dangerous" to novices, seminarians, and professed religious, including priests.

St. Francis de Sales, despite his well-known mildness, fared little better. For some time he lay under an accusation of sexual irregularity. Then his *Introduction to a Devout Life,* bringing the doctrine of sanctity to laymen, was attacked by priests, religious, and bishops.

Yet according to Pope Pius XI, Providence raised up this holy man for the very purpose of restoring and preaching this doctrine. His mystical work, *The Treatise on the Love of God,* like the writings of St. John of the Cross, suffered an eclipse and lay under a rebuke, through its being confounded with the work of false mystics; until in our own time the Holy See has elevated its author also to the dignity of doctor of the Church.

Catholic universities although founded to teach truth, have been known to fail in this duty. It was the great University of Paris, together with the Inquisition and an Archiepiscopal court, that condemned for heresy and witchcraft the maid who is now honored by the Church as St. Joan of Arc. The same university — and with this example, the most astonishing of all, I will close this list of cases — condemned the works of St. Thomas Aquinas, who, but a few years before, had been such a light in its lecture halls, and is now honored as the common doctor of the Church. This condemnation was decreed by Stephen Tempier, the Archbishop of Paris. The saint's writings were also condemned by the University of Oxford and by two successive archbishops of Canterbury.

But by 1323 — less than a century after his death — Thomas was canonized; and Pope John XXII, who proclaimed his sanctity, said also that "his philosophy can have proceeded only from some miraculous action of

God." The doctors of Paris, Oxford, and Canterbury, like the people of Bethlehem in an earlier time, had been unable to recognize the divine action.

Such examples could be multiplied indefinitely, but I will bring them to a close by quoting, from St. Augustine's *Confessions* (10:23), an explanation of why the truth so often calls forth hatred from those who profess to love the truth:

> Why does truth call forth hatred? Why is Your servant treated as an enemy by those to whom he preaches the truth, if happiness is loved, which is simply joy in truth? Simply because truth is loved in such a way that those who love some other thing want it to be the truth, and, precisely because they do not wish to be deceived, are unwilling to be convinced that they are deceived.
>
> Therefore they hate the truth for the sake of that other thing which they love as if it were the truth. They love truth when it enlightens them, they hate the truth when it accuses them. Because they do not wish to be deceived and do wish to deceive, they love truth when it reveals itself, and hate it when it reveals them. Thus it shall reward them as they deserve: those who do not wish to be revealed by truth, truth will unmask against their will, but it will not reveal itself to them.
>
> Thus, thus, even thus, does the human mind, blind and inert, vile and ill-behaved, desire to keep itself concealed, yet desires that nothing should be concealed from itself. But the contrary happens to it — it cannot lie hidden from truth, but only truth from it. Even so, for all its worthlessness, the human mind would rather find its joy in truth than falsehood. So that it shall be happy if, with no other thing to distract, it shall one day come to rejoice in that sole truth by which all things are true.

Priests who are persecuted need not be alarmed; the alarm should be felt by those who are not persecuted. Suspicion should attach to the unpersecuted priest, to the priests who are comfortable, worldly, admired, and flattered on every hand. What are they preaching? Certainly not the foolishness that is such a stumbling-block to the natural man; not the folly of the cross. But to those who preach Christ and Him crucified, persecution is not only a sign of good doctrine, but a positive benefit to their own spiritual life and their ministry for souls. Father Jean-Pierre de Caussade, S.J., compares those who contradict us — our "enemies" and "persecutors" —

to oarsmen who row passengers into port. It is a curious thing about oarsmen that, although looking in one direction, they move in quite an opposite one.

So those who oppose us, as we try to live or teach the supernatural life according to the Gospel, are in reality giving indispensable assistance to our own efforts. They are helping in the work of our purification, which is the underside of sanctity. They are forcing us into closer union with Jesus suffering and crucified, thus to help "fill up what is wanting in the suffering of Christ" (Col 1:24), and thereby win, both for others and for ourselves, the most precious satisfactions and graces. They are rowing us into the port for which we long. And the more diligently they work, the more swiftly do they propel us to what alone we desire.

A Sign of Contradiction

Faith in the Church

The next four selections grew out of the conflicts between Father Hugo and Church authorities over whether his writings and preachings on Christian holiness were consistent with official Catholic doctrine.

Like other pioneering Church figures of this century who were silenced and misunderstood only to be vindicated by the Second Vatican Council, Father Hugo approached these conflicts with an attitude of humility and a sense of suffering for Christ and the Gospel.

Although living in the shadow of suspicion, Father Hugo never succumbed to the temptation to use the media or to form pressure groups to denounce Church authority. Instead, even in his private letters, he is shown offering up his struggles to Christ and trusting that, despite the ignorance and the petty vanity of some Church authorities, he would be vindicated by the wisdom of the Church acting under the guidance of the Holy Spirit. These selections are, then, instructions in faithful service to the Church and obedience even in dissent.

The right conception of faith is this: a belief in God, in what God teaches, in the Church only as proceeding from God and authorized by Him. It is a misconception of faith to think that faith means belief in men — even in *Churchmen.* Even the pope is not the formal object of faith.

Of course, as I said, true faith means also belief in the Church — as coming from God. And the Church is human as well as divine. Are we to have faith, theological faith, in the human element of the Church? No, not in the human element as such. Yes, in the human element as caught up, united to, absorbed in, the divine.

Unfortunately in the Church, although all are called to be sharers in the divine life even as Jesus, the Son of God, shared our human life, all do not respond to this initiation or live up to their sublime dignity. Even in the hierarchy — should we say *especially* in the hierarchy, whose members, as private men, are so easily carried away by vanity in the eminence of their worldly position — it will happen that Christians will not live up to the vocation to which they were called.

And so it is a trial of faith to learn that all priests are not men of God — that hence they do not always take God's view of things. It will be an even greater trial to find, alas, that often Churchmen and priests are not even men.

Would this revelation destroy faith? I think not. It should purify it — pull it away from all human supports, give it to the Lord to Whom alone it belongs. As for the Church, it should be given to the immanent divinity, the divine principle in the Church, the human insofar as this reflects, speaks for the divine.

Our faith ought not depend at all on men: we should be like St. Francis of Assisi who could ask the blessing of a sinful priest. For a priest is a channel, not a source. What is it to me if the priest who hears my confession is a sinner? His sin ruins himself but does not impair the divine character given to him. I will pray for him, I will do penance for him. But in the end he is accountable for his own conscience.

Letter to Dorothy Day, September 19, 1945

Who's in Charge?

In speaking thus of authority in the Church, it should be clear that the term cannot be understood here as it is in society generally.

Said Jesus: "You know that those who are supposed to rule over the Gentiles lord it over them, and their great men exercise authority over them. But it shall not be so among you; but whoever would be great among you must be your servant, and whoever would be first among you must be slave of all" (Mk 10:42-43).

He illustrated this teaching by washing their feet at the Last Supper, telling them to do likewise. Authority in the Church, therefore, differs vastly from that of political establishments or the military, although such models, unfortunately, have been followed, providing distorted images. For the authority that Jesus exercises and transmits He gives us the image of servant, and servants in His day were slaves, referring all obedience back to the Father.

He speaks of Himself as physician, shepherd, teacher. Each of these is an authority figure, but all exercise authority benignly: The physician's power is used to heal, the teacher guarantees knowledge. The good shepherd, who "gives his life for his sheep," recalls the highest degree of caring, even to heroism. The conscientious physician also spends himself in healing, as does the true teacher in communicating wisdom.

The reverse of these images tells the manner in which Christians are expected to regard those in authority. With filial obedience, not as robots or with the mindless obedience expected of slaves or conscripts; aware of being afflicted with the malaise of sin, yet willingly carrying out remedial measures offered for their own welfare; or as pupils ready to profit by the knowledge of a dedicated teacher.

The idea of a shepherd, however, may suggest that subjects are to obey as sheep — not a very acceptable image for adults in our day. Yet here the picture of shepherd merges with that of teacher, and it may be remembered that the word docility, which is what shepherds expect of their sheep, signifies in its Latin origin *teachable*. Is there any person who desires not to be teachable?

To Peter, Jesus said, "Feed My lambs. . . . Feed My sheep" (Jn 21:15, 17). And "whoever does not receive the kingdom of God like a little child shall not enter" (Lk 18:17).

Again, the Church provides useful guidance by the works of approved theologians elucidating her teaching, but is never finally bound by their conclusions. Foremost among these are special teachers designated as Doctors of the Church. Although they have no guarantee of inerrancy, they are, because of their knowledge, orthodoxy and holiness, specially designated to interpret the teachings of the Church.

Many also are skilled in the practical ways of holiness and in the Church's moral teaching, and because of their wisdom and experience can lead eager pilgrims securely to God. The counsels of Augustine, Bernard, John of the Cross, Teresa of Ávila, Francis de Sales — to mention a few — are beacon lights along the way of Christ and, because they have been recognized by the Church, they are reliable interpreters of her teaching.

Indeed, since all Christians are "temples of the Holy Spirit" (1 Cor 3:16), everyone should be able to find appropriate counsel among friends and associates, as well as superiors. The paramount quality needed in such intimate counselors — whether lay, religious, or clerical — is that they possess, or earnestly seek, *the mind of Christ.* "Where there is no guidance, a people falls; but in an abundance of counselors there is safety" (Prv 11:14).

Your Ways Are Not My Ways, vol. II

'We Have Powerful Enemies Everywhere'

Of course it is hard for others to understand the need for this particular retreat — they interpret matters in terms of their own mentality. So much the more the need to stand fast. Undoubtedly, the devil will intervene at every possible point to spoil and dilute the doctrine. He certainly finds it odious.

We have so many powerful enemies everywhere, and there is little chance, humanly speaking, that we could get a favorable hearing now. It almost seems that the more delay the better. Sometimes we are tempted to become impatient at the Church's delays in making decisions. Yet how wise are these delays, and how beneficent! Only in this way can personal prejudices and venom be removed from judgment. So we must pray that our enemies are not able to force a precipitate judgment.

Letter to Dorothy Day, August 7, 1943

My Bishop's Hands

Despite rumors to the contrary, I had never been "silenced"—a word sometimes used but really having no canonical meaning. Even as a curate I could be free to conduct retreats only in vacation times — which were of uncertain occurrence for a curate!

Since I had once placed my hands within my bishop's and promised obedience, I did so and was never seriously tempted to do otherwise, going where I was sent: it was to God that I had committed my spirit.

The radical, Dorothy Day, encouraged me in this obedience. She expected it, never suggesting an alternative, evidently pleased that I was honoring my promise, visiting me in all my places of "exile."

Your Ways Are Not My Ways, vol. I

'Religion Without Obedience Is Simply Self-Delusion'

This is a prophetic text, and it is again one which clarifies Father Hugo's attitude on the importance of obedience both in the Church and in the broader society. It was occasioned by the Catholic Worker movement's efforts to define its social philosophy in the post-World War II years. He is responding in particular to the writings of Catholic Worker editors Robert Ludlow, a convert with a devotion to Gandhi's ideas of social change and reconstruction, and Ammon Hennacy, a flamboyant individualist with roots in the syndicalist and anarchist traditions of the American labor movement.

Father Hugo shared Ludlow and Hennacy's distrust for government and big business, which he agreed were expanding powers gained during wartime to seize more and more control over areas that were rightly the domain of personal conscience and religious liberty. He also agreed with them that when faced with unjust laws and social conditions, a Christian has the duty to follow God and not the rules of man.

But he rejected the implication by Ludlow and Hennacy that dissent and disobedience should be the basic posture of the Christian toward those in authority, including those in authority in the Church. Such an attitude, as he saw it, was influenced more by American ideals of an exaggerated and rugged individualism than by the Gospel. The liberty of the children of God (Gal 5:1,13) nevertheless meant that personal conscience and freedom must be checked and balanced by the authority of the Gospel and its interpretation by the Church.

To reject all authority, as the Catholic Worker anarchists proposed, was to wrongly exalt the individual as the sole arbiter over right and wrong, and it would, Father Hugo indicated, ultimately undermine all authority and replace it with a dangerous and radically individualized idea of personal freedom and conscience. Obedience to established authority in the Church would keep lay people and clergy and religious in communion with the truth of the Gospel, and would prevent them from confusing their own intuitions and prejudices with the "mind of Christ."

Father Hugo also saw that social justice and peace work, not to mention attempts at change within the Church, would have little moral authority or persuasive power if based on the solitary judgments of individual consciences, cut free and acting alone and apart from the authority of the law of God and the Church.

In a sense, this selection marks Father Hugo's prophetic rejection of a style of dissent and radicalism that has become a norm among many in the post-Vatican II Church. As he predicted, untethered from concern for the ordinances of God and the magisterium of the Church, dissent has become for many in the Church "a habit" more than a principle and "the objector is soon objecting to everything" even "authority itself."

✦

I have been concerned by the direction *The Catholic Worker* has taken since Bob Ludlow joined you, and even more so after Ammon Hennacy became a definite member of your staff. I was at first puzzled, then disturbed, by their discussion of Catholic anarchism. Their lengthy articles have not persuaded me that the two notions are compatible.

At the head of such discussions you should place the text: "Let everyone be subject to the higher authorities, for there exists no authority except from God, and those who exist have been appointed by God. Therefore, he who resists the authority resists the ordinances of God, and they that resist bring on themselves condemnation."

There is more to the passage, which you can read in Romans 13, and I rather think that St. Paul was in sufficiently good standing as a Christian to have some voice in this discussion of Catholic anarchism. It is perhaps not without significance that he wrote these words during the regime of Nero.

No doubt there are abuses of authority; but there is also a duty of obedience on the part of the subjects. I understand the difference between religious with a vow and the laity in this obligation. Nevertheless, allowing for this, and allowing also for the imperfections of superiors, of which I have had myself sufficient experience, it remains that *Catholicism without obedience is a contradiction and religion without obedience is simply self-delusion.*

Since there are abuses of authority, conscientious objection to unjust laws may at times be necessary. Yet it is dangerous for a subject to simply assume the office of judge of his superiors. Perhaps this is why theologians, while understanding the need for protest against unjust laws, are cautious about approving it in practice.

Conscientious objection may readily become a habit. Once started, like a tear in a piece of cloth, it is hard to stop. The objector is soon objecting to everything. He feels that he must vindicate his unusual stand, and he does so by finding fault with everything that the authorities do. In the end, he will use any type of material or propaganda to throw discredit on the authorities, and by implication on authority itself. This seems to me the direction of the Catholic Worker over the past years.

I am sorry to write thus. I still admire you and love you for the love that you have ever shown the poor. But love, however exalted, must stem from the truth. In departing from the truth, you depart also from genuine love.

Letter to Dorothy Day, November 17, 1955

'Progressives' and 'Conservatives' Are Both Irrelevant

All of Father Hugo's writings on theology were occasional writings — writings inspired by the issues and stresses of the day. Thus, he did not leave behind any theoretical statement of his beliefs about how theology should function in the Church and how theology should speak to society and challenges to traditional teaching. But these final selections suggest a reliance on Cardinal John Henry Newman's work on the growth and development of Christian doctrine and an impatience with the presumptions and fashions in some of the theological currents of his day.

Father Hugo had a reverence for Church tradition and believed that in order to speak to the questions of the world today, theology had to return to the sources of Church teaching — the Bible and the writings of the Church fathers and doctors. It is also worth noting that his only full-scale book of theology, "St. Augustine on Nature, Sex and Marriage," was a defense, based on a return to the sources, of the Church's teachings on birth control and sexuality, at a time when these teachings were under attack by some of the most prominent theologians in the Church.

⁂

Dom Aelred Graham has written that, "In religion *conservative* or *progressive* are irrelevant categories. The categories that really apply are *radical* or *superficial*." What is desirable is the radical Christianity that goes to the root (*radix*) of truth. And in Christianity the root is divine truth, possessed in faith, working to bear fruit in love (Gal 5:6).

The search for such radical truth is the paramount goal of theological inquiry, and it must be sought without allowing ourselves to be pulled this way or that by temperamental inclination or party prejudice. Truth cannot be a party slogan but must be accepted from whatever source it comes.

While there are polarities within truth, these must be brought together in harmony and oneness, for reality is one; and truth, as St. Thomas says, is conformity of the mind with reality. Certainly the purpose of all true religion is to bring about oneness among humans and between them and their God.

Accordingly, when words like "conservative" or "progressive" are used as they are today, for political labels, they are indeed irrelevant in religion. Nevertheless, there is a central and inescapable polarity in the Christian religion which can be described only in the terms, understood theologically, *traditional* (or *conservative*) and *progressive*.

As Catholics and Christians we must all be traditional, hence also conservative, in our commitment to live and think by the truths of the Gospel in every age. At the same time we are under a compulsion to relate these truths to the problems of the age in which we pass, that our faith may not be dead, preserved as a mummy, but a living and transforming presence in every generation.

In other words, there must be a growth, both in doctrine and worship. As we move among the changes of any age, and the chaos of our own, we need to develop a spiritual discernment and ability akin to the skill of a tight-rope walker. And this can be difficult and hazardous, especially at times of great unrest like that which followed the Second Vatican Council.

Your Ways Are Not My Ways, vol. I

The Church Did Not Begin with Your Generation

Therefore every scribe who has been trained for the kingdom of heaven is like a householder who brings forth out of his treasure what is new and what is old (Mt 13:52).

This tradition which comes from the Apostles develops in the Church with the help of the Holy Spirit. For there is a growth in the understanding of the realities and the words which have been handed down (Second Vatican Council, *Dei Verbum,* 8).

One would almost think that Augustine is a contemporary. At least his ideas are considered newsworthy by magazines like *Time,* while those of many contemporaries are not. To be sure, while Augustine still has his disciples and friends, by no means every mention of him is favorable. Today, in fact, there seems to be a sort of concerted effort to vilify him, or at least to undercut his influence.

In one important respect, he offends the modern world, or a segment of it — the segment that believes that many of the problems of today can be solved by contraception. Augustine appears to stand in the way of such a solution. His ideas of marriage and sexuality seem outmoded, if not false. And these affect his whole view of life, which, we are told, tends to be pessimistic and rigoristic.

Some might ask: Who cares? What difference does it make for us today what Augustine taught in the fifth century? Much water has gone under the bridge since then. The Church itself is now in the throes of what Pope John XXIII has called an *aggiornamento,* a renewal or a bringing up to date. We must solve our problems, it is said, by our twentieth-century conscience.

With all respect and admiration for Pope John, however, the Church of Christ did not begin with him. One can read contemporary works on moral and theological problems without realizing this — even when carefully footnoted, their earliest reference may be to Karl Rahner or Teilhard de Chardin. The past can be disregarded by twentieth-century man, arrogant in his possession of vast knowledge; or else it can be filled in with a few broad and frequently inaccurate brush strokes. *Aggiornamento,* for some at least, appears to mean a complete break with the past and a wholly fresh start.

Certainly, men today have certain obvious advantages. Rahner and Teilhard and other contemporary thinkers do stand atop a vast accumulation of scientific knowledge. Alongside these stores even men like Augustine and Aquinas in many respects seem primitive. Nevertheless, while our contemporaries may in a sense judge the doctors of the past, these in turn will join in pronouncing judgment on our contemporaries. Catholic doctrine is a living, evolving truth. It changes, but it also remains the same.

In doctrinal development, the Church assimilates elements from every age, including pagan elements, always retaining its own identity. Some elements are taken into the "organism" of the Church, others are rejected as inassimilable. We must make this distinction in matters of the mind, especially in the question of developing theology.

Accordingly, Augustine and Aquinas along with others will be judges of our contemporaries, despite the advantageous position of the latter. Christians of past ages will be called upon to decide whether material submitted by the moderns is assimilable, whether it is to be retained or rejected, whether it is consistent with the unity and continuing identity of Catholic truth.

To facilitate this living process, we ourselves should try to discriminate between what is digestible and what is not. Our age, despite its pretensions, has also its fashions in thought, although the current fashion may seem to us like the final stage of evolutionary progress. Within a short time there will be several other evolutionary "mutations."

Consult the books of a few years ago and you will find other "advanced" ideas, now forgotten. A strange thing about most of these ideas is their repetitiousness. As often as not, they can be traced to pre-Socratic sages.

C.S. Lewis, in the dedication of one of his books, thanks a former teacher for telling him that the age in which we live will some day also be considered a period. We would be wise to bear this in mind. It would keep us from running off after every new style in thought. It would caution us that what we now praise as the latest may very soon be dated. Precisely here, knowledge of the past can be of help in discerning what belongs to the inner identity and coherence of Christian truth.

Christian theology is a unified but growing body of truth, the fruit of the Church's endless meditation on Sacred Writ. Augustine made the first really significant contribution to this corpus in the West. In reexamining his work we must determine how far it belongs to his own time, how far he has contributed to enduring truth, how far his teachings are part of our developing knowledge, how far they diverge from it.

Augustine was very much a man of his own age, so different from our own. Manichaeism, Donatism, Pelagianism, and a persisting undercurrent of paganism were his constant preoccupation. In meeting these errors, as he reflected on the Scriptures, and in zealously carrying out his pastoral office of preaching to the people of Hippo, he formulated the principles of what was to be called Augustinian thought.

Yet in serving his own age so well he became a man for all ages. His thought transcends the local and temporary because, in the first place, seeking solutions to his contemporary problems, he tried to bring to bear on them the universal light of the Gospel. Moreover, certain heresies and errors, while they have local variations — and we easily become impatient reading the vagaries of past ages — reveal perennial attitudes of the human mind, persistent tendencies, and recurrent temptations. This is true of the systems combated by Augustine: they are not quite as dead as we would like to think. Consequently, his thought can be of help in meeting these attitudes in other times, including our own, in which some of these wraiths exhibit surprising vitality.

Even the greatest theologians cannot escape an admixture of human error. Such errors result not only from the personal and human limitations of the thinkers, but also from the restricting limits of knowledge and science of the era in which they live. The social and cultural milieu is the matrix in which theology on its human side is formed and developed. It is the task of reflection and study, separating error, to channel authentic elements into the swelling mainstream of theological truth. Accordingly, the final value of any work is determined by the degree to which it is absorbed into the main tradition.

Through Christ we plunge into "the depths of the wisdom and knowledge of God" (Rom 11:33). No man, whatever his genius, can contain it fully. It is the task of us all, led by those gifted in the mind and endowed with spiritual vision purified by holiness, to seek constantly to extend our comprehension of this mystery.

St. Augustine on Nature, Sex and Marriage

V
Mysticism in Action:
Catholics in the Public Square

The Failure of Christian Effort

Father Hugo's writings on Catholic social justice issues are best seen as extensions of his writings on holiness and spirituality. His insistent theme is that Catholics' efforts to change the world had thus far failed because of their "worldliness" — their lack of faith in God's providence, and their unwillingness to root out the sinfulness in their own lives. This generation, Father Hugo observed, has seen the rise of Catholics committed to fighting injustice and sinful social conditions. But many of these same people have lost sight of Jesus' call for a revolutionary transformation of their own hearts. Too often, he complains, Christians struggle to change social conditions, but overlook the truth that they must also change themselves.

By now the world should be aflame with Christianity. "I have come to cast fire on the earth and what will I but that it be kindled" (Lk 12:49).

The failure, of course, is one of Christian effort, not of Christianity. The religion of Jesus still fulfills the deepest aspirations of men and women. It alone can respond fully to the individual's desire for personal happiness. It is the answer also for the world's cry for social justice, charity and peace.

The fault is with us Christians. God has called us to collaborate with Him in the sanctification of the world and, through the merits of His divine Son, preserved in the treasury of the Church, has mapped out a program for us with elaborate detail.

It is we ourselves who have been wanting; and the reason is that our flesh, greedy for itself and proud, is unwilling to submit to the law of the Spirit, through which alone can Christian life and Christian society be realized.

A social problem is symptomatic of social disease, just as a skin eruption is symptomatic of bodily disease. Poisons in the body become localized or "come to a head," in tumors or wellings or inflammations of some kind. Just so the evil humors of society "come to a head" in wars, economic crises, and social diseases. The problems that agitate the minds of people today are symptoms of deeper ills. At the same time they are evidence that we Christians, in spite of Almighty God's commission, have not carried the good news to all people of good will.

Christianity is a leaven; if the world is still unleavened, is it not the fault of the very enterprises of which we are so proud? That the forces of paganism and not those of Christianity have gained control of the world, compels us to admit that there is a lack of inner force in those agencies that have for their purpose the promotion of Christian principles and the Christian way of life.

To admit that Christianity is not being made to penetrate the remote places of human affairs is at the same time to affirm that an uncomfortably large number of Christians are lifeless.

The Catholic Worker (September 1941)

A Religion of Our Own Standards

"We are dying of complacency and insipidity, of vulgarized and minimized truths, of a religion reduced to our own standards." These words of Jacques Maritain are not merely an opinion; they are rather a statement of fact. If Christ is in truth the Prince of Peace — and it is the Holy Ghost that says He is — then all the turmoil and unhappiness in men's hearts must be there only because they have not lived fully in accordance with the truths of the Gospel.

Further, the discord and distress of the whole world must likewise be due to the fact that people have rejected, or insufficiently realized the teachings of Christianity.

The Catholic Worker (May 1942)

Death of a 'Practical' Catholic

A Catholic organization may have life in the sense that all the members are *practical* Catholics, but it may be at the same time lifeless, spiritually inert. For a *practical* Catholic is too commonly a person who uses a veneer of external practices to cover a lukewarm heart and purely natural principles of action.

As a result, his organizations, while perhaps promoting successful dances or athletic teams, are not concerned with the spiritual progress of members or with the task of spreading the Christian way of life.

No one would deny that there are groups working zealously for the Church and helping to spread God's kingdom on earth. Nevertheless, there are other groups whose zeal is pretty well used up in bridge and beer, bowling, bingo, and bazaars. Spiritually, however, such organizations have no significance. While describing themselves as Catholic, they accomplish nothing for God or the Church. Very often, indeed, they are corpses that actually encumber the work of the true apostolate.

In the Vineyard

Spiritual Aptitude Test Scores

Consider the Catholic educational effort. In view of the enormous amounts of money expended in building up a Catholic school system, and of the large personnel engaged in maintaining this system, it would be reasonable to expect the present age to be the most Christian that the world has ever known and our country to be the most Christian of all nations. In fact, however, anyone who speaks of society today, or even of our nation, as Christian, is guilty of an abuse of language scarcely short of falsehood.

For the sake of argument, we may limit our attention to those who have been directly influenced by Catholic schools. Is there among these, proportionately, greater zeal than among those who have not enjoyed such advantages? Do young people coming from Catholic schools, in their zeal for Christ's cause, rival the devotion of the Hitler youth to the Nazi cause?

The final spiritual test of Catholic education is whether it produces fervent, zealous Catholics, on fire with the love of God, seeking after the perfection of Christian life, seriously attempting to imitate the virtues of Jesus Christ. When this end is not accomplished, then something has happened to intercept the power of divine truth.

In the Vineyard

The Illusion of Christian Effectiveness

We have set aside spiritual norms, which are alone of value in estimating spiritual efforts, and now form our judgments according to the worthless external standards of an age given over to frantic activity and noisy advertising.

God's work is interior, spiritual, supernatural, and "the sensual man does not perceive the things that are of the spirit of God, for it is foolishness to him and he cannot understand, because it is examined spiritually" (1 Cor 2:14).

Catholic organizations go tirelessly from city to city, state to state, for meetings and conventions and councils. They conduct learned discussions, usually over sumptuous dinners in elegant hotels. The dinners are arranged, no doubt, to sustain the delegates through their difficult work; while to relieve frayed nerves, discussions are punctuated by frequent recreational features.

There is an air of bustle about all this, and a delusion of accomplishment. Speeches are multiplied, papers are read showing what ought to be done, or congratulating those present on what they are supposed to have done already; then plans are made for the next convention. Because of all this noise and activity people fancy that they are making huge advances for Christianity.

Of course, there is nothing intrinsically evil in all such things. The point is that they are fruitless supernaturally; for spiritual work must employ spiritual means. "Prayer is good with fasting and alms more than to lay up treasures of gold" (Tb 12:8). More would be gained for an organization by prayer and fasting than by luxury and display.

When the Apostles had important work on hand, the Acts tells us, the procedure they followed was prayer and fasting. A discussion in which earnest Christians sincerely seek the guidance of the Holy Spirit in promoting apostolic work might have as its fitting preparation a day or so of fasting. It might be conducted in a spirit of mortification, silence, and recollection, with all participants making a holy hour each day, and really generous souls doing a great deal more.

In the Vineyard

Nero's Fiddle

The picture of Nero fiddling while Rome burned is still used to shock children. Such fiddling has become a characteristic occupation of our times. Americans lost a democracy because they gave themselves over to pleasure while unscrupulous people robbed them of their country and exploited its resources. People today, in the face of terrible sufferings that have overtaken their fellows and may soon overtake us all, lose themselves in their own pleasure and self-interest.

Surely this is not different from the manner and spirit of Christians who, knowing from St. Paul that "all creation groans and travails in pain" awaiting for Christ (Rom 8:22), nevertheless engage their attention and affections with trivial occupations, with pleasure and other selfish private interests, refusing to make any sacrifices for a work that can advance only through supreme sacrifice.

Yes, God expects even supreme sacrifices. He does desire that we give up our bourgeois comfort and smugness. "In this we have come to know His love, that He laid down His life for us: *and we ought likewise to lay down our life for the brethren*" (1 Jn 3:16).

Apostles nowadays are too much occupied with the things of the world. They are earthly minded, like the first Apostles before the coming of the Holy Ghost. They are bewitched by the trinkets of a pleasure-seeking world, and defend their indulgence with the maxims of paganism. Strongly attached to the pleasures of the world and guided by a too human prudence, they do not understand that, by the very terms of our Lord's invitation, they must leave all to follow Him.

Their love for earthly things may seem trivial, but if it could only be diverted to the love and service of God, what a difference there would be in the world! To be occupied with the pleasures of a pagan world is the Christian's way of fiddling while the world groans and travails for Christ.

Attachments to the goods of earth mean that huge quantities of love are given to creatures by Christians who are bound to love their Creator with their whole heart.

Moreover, this love for the world — this paganism — as it is a cause of war, and not an effective defense against war, so it is also, no mere trifling occupation, but a veritable cause of the lifelessness and powerlessness of Catholic organizations. As it diminishes their love, it diminishes their life. For alas, "if anyone loves the world, the love of the Father is not in him. . . . My dear children, let us not love in word, neither with the tongue, but in deed and in truth" (1 Jn 3:18).

The Catholic Worker (November 1941)

The Fatal Delusion of Our Times

The history of the twentieth century, the bloodiest and the deadliest in the history of humanity, can be written as the story of a time when a succession of collectivist and individualistic ideologies, sought to usher in the "brotherhood of man" without acknowledging the reality and the necessity of God. These next several selections represent Father Hugo's prophetic reminder that it was not without good reason that the prophets of Israel, and later, Jesus and the Apostles, taught that the love of God can never be sequestered from the love of neighbors.

<hr />

There is no shortcut to the love of neighbor. In our day there are some who mistakenly fancy that it can be attained without the love of God. It is a fatal delusion, responsible for nullifying all the fine talk of the modern world about the brotherhood of man. It is sober fact that there is no other way of creating love among neighbors than by cultivating the love of God.

Cut the love of neighbor from its moorings in the love of God, and you have what we Americans love to call "service," that is, willingness to "love" and "serve" others as long as self-interest finds it profitable to do so. Such "service," employed as a substitute for the charity of the Gospel, has in fact brought us back to the law and condition that obtained before the coming the Gospel, namely: Love those that love you, hate those that hate you. Such is the law observed today. It is not the one whose observance brings peace.

Dutiful and affectionate children, genuinely concerned for the welfare of their parents and home, are united by this common love also to one another — the love of their parents creates peace among themselves. It is otherwise with children who do not love their parents: they are prone to regard family possessions jealously and selfishly, thus becoming divided among themselves. Similarly those who love God and place His interests above all else are united among themselves and enjoy peace. But those who have not love for God soon also become divided against each other over temporal goods.

Peace is measured by charity. Hatred and discord, on the contrary, in proportion to the violation of the Gospel law. Do not people become rich by defrauding others of material goods, by robbing the laborer of his wages, by exploiting the poor and defenseless? It is precisely in this way that there arise industrial wars, class wars, international wars. The cure, obviously, lies in cultivating an attitude of soul which regards material goods with indifference and is able to use them unselfishly and for the glory of God.

The greater is the attachment to material goods, the more irreconcilable will be the divisions among people and the more furious their conflicts; as with pirates, the greedier they are, the more violent and murderous will be their assaults.

Here is why wars get worse: their progress in destructiveness and horror is directly related to the increasing abandonment of divine law. It is not because of advances in science and technology — science and technology are but instruments — but rather because people, drifting further and further into forgetfulness of God, become at the same time more attached to the goods of earth. Ever more ruthless in their determination to secure these goods together with the paltry joys that come from them, they do not stop short of destroying whoever stands in the way of their satisfying themselves.

To carnal people, that is to those who pamper the desires of their fallen nature by pursuing the goods of earth, genuine supernatural love of neighbor is impossible. To such also peace is impossible.

In our day it was precisely through material goods that the false prophets of materialism thought that universal peace and prosperity were to be obtained. So proud of the ingenuity which, with the aid of science created new inventions, produced them in great quantities, and opened up ever new sources of supply, these blind leaders of the blind boasted that through technical and material means mankind would attain to universal happiness. They saw in the developing systems of communication and transportation the means by which people were to be brought together in one universal brotherhood.

In reality, however, the increase of wealth put people more furiously at one another's throats, caused class war and international conflicts, and resulted everywhere in poverty, unemployment, and misery. The new developments in transportation and communication, as well as all the other marvelous inventions of science — railroads, gasoline engines, airplanes, radio, telephone, etc. — became the very means by which the peoples of the earth locked themselves, not in the embrace of brotherhood, but in the most horrible slaughters that the world had ever seen.

The Gospel of Peace

There Is No Such Thing as Personal Ethics

It is usual to mark a division between personal and social ethics. But Christian morality, precisely because it is personal, is inescapably interpersonal as well; and therefore already communal because it issues from love, which can only be personal, while the love of God and neighbor are but one love.

For the Christian, personal morality is also social, and social morality — which is not mere obedience to rules or laws — arises from the love of God and gains a social dimension as it expresses itself inevitably in the love of neighbor.

In God's plan society is laced together by an endless network of loving bonds. Faith, opening up to the Christian a vision of the kingdom of God, reveals that this kingdom is peopled by brethren living in loving union.

There can be no mere individualistic or sacral or ritualistic piety concentrated solely on God while unconcerned with neighbor. In becoming individualistic it would simply wither and die, leaving behind only a shell of externalism. "If anyone says, 'I love God,' and hates his brother, he is a liar; for he who does not love his brother whom he has seen, cannot love God whom he has not seen" (1 Jn 4:20).

A special advantage of the image which Jesus favored — the kingdom of God — which otherwise might seem irrelevant today, is in keeping us mindful that our union with God is not merely of the alone with the Alone, but in fact a communion and a "fellowship with one another" (1 Jn 1:7).

Your Ways Are Not Ways, vol. II

Your Own Private Revolution

Father Hugo, in these next selections, hammers away at the key theme of his social writings — that Christians can never hope to rid society of injustice unless they root out the sin, ungodliness, and disobedience in their own hearts.

✥

This is the law that governs the spiritual growth of Christian society and there is no other way of bringing it about: Only by becoming more and more intensely Christian ourselves can we hope to make others Christians.

Alas, Catholics engaged in Catholic action, when reading the papal encyclicals almost universally pass over, as something to be taken for granted, those sections where it is laid down that the first step in bringing about social reform is to set about our own moral and spiritual reform. When we consider how far we are away from the perfection that Our Lord sets before us, then we will understand that such reform is not to be taken for granted, even in those who consider themselves excellent Catholics.

Catholic action in the Catholic sense is the bringing into play of the innermost powers and resources of Christianity. It presupposes, therefore, a deliberate cultivation of the Christian life and is indeed nothing else than a blossoming forth of that life.

Accordingly, the apostles' first concern must be not to increase their activity, but to develop their interior lives. Their first care must not be for others but for themselves. As a doctor helps others best by first perfecting his own skill, so the apostle helps others best by first perfecting his own spiritual resources.

Though they strain to go through the world bringing Christ to others, they must first bring Christ more and more intimately to themselves — or themselves to Christ. In the measure that they refuse to concern themselves directly with others and devotes themselves to perfecting their own personal union with Christ, this is the measure in which they will be spiritually useful to others.

"He that abideth in Me, the same shall bear much fruit" (Jn 15:5). It is the knowledge of this truth that enables individual saints to do so much for Christ. It is the ignorance of this truth, or the refusal to accept it, that is responsible for the fact that whole organizations, comprising vast numbers of Christians, nowadays fail to accomplish anything for Him.

The Catholic Worker (June 1942)

The Only Reason to Act

Because all people are obliged to the summits of perfection by the law of God, they certainly may, and must, refuse to perform any actions that make the fulfillment of that law impossible. "If it be just in the sight of God to hear you rather than God, judge ye!" (Acts 4:19)

The supreme duty of a Christian is the imitation of Christ. Those who are "sons of God" are recognizable as such in the degree of their likeness to Him who is their brother and the "first-born among many brethren" (Jn 1:12, Rom 8:29)

Therefore, any condition in society that hinders the imitation of Christ stands condemned by His law. Any arrangement which prevents people from taking up this great spiritual undertaking, which is expected of all, has no validity, no force, no sanction in eternal law.

Any situation created by people, together with whatever circumstances result from their actions, which are opposed to the fullness of Christian life, are iniquitous; and it is therefore a duty to change or modify them until they serve the divine plan. Human society and secular governments, for all their preoccupation with terrestrial ends, have the duty to assist their members and subjects in obtaining their final spiritual end and beatitude.

The Gospel of Peace

Mystics in Action

A brief, but evocative description of the Christian life, which for Father Hugo is to be a life of action flowing from contemplation, a life of love in union with God and with faith in God's providence and hope in His promises.

Beyond the recognizable region where we can reach and to some extent control events through God's express will, there is a vast expanse of happenings, both good and evil, like the weather, or the action of others, over which we have little or no control.

In this twilight zone St. Francis de Sales shows us how we can also find, in faith, what he calls "the will of God's good pleasure," that is, His providential direction of all events. Here is where, especially, we can utilize the notion of the sacrament of the moment: each event is an outward sign of the divine presence which we can find only in the darkness of faith.

Even harsh, cruel, and unjust actions can yield us indications of God's design, so that, through good or ill, we can live in continuous union with the will of God. This is what we may call the authentic mysticism of action, living in union with God in prayer and in action. Here is the place where prayer, in the quest of God, does in fact spill out into the activity, to bring about a sanctifying mixture and a true mysticism.

Your Ways Are Not My Ways, vol. I

The Work of the Apostolate

Apostolate — the mission of the Christian in following Christ and the Gospel — is a word that has sort of fallen out of favor, or at least out of usage, in the years following the Second Vatican Council. But "Apostolicam Actuositatem," the Council's decree on the apostolate of lay people, summed up several decades of intense reflection among theologians and others on the meaning of the Christian life which began in the early years of this century. Father Hugo was deeply influenced by this period and himself made an important contribution to the Church's understanding of the mission of disciples today. These next selections share his insights on the ultimate meaning of Christian living.

⚜

The work of the apostolate — it cannot be repeated too often — is simply to bring the divine life of grace and love to others. To succeed, Catholic action requires, not that its agencies have luxurious headquarters or brilliant affairs, but that it bring into the world an increase of the divine life. The Son of God took our humanity that we might share in His divinity. Therefore, the apostolate must have as its aim, working through the humanity of Jesus, to bring to more people a greater share of divinity.

The Catholic Worker (June 1942)

Supernatural Living

The kind of life which must be possessed by those working in the apostolate, which they desire also to give to others, is supernatural life. This they obtain in grace and it is rich and full within them in proportion to their possession of grace.

The life of grace, as the Scriptures teach us, is the same as the divine life: it is a participation in the divine life (cf. 2 Pt 1:4). As the branches obtain life from the vine, this is the example that Jesus Himself gives us, so do our souls obtain divine life through the sacred humanity of Jesus. Therefore, with the Church we pray to the Father that He will make us, as the priest says at the altar, "sharers in the divinity of Him who became a partaker in our humanity, namely Jesus Christ, Our Lord."

God, then, is life. Likewise, "God is love" (1 Jn 4:16). As our supernatural life is a sharing in the divine life, so our love is a sharing in the infinite love of God. Supernatural life makes itself manifest in love; and life is strong in the measure that love is ardent. For life is given to us in grace, and grace, if we are docile to its attractions, would unite us more and more intimately to God in love.

Thus the love of God is not a mere natural exercise of the human will, it is not something that we create within ourselves. It is a gift, a real participation in the divine life of love. Of course the fact that charity is a gift of God does not exempt us from effort. We are ourselves in a very large measure, responsible for the degree and intensity of our love, for charity is a reward merited by our correspondence with grace.

If life is love, then lifelessness is lovelessness. Herein lies the significance of the worldliness and self-seeking in Catholic organizations, of their preoccupation with amusement and recreations, of their dependence for success on merely natural baits and enticements.

Whatever weakens love, weakens life. Attachments for creatures, even when they stop short of what is sinful, can divert our affections from God to squander them on worldly trifle. And thus lessening our love, they at the same time diminish our life, for life is love.

Not that there is anything wrong with creatures, not that they are evil. But they can absorb our affections, so that love of God and zeal in His service are dried up within us. Every lessening of love is a lessening of life.

Our conclusion must be, even though we may be tempted to rebel against it, that our spiritual apathy and ineffectiveness is caused by a want of love for God. "This people honors Me with their lips but their hearts are far from Me" (Is 29:13).

The reason for the failure of our effort is no mere technical defect in organization, no lack of means or inferiority in personnel. It is a deficiency of heart, of desire, of love. In view of our failure to capture the world for Christ, what other conclusion is possible? For the victory should be ours: "I have overcome the world" (Jn 16:33).

The Catholic Worker (October 1941)

Detachment and Turning

In these final selections, Father Hugo makes a plea for a reconversion of Catholics, a rededication to the cross of Christ and to lives of holy self-denial. To change the world, he says, Catholic activists must truly be willing to sacrifice all that they have — their comforts, their habits, their priorities — to take up His cross and follow Him.

In one word, the cause of lack of fervor, and the reason why Catholic organizations are ineffective in their fight against paganism, is *worldliness*. This it is which inwardly and secretly destroys the life of Christians and nullifies the spiritual effect of their work.

We lack life because we lack the love of God, and we lack the love of

God because we are filled with the love of creatures. That is what worldliness is — a merely natural love for the creatures of the world.

This earthly love, innocent as it may seem, has an immediate and disastrous effect on our spiritual lives, for we have but one heart with a finite capacity for love and the love that we give to creatures weakens and reduces the love that we have for God. Not that there is any opposition between creatures and Creator, but there is a rivalry for man's love.

Almighty God desires that we love Him with our whole hearts. Merely to keep the first and greatest commandment, the Christian must be unworldly, must practice what the spiritual masters call "contempt for the world." Not because he believes that the creatures of this world are evil, but because his love belongs, not to creatures, but to their Creator. Detachment from creatures, moreover, is an *elementary condition* of Christian life.

That explains why St. Thomas defines all sin simply as a turning from God and a turning toward creatures; which shows that the degree of one's turning from God is the degree of one's worldliness or, perhaps, sinfulness.

This is also why Dom Jean-Baptiste Chautard, O.C.S.O., in The *Soul of the Apostolate*, reverses the formula of St. Thomas and defines the Christian interior life as a turning from creatures and a turning toward God, so that the degree of one's turning from creatures is the degree of one's love for God. In other words, the progress of the soul toward God and its removal from creatures are opposite sides of the same movement.

Jesus himself speaks of them as one thing. Replying to the rich young man who had faithfully kept the Mosaic code, He said: "One thing is yet lacking to thee." Then he states what appear to be two things, first, "Sell what thou hast," and secondly, "Come, follow Me" (Lk 18:22). To follow Christ we must first deny ourselves, we must first renounce all that we possess, at least in affection. We must first hate even our own life.

In order to manifest the life of Jesus, we must bear about His death in our body. "For we the living are constantly being handed over to death for Jesus' sake, that the life of Jesus may be made manifest in our mortal flesh" (2 Cor 4:11).

How shallow and senseless it is, therefore, to talk of "glossing over" self-denial and detachment. He who refuses these practices will certainly not rise very high in the love of God.

Any programs of Catholic action that neglect this condition, no matter how admirable they may be in themselves, are foredoomed to failure. Discussion clubs, programs of youth activities, efforts to enhance liturgical life, whatever merit they may have on paper or in the abstract, cannot be fruitful spiritually if their advocates are afraid to face and insist upon the negative conditions that have been fixed by divine law, as the means of producing spiritual fruit.

If people will have the life of Christ — His love, His joy, His peace — then they must accept Calvary and the cross. There is no Christianity without the cross, and those who accept Cana but reject Calvary separate themselves from the divine Master at the very outset of the way. If modern youth, or modern men and women in general, are not willing to take up the cross, then they simply cannot possess Christianity.

The warning that St. John of the Cross gives to the worldly of his day is just as necessary in our age: "He who seeks not the cross of Christ seeks not the glory of Christ."

In the Vineyard

The Radical Cross

Radical Christianity is discovered only at the cross, but who desires to be crucified? Like Peter and the other apostles — before the coming of the Holy Spirit! — we all tend to prefer a Christianity without the cross, "airfoam Christianity," as it was satirized by Ed Willock in an outrageous cartoon showing a contented Catholic snuggled down on a cross spread with that seductive cushioning. Many attempt a life of vigorous and dedicated action, while failing to realize that such action is authentically Christian and efficacious only when grafted to the Tree of Life on Calvary.

Your Ways Are Not My Ways, vol. II

Dying to Self

Would you have supernatural life and joy and riches and love? The way to get them is clear. You get eternal life by death to your life here on earth. You get joy through meekness in affliction. You get riches by renouncing all things. You obtain love by severing yourself from the love of earthly things.

If you desire to advance in the love of God, if you wish to promote the work of Christ, by spreading the divine life and love in the world, you see how it is to be done in this law fixed by God. It is not to be done by your speeches or articles or books.

What alone can give supernatural value to your work is fidelity to self-denial and penance, the minute self-sacrifice of a life that is wholly consecrated to God, increasing detachment from the world and its vanities, meekness in bearing injury, patience and humility and endurance in trials.

Detachment, mortification, trials — these are like a pruning knife in the hand of God, who, like a good gardener, uses them to get more fruit from us. The gardener prunes his trees in order to make them increase. He cuts them shorter in order that they may grow taller, he thins them out in order that they may grow more thickly, he cuts off the fruit that he may get more fruit, he cuts off living branches in order to increase the tree's vitality.

The same laws operate in the supernatural world: "I am the true vine and My Father is the vine-dresser. Every branch in Me that bears no fruit, He will take away and every branch that bears fruit He will cleanse, that it may bear more fruit" (Jn 15:1-2).

Alas for the soul that does not submit to the pruning knife: its fruit, at best, like that of a tree grown up without care, will be scattered and dwarfed and tasteless.

Mortification and renunciation are man's part of the work of sanctification; and much grace is necessary for us even to accomplish that. This is the work that God has put into our hands and, if it is neglected, there will be no growth or fruitfulness.

It is all very well to dream of the treasures of heaven. But they are in God's possession, not in ours; to get them, we must stop dreaming and set to work; and our work is to cast out of our hearts the treasures of earth.

There is another idea that needs to be refuted: the notion that penance is gloomy and that insistence on mortification is pessimism. Or rather, we should admit the truth of this contention, for pagans are those who live by the rule, "Take thy ease, eat, drink, and be merry" (Lk 12:19). It is sad indeed for them to be deprived of their only pleasure!

It is different for those who live for God — who, spurning the consolations that come from creatures, listen to Him who said, "Come to Me . . . and I will refresh you."

For these, penance is not a cause of gloom — it is a means ready at hand for acquiring the one true joy. "Now all discipline seems for the present to be a matter not for joy but for grief; but afterwards it yields the most peaceful fruit of justice to those who have been exercised by it" (Heb 12:11). Therefore, "let us run with patience to the race set before us, looking toward the Author and Finisher of faith, Jesus, who for joy set before Him, endured a cross" (Heb 12:1-2).

The Catholic Worker (April 1942)

Our Lady, Queen of Apostles

Father Hugo's affirmation of the ancient wisdom of the Church, summed up best perhaps by St. Bonaventure: "If you seek Christ without Mary, you seek Him in vain."

Necessary and indispensable to bringing Christ to men and women is a true devotion to Christ's Mother. In the words of St. Louis Grignon de Montfort: "It is through the most Holy Virgin Mary that Jesus came into the world and it is through her that He has to reign in the world.... Jesus Christ is not known as He ought to be because Mary has, up to this time, been unknown."

Jesus is Truth, the very Word of God (Jn 14:6, 1:1). Now the Word became flesh, the Scriptures say. Let us remember, further, that He became flesh through Mary. That is to say, divine truth entered the world through Mary. This was according to a plan and a decree formed by God from all eternity. Since there is no shadow of change in God, Mary must still be the means of bringing divine truth to the world.

Jesus is Life (Jn 14:6). God's truth is not abstract, but living. To know God is to live. "The words that I have spoken to you are spirit and life" (Jn 6:63). The Word of Truth is Himself a living person and He has come into the world to give people some share in the divine life: "I am come that they may have life" (Jn 10:10).

It was, however, only through Mary that this divine life came to our humanity. She was, by God's will, the instrument through which life came into the world. And it is still through Mary that life must come into the souls of men and women.

You and I have a supernatural life through Mary and all our future growth in that life shall likewise be through her. It is a cold doctrinal fact that, if Christ is to reign in the world, He shall do so through Mary.

It is certainly true that the world can be saved, even on the temporal level, by Christianity. But not by the diminished Christianity that we Christians have been practicing. If Christianity is to come into the world, it can be only through Mary. Once again, however, it is not through such lukewarm and false devotion to her as is now found among us.

The following words, which Father Frederick Faber spoke of English Catholics at the turn of the century, can be applied equally to us:

> Here in England, Mary is not half enough preached. Devotion to her is low and thin and poor. It is frightened out of its wits by the sneers of heresy. It is always invoking human respect and carnal prudence, wishing to make Mary so little of a Mary that Protestants may feel at ease about her. Its ignorance of theology makes it unsubstantial and unworthy. It is not the prominent characteristic of our religion which it ought to be. It has not faith in itself.

Hence it is that Jesus is not loved, that heretics are not converted, that the Church is not exalted; that souls which might be saints wither and dwindle; that the sacraments are not rightly frequented, or souls enthusiastically evangelized. Jesus is obscured because Mary is kept in the background. Thousands of souls perish because Mary is withheld from them. It is the miserable, unworthy shadow which we call our devotion to the Blessed Virgin that is the cause of all these wants and blights, these evils and omissions and declines.

Only those who seek to live according to the cross are capable of being true clients of Our Lady. In "The Secret of Mary," a pamphlet in which St. Louis Grignon de Montfort gives a brief summary of this devotion, he points out those who are to be given this secret, namely, "those persons who deserve it by their prayers, their almsgiving and mortifications, by the persecutions they suffer, by their detachment from the world, and their zeal for the salvation of souls."

True devotion to Mary will ever remain a secret hidden from the carnal person, the natural person, the Christian who refuses the cross. Again St. Louis Grignon de Montfort writes: "If then, as is certain, the knowledge and the kingdom of Christ are to come into the world, it will be by the necessary consequence of the knowledge and the kingdom of the most Blessed Virgin Mary, who brought Him into the world for the first time and will make His second advent full of splendor."

The Catholic Worker (July-August 1942)

God's Law and the Law of the Land

Father Hugo never sketched anything approaching a systematic program of Catholic political action. In the following selection he outlines the basic position that Christians should take toward government authorities and civil laws. In the concluding selection on Dorothy Day, he takes up her basic critique of the workings of American society from the standpoint of the Gospel and Catholic teaching.

❧

Let everyone be subject to the governing authorities. For there is no authority except from God, and those that exist have been instituted by God. Therefore he who resists the authorities resists what God has appointed, and those who resist will incur judgment. For rulers are not a terror to good conduct but to bad (Rom 13:1-2).

People of faith will have no difficulty tracing the will of God in laws that assist them and all the members of the community in finding their true human welfare and establishing a just society. And they will readily trace the divine will in all the laws that support them in their concern and love for others. Even such apparently minor ordinances as traffic laws will not be unimportant in this respect, since love would have him do all that he can for his neighbor, as well as for himself — *Love is the fulfilling of the law* (Rom 13:10).

On the other hand, unjust laws cannot manifest the will and holiness of God and therefore lack moral force. Hence, we learn that when Peter and the other Apostles were told not to preach Christ, they answered, "We must obey God rather than men" (Acts 5:29).

Yet this same Peter wrote to the first generation of Christians, "Be subject for the Lord's sake to every institution, whether it be to the emperor as supreme, or to the governors, as sent by Him to punish those who do wrong and to praise those who do right" (1 Pt 2:13-14).

Peter therefore vindicates the right and duty of conscientious objection against unjust laws, without rejecting legitimate authority.

What Henry David Thoreau called civil disobedience, therefore, if genuinely based on conscience, is not disobedience at all but rather, like Peter's act, obedience to the higher authority of God.

Jesus himself, while enjoining obedience to the authority of the Pharisees (Mt 23:3), rejected many of their regulations as mere traditions of men without value before the Father (Mk 2:23; 7:3, 9).

This He did in spite of an apparently contrary instruction elsewhere: "The scribes and Pharisees sit on Moses' seat; so practice and observe whatever they tell you to do, but not what they do" (Mt 23:3).

It may be objected that, if the practice of conscientious objection were to become general it would lead to chaos and anarchy. This is true. Therefore, for the sake of civil order it should be exceptional or happen not at all. Yet if it becomes necessary to exercise such disobedience frequently, this is rather the fault and responsibility of those in authority rather than of the subjects.

Obedience is a two-edged sword imposing duties and responsibility on those exercising authority as well as on those living under it. If the latter are expected to obey, the former must see to it that their ordinances are just. Otherwise, their ordinances lack moral force. A multiplication of injustices, that is, of authority serving special interests instead of the common good, invites anarchy.

To seek the divine will through the ordinances of human authority may be compared to hearing the paradisal melodies of Mozart on a desert island through the distortions of a damaged instrument. Our expectations must be modest. Even Jesus seemed to be looking into a gray obscurity when He prayed, "If it is possible, let this chalice pass from Me." We cannot expect greater clarity for ourselves.

Your Ways Are Not My Ways, vol. II

Dorothy Day, Apostle of the Industrial Age

In his retreats and in his writings, Father Hugo returned again and again to the witness in Christian living offered by Dorothy Day, who was, in many ways, one of his spiritual godchildren.

For Father Hugo, Dorothy Day was a saint for this age, a convert who had embraced the contradictions of trying to live an apostolic life in the heart of the world's richest and strongest nation. In her writings in The Catholic Worker, she referred to Father Hugo as a dear and precious friend, and as a defining influence on her spiritual life.

In the years after her death, Father Hugo was a zealous guardian of the truth that Dorothy's special witness to this century had been shaped by his retreat and its teaching of radical Christian holiness. Father Hugo noted ruefully that an "elite of 'intellectuals' " and self-anointed interpreters of Dorothy's life "distrusted her spiritual judgment" and rejected the spirituality of detachment, self-sacrifice, and obedience to Christ that had been at the heart of her work.

In his last book, the privately printed "Your Ways Are Not My Ways," Father Hugo insisted that such disdain came from a confused generation of Catholic activists — some of whom, in his estimation, had fallen under the spell of "the new morality" that rejected traditional Church moral norms in favor of norms established by the prevailing culture. Such people, he claimed, had made social action their religion; or, as he put it, they preferred "the secular mystique of activism rather than . . . the authentic mysticism of prayer and love." To such critics, whom he called "the unseeing and the latecomers," any talk of suffering with Christ, renouncing the world for the higher calling of life in Christ, was foolishness. But Father Hugo continued to maintain that work for social justice "is authentically Christian and efficacious only when grafted to the Tree of Life on Calvary."

Four years before her death, Dorothy asked Father Hugo to preach the homily at her funeral. But when she died, November 30, 1980, he was unable, for a variety of reasons, to attend the funeral. The following reflections call attention to the great influence of Father Hugo's teaching on Dorothy's life. They also summarize his ideal of the apostolate — mysticism in action.

I knew Dorothy Day since about 1940, when she came to Pittsburgh to make a retreat that I was conducting. The retreat had been planned for a group of young Catholic actionists. This was soon after Dorothy had become a Catholic and was looking for a deepening of her Christian faith.

She came at the suggestion of Sister Peter Claver, a Trinitarian, who was working among the poor in the New York area. Sister Peter was the first devout and knowledgeable Catholic that Dorothy had become acquainted with. She told Dorothy about the retreats we were giving, and gave her some notes. Dorothy read these promptly and came right back asking: "This is what I want: where do I find these men?" After the retreat she said, "I have at last found what I have been looking for in the Church!"

Subsequently, Dorothy came to the retreats many times, taking copious notes, which would often turn up later in her "On Pilgrimage" column in *The Catholic Worker,* and leading a constant stream of Catholic Workers to the retreat in Pittsburgh. She also invited me to conduct retreats at the Catholic Worker farms in Easton, Newburg, and Tivoli.

She called the retreat "the bread of the strong," said that it was "like hearing the Gospel for the first time" and a "foretaste of heaven." Sister Peter Claver once wrote, "The retreat is what made the wheels go round in the Worker movement. It is what made Dorothy holy."

The last retreat that she attended was in August 1976, at Mount Nazareth Center, Pittsburgh, through the hospitality of the Sisters of the Holy Family of Nazareth. In *The Catholic Worker* for March-April, 1978, she wrote: "I must not forget to mention the influence of Fr. John J. Hugo in my life. He gave retreats in the early days of the Worker that so aroused the ire of other priests that his books, his 'doctrine,' were put 'on the shelf,' as it were, for many years. He was young and preached so thrillingly severe a doctrine of 'putting off' the world and 'putting on' Christ, and upheld the pacifist cause so ardently, that for years he was shifted from parish to parish in his diocese. A truly consistent person, he kept his calm over the years, and is now giving scriptural retreats again."

For almost forty years, therefore, I was in communication with Dorothy in her deepest self, that is to say, in her spirituality, which has made all her other gifts so fruitful. What I wish to do now, as we mourn her passing from us, is to review her life briefly, considering the manner in which she has helped so many, both within and outside the Church: for her influence has been worldwide.

In Dorothy Day's life and thinking I see three convergent tendencies, all rooted in an unusual depth of Christian love.

The first and perhaps the best known of these is her compassion for the poor, the suffering, the downtrodden, the *anawim*, "the little ones," so beloved by Yahweh in the Old Testament and by His Son in the New.

Concern for the poorest has been dramatically shown in the Houses of Hospitality which, with Peter Maurin, her partner in this work, she established in the depressed areas of many of our large cities. These houses have also inspired other groups who, in response to this challenge, are also devoting themselves to helping especially the urban poor.

These poor are the offscourings of our industrial society, the flotsam and jetsam of the injustices arising from the overcentralization and maldistribution of our economic system. Dorothy's work of charity, therefore, besides bringing immediate aid to those in need, has served also to draw attention to the flaws of our system.

No doubt, as Dorothy well knew herself, the houses of hospitality are an inadequate remedy for the widespread evil. Yet there needs to be someone at hand to care directly and immediately for the manifold emergencies occurring every day, and especially to help those considered unacceptable even by social agencies — alcoholics, tramps, prostitutes, the emotionally and mentally deranged — all the unwanted of our society.

For Dorothy the phrase "deserving poor" was meaningless and near blasphemous. All who are in need deserve our love, and indeed our Father in heaven, of whose generosity she liked to speak, loves us all, although we are all "unworthy servants" (Lk 17:10).

If Dorothy's policy — or lack of any policy, as it seemed to some — appeared irresponsible, she knew that she was in the good company of Him who was criticized for his interest in the lame and the halt, as well as for seeking the company of "publicans and sinners." In *The Catholic Worker*, which had a readership of more than 90,000, Dorothy was continually drawing attention to the plight of such people and to all the problems and injustices that shatter the lives of so many in our society.

Yet despite her wish to direct attention to the social problem, and help to solve it, her love of the poor was not merely abstract and humanitarian; she was not merely a philanthropist. Her love was direct and personal.

This may be illustrated by a story told of her as she was guided by civic minded citizens through San Francisco to see the Golden Gate bridge. She met civic pride over this great engineering feat with the question, "Isn't this where the sixteen workers fell into the bay and were killed?"

Dorothy valued people over things, a characteristic not common in our society.

In this connection she frequently quoted a remark made in the retreat, "The love you give to the one you love least is the measure of the love you will receive from God." This is of course but a paraphrase of the Lord's own, "The measure you give will be the measure you get" (Mt 7:2). Dorothy was concerned that no one be excluded from love.

Another characteristic of Dorothy Day is what is commonly called her pacifism: which, however, seems too pale a word to describe her utter abhorrence of war. When she spoke of war, her eyes would narrow, her jaws set, her whole body became taut. Her loathing for this manifestation of human power was complete.

To some she would appear irrational and fanatical, so conditioned have we become in this "enlightened" age to seeing our young, armed with every destructive weapon that science and technology can devise, marching bravely forth to destroy one another. To such a height have reason and civilization brought us!

For Dorothy Day, I believe, the rejection of war was indeed beyond reason, especially beyond the shadowed reason by which nations and leaders choose to govern our lives.

For Dorothy the rejection of war was a matter of religion, an act of faith. "The just one lives by faith" (Rom 1:17). Indeed, it was her supreme act of faith in the goodness of God, who is love, and who makes love, entire love with the whole heart, at once the fundamental law of life for His rational creatures and the fulfillment of their deepest desires. This love, centered in God and reflecting His glory, embraces all His creatures; and if it starts with loving one's neighbor as oneself, it culminates in "A new commandment I give to you, that you love one another; even as I have loved you, that you also love one another" (Jn 13:34).

If in this matter Dorothy Day seems too far ahead of the human race, and the Christian community as well, both the race and the community need to catch up. We have reached a time in history when the very survival of the human race depends on acceptance of the fundamental law of God, the law of love.

Although many Catholics incline toward pacifism, few will go the whole way to absolute pacifism. The doctrine of "the just war," approved by St. Augustine and St. Thomas Aquinas, is an obstacle difficult to surmount. Hence Catholic opposition to war, except for the statements of a few popes, becomes conditional and blurred.

Dorothy was an absolute pacifist. She believe that violence cannot accomplish true peace. She gave her assent in sheer faith to the words of Jesus, "All who take the sword will perish by the sword" (Mt 26:52).

Dorothy Day's pacifism was not merely sentimental, nor merely doctrinaire. It issued from a love expressing itself in universal compassion. Her hatred of war was of a piece with her efforts to reduce the misery of the little people in our great urban ghettos.

Like her Master she had compassion on the multitudes. She saw that in every age, and especially in our "advanced age" of technological warfare, it is the poor, those already oppressed, who suffer first and most, both as soldiers and civilians. They suffer in the destroyed cities. They are the ones in the long lines of refugees, carrying their few possessions on their backs. They are the first to be conscripted into our armies.

Modern war with its mass killings is the ultimate, encompassing immorality, the source of all other immoralities. We deplore urban violence, even television violence, while training generations of our young in how to kill their fellows. We worry about the spread of sexual immorality; yet how can those who are formed without respect for life show respect for the source of life?

True, in a capitalist society we profess a belief at least in the "sacredness" of property. But this is no adequate basis for morality and, in practice, is like trying to save a wooden house in a general conflagration. Without respect for human life — which in practice means compassion for all our fellow humans — there is no human good or value on which we can anchor human morality. "Be compassionate as your Father is compassionate" (Lk 6:36).

Dorothy's pacifism will be a continuing reminder of how all Christians should feel about the horrifying actuality of war. It will be, I think, her greatest contribution to the Church, the body of Christ, which she loved.

And here we come to the third purpose which marks the life of Dorothy Day and joins with her anti-war effort and crusade against social injustice: It is not enough to give alms. Those in need must be provided with a secure livelihood as the basis for a life of human dignity.

The Catholic Worker movement has by some been thought of as a band of starry-eyed do-gooders without any real program. In fact, with Dorothy Day leading, they offered an alternative to the dominant socio-economic trends of the day.

The program adopted by Dorothy, intended to remove the causes of injustice and to neutralize the forces leading to war, is, if modest in appearance, breathtaking in its ambition. We should not be surprised, therefore, that the success of this effort of the Catholic Worker has not been notable. The difficulties in the way of its success are immense.

Two economic systems, capitalism and socialism, strive for dominance in the world, and people generally tend to see the solution of our socio-economic woes in one or the other of these two systems. In the West we oppose socialism and communism, which we see as a threat to our way of life. To be sure, we also recognize certain flaws in capitalist society. These we seek to cure by an endless series of band-aid solutions. Few in the West, even among those invoking Christian social principles, have attempted a really drastic criticism of capitalism or even admit that such a criticism is needed.

In becoming a Catholic Dorothy Day moved away from the social-ist solution, but she never fully adopted the capitalist system. She re-mained between them recognizing a third possibility: a society in which the economic system is decentralized, allowing for smaller units of ag-riculture and business, and encouraging the independent initiative of individuals. By decentralizing the economy, ordinary people can escape an almost serf-like (with many comforts of course) dependence on their masters, whether socialist or capitalist, and become responsible for their own destinies.

Dorothy Day was not an ideologist, she recognized her ideals in prac-tice by promoting a tendency toward small farms and small businesses to enhance the dignity and independence of the little people. Here is the rea-son for the communal farms established by the Catholic Worker. These in turn would prepare individuals to live on family farms. And of course de-centralism would encourage small businesses as well as small manufactur-ers. It is a tendency but not an ideology.

Dorothy kept up a constant struggle against all the injustices and abuses of the capitalist society in which she lived. She would help the little people in legitimate enterprise. We should not forget that the whole purpose of Catholic social action is to provide everyone with the means essential to a dignified human life. This was also very much Dorothy's goal.

"In the evening of life we shall be judged on love." This saying of St. John of the Cross is not merely a pious platitude. It is quintessential theol-ogy and comes to us from Jesus Himself in the preview He gives of judg-ment (Mt 25:31-40):

> When the Son of Man comes in His glory, and all the angels with Him, then He will sit on His glorious throne. Before Him will be gathered all the nations, and He will separate them one from

another as a shepherd separates the sheep from the goats, and the sheep He will place at His right hand, but the goats at His left.

Then the King will say to those at His right hand, "Come, O blessed of My Father, inherit the kingdom prepared for you from the foundation of the world; for I was hungry and you gave Me to eat, I was thirsty and you gave Me drink, I was a stranger and you welcomed Me, I was naked and you clothed Me, I was sick and you visited Me, I was in prison and you came to Me. . . . Truly I say to you, as you did it to one of the least of these My brethren, you did it to Me."

"In the evening of life we shall be judged on love." It was to this love for the least brethren that Dorothy devoted her life. In this love were rooted all three of the tendencies, or branches, described above, that filled her life.

We do not presume to canonize Dorothy, but surely we may declare the basis of our great hopes for her. She herself provided us with a way of doing this. Just three weeks before her death, Sister Peter Claver had a joyful, if very short, visit with her. Sitting together in Dorothy's little room at Maryhouse, the Catholic Worker house in New York City, they talked, as long-time friends do, of the past and experiences shared.

Dorothy held on her lap a book of the retreat conferences that I had sent to her. Holding them she turned and fondled some flowers in a little vase, and said, "I am still sowing." When I heard this I rejoiced because I realized that she was still reaching into the retreat for "the bread of the strong" as she approached the Day of the Lord, the day of harvesting.

She was recalling the central and climactic idea of the retreat, taken from the Lord Himself as He approached His own death — and resurrection: "Truly, truly, I say to you, unless a grain of wheat falls into the earth and dies, it remains alone; but if it dies, it bears much fruit" (Jn 12:24).

Jesus is Himself the first and perfect Grain of Wheat: in His dying we all may have eternal life. Yet we, too, are grains of wheat; and all the good things that the Lord has given us are grains of wheat. And we are called, sooner or later, to "sow" them, that is to relinquish them to the Lord to gain an eternal harvest.

As Dorothy looked back over her life, so generously given to that "harsh and dreadful love," a life she herself candidly described as a "long loneliness," now diminished and completed with an irreversible disease, she was able to see it all, in faith, as a sowing. And sowing is done with the hope of reaping a harvest. As the Psalmist put it, "Those who sow in tears, reap with shouts of joy!"

Dorothy was buried in a homespun dress and laid in a plain wooden casket provided by the Trappists. Around her neck was a wooden chain holding an icon. On the casket was one flower, saying *Resurrection*.

He that goes forth weeping, bearing the seed for sowing, shall come home with shouts of joy, bringing his sheaves with him (Ps 126:6).

The Pittsburgh Catholic (December 12, 1980)

VI
How to Fight a War:
Conscientious Objection
and the Nuclear Age

Catholics and War

Father Hugo's writings on war and peace were forged in the Second World War. With the great cities of Europe under siege and bombardment, with the passions of fear, hatred, and uncertainty excited on a mass and global scale, Father Hugo preached against the Allied war effort in the name of what he called "the Gospel of Peace."

To say that he was a lonely voice at the time would be a vast understatement. The American Catholic bishops had joined their brothers across the seas in calling the conflict a "just war" and giving their blessing to the Allied cause. Tens of thousands of the U.S. Catholic faithful were fighting and dying alongside their countrymen in the battlefields of Europe and the South Pacific. Catholic clergymen were highly visible in their patriotic and moral support for U.S. troops and the war.

Father Hugo was among a handful of dissident voices opposed in conscience to cooperating with the war effort. His own conscientious objection grew out of his belief that the Gospel calling of all Christians was to holiness and perfection. He professed respect for the Church's traditional "just war" theory, but he said that the traditional criteria used to determine a war's justice had not been met in the case of World War II. He said that even if it was granted that the Allies had a "just cause" for war against Germany and Japan, the warfare could not be justified because the tactics of "total war" — bombing entire cities instead of just military targets — violated Church requirements that warfare be "proportionate" and strictly protect innocent civilians from casualties. The U.S. use of the "bomb" at the end of the war only solidified his conviction that the ways and means of modern warfare made it impossible for any war to satisfy Catholic moral criteria. But Father Hugo also believed strongly that Catholics were called to follow "the higher way" of the Sermon on the Mount. Simply put, for Father Hugo, war and violence were not Christ's way and hence they could not be the way of His followers.

Father Hugo's work made a lasting contribution to the Church's the-

ology of peace. But the texts presented here are not merely of historical import. They show the daily implications of the "radical Christianity" that Father Hugo preached. Moreover, the issues they touch — the relationship between the religious freedom of the Christian and the demands of the state, the duty of Christian conscience when confronted with unjust or immoral laws, the moral life of nations — are as pertinent today as they were a half-century ago.

These first several selections show the stamp of St. Thomas Aquinas, as Father Hugo argues in patient and rigorous Thomistic fashion against the claim that good Catholics cannot be conscientious objectors to war.

≈≈✿≈≈

Catholics who regard it a duty to serve their country in the armed forces look askance at their co religionists who have taken up the position of "conscientious objectors" to the war. Indeed, it has become customary for many, even responsible writers and editors, to cast slurs on the those who for conscience's sake oppose uncompromisingly the monstrous evil of modern war. Because Catholics as a whole — so the argument runs — have failed to adopt conscientious objection as the characteristically Catholic response to war, therefore it must be wrong and un-Catholic.

That is the mode of argument fortunately not common among Catholic theologians. If it were, then we could acquiesce in any widespread abuse among Catholics simply because it is widespread: or we could dismiss any Christian ideal that is rarely realized in the lives of Catholics, as for example the Franciscan ideal of poverty, simply because it is rarely realized. By the same token, if votes determine truth then we Catholics would have to adopt birth control and divorce as institutions characteristic of our age and genius.

Msgr. Fulton Sheen has said more than once that "right is right though nobody is right, and wrong is wrong though everyone is wrong." Since when has Catholic theology adopted the method of deciding controversial issues by counting noses on the respective sides?

People, even Catholics, have been known to abandon ideals, not because the latter were wrong, but because they themselves shrank from the consequences of defending unpopular and unacceptable truths.

When in an entirely Catholic country, Henry VIII began to tamper with Christian marriage and scale down papal supremacy, he was opposed by just one Catholic layman, a handful of Carthusians, and one bishop.

It was urged against Thomas More, the one layman, that all the priests and bishops, with the exceptions mentioned, were on the opposite side of the quarrel, that the universities and the whole of Catholic England had accepted the king's innovations, and that they could not all be wrong. Even More's family and friends considered him odd, deluded, obstinate, and it did indeed seem inconceivable that everyone including priests and bishops should be wrong except this small group of men.

Yet the passage of four centuries, climaxed by a canonization process, has shown that all of Catholic England was actually wrong, while only St. Thomas More and St. John Fisher, the bishop, and the Carthusians were right.

More was a conscientious objector: that is, he objected to the infringement of the state upon certain sacred rights, although no one else could see this infringement. Incidentally, he was also a pacifist.

His case is parallel to the one we are considering; for the modern conscientious objector, while not denying the duty of obedience to the state, considers that the state today, in its declarations and conduct of war, is again trampling underfoot sacred human rights. Nor is the controversy decided against the conscientious objector simply because, as in More's day, the mass of people prefer to go along with the all-powerful state.

Oddly, among Catholics there is no public discussion of the matter at all. There is absolutely no debate in the Catholic press over the most important moral and spiritual issue of the day. Catholics have left the matter entirely in the hands of officials with little or no Christianity, and they are apparently satisfied to accept the moral decisions of these rather dubious ethical authorities. Still, as soon as one begins to examine modern war in the light of conditions set down by theologians, doubts begin to arise in the mind. Only by suppressing discussion, or refraining from it, can a semblance of unanimity be obtained.

A person is required to obey his or her superiors and not to judge them. For this reason it is concluded that the Catholic's duty in war is also obedience and that he consequently has no choice when he is called to arms by lawful authority.

Certainly the Christian is bound by obedience. Yet if the obedience demanded is such as to dispense or prevent him from forming his or her conscience aright, then it is the kind that goes with modern state-worship and it is not the obedience of Christianity.

Christian obedience is itself a duty of conscience. Its obligation must be recognized by conscience and freely acted upon before it becomes meritorious. Its genuine expression demands a great refinement of conscience, and it is not to be confused with timidity, fear, servility, or expedience.

Indeed, at first glance there is something suspicious about the universal appeal to obedience in an age which, as Pope Benedict XV pointed out in his discussion of the causes of war, is chiefly characterized by a spirit of disobedience and rebellion. In any event, religious obedience does not exempt men and women from judging the world and the morality of their actions. Were it to suppress conscience and deprive them of inalienable rights, there would be truth in the contention that religion is an opiate.

Furthermore, Christian obedience is circumscribed by certain definite limits. One of these is well known, namely, that we are obliged to obey in all things except sin. Hence subjects are not bound by the unjust laws of civil authority.

Here is exactly the crux of the present matter: The Catholic cannot claim exemption from the just laws of legitimate authority. But he can without fault disobey unjust laws even when these are framed by lawful authority. In such a case he has a *positive duty to disobey.*

This is shown by the martyrs who, obedient enough to Caesar in all that pertained to him, accepted death rather than obey him where his ordinances conflicted with the laws of Almighty God. The dying words of St. Thomas More were, "I die the king's good servant, *but God's first."*

The duty that the Christian has to obey in the case of just laws is balanced by his or her *duty to disobey* in the case of unjust laws. If a Catholic considers a war unjust, he not only has the right to be a conscientious objector; he has a very serious duty to be one.

Especially when nations are not Christian there is a need for great care in scrutinizing their ordinances. Obviously, too, the standard of judgment should be Christian. Surely then there is a grave necessity for vigilance in our country, where thought is dominated by neo-paganism and political practice is deeply infected by liberalism, a system that was formally condemned by the Holy See long before its condemnation of Nazism.

There are other important limitations to be attached to obedience. As St. Thomas Aquinas observes in his *Summa Theologiae* one is not obliged to obey a superior in matters over which the latter has no authority. Accordingly, says the saint, no person is bound to obey a human superior *in those things which pertain to the interior movements of the will.* In such matters obedience is due only to God.

Yet even when it is granted that Catholics in certain circumstances may refuse obedience to civil authorities, it is nevertheless urged by opponents of conscientious objection that this right cannot be exercised in the present situation because of public statements made by the bishops concerning the war.

These statements, it is alleged, should serve as a guide to Catholics for forming their consciences; and since many bishops have expressed approval of Allied war aims and their belief in the justice of World War II, the conscientious objector should lay aside scruples and do as he or she is told. Once these statements are made public, it is said, there is no further grounds for believing that the war is unjust.

This would be true if the bishops, in setting forth their views, were acting in virtue of the infallibility promised by Christ to His Church. But they clearly are not, and therefore, although their statements should be given the attention they deserve by reason of the dignity and authority of their writers, still they cannot be taken as a final resolution of the problem of conscience.

If the bishops were to lay down some definite doctrinal pronouncements or some precise legislation binding in conscience, the problem would be greatly simplified for Catholics. But they have not done so; their statements are expressions of their own view; and many bishops have not thought fit to make public statements on the war at all.

Of course it is extremely doubtful whether it falls within the scope of episcopal authority to make final doctrinal pronouncements or set up coercive legislation in this matter. As human authority cannot legislate for consciences, so it is the opinion of the best theologians, including St. Thomas, that even ecclesiastical law cannot directly enter the sacred precincts of conscience and compel the will.

Some Catholic writers, for example Gerald Vann, O.P., in his *Morality and War,* deny that even the Holy See can make a decision as to the justice of a particular war. But this much is certain: such a decision can never be made by any authority less than the Holy See or the bishops in conjunction with that See. No doubt all Catholics would welcome a final, authoritative answer to these difficulties; but as long as it does not come, they are left to make their own decisions.

A Catholic therefore, convinced by private study of the injustice of this war, can dissent from the views expressed by the bishops in their public statements without offending against obedience or showing any want of the respect and reverence due to episcopal authority.

Enlightened by the lessons of history as well as by his study of religion, he is simply recognizing in practice the doctrine of limited episcopal authority and jurisdiction. As Jacques Maritain writes in *The Things That Are Not Caesar's,* "a number of prelates do not constitute the Church and do not bind the Church, as the judges of Rouen have clearly proved." The prelates here referred to are the French and English bishops who condemned Joan of Arc for heresy and witchcraft. Within a lifetime their decision was reversed by the Holy See, and in due course she was canonized by the same infallible authority.

There are four grounds upon which a Catholic may be a conscientious objector:

First, he may regard conscription as immoral, since it deprives people of their right to follow a vocation, forces them into a life of celibacy for which they have no aptitude or call, and therefore interferes with, and seriously injures, Christian marriage and Christian family life.

Second, he may be convinced that all the conditions necessary for a just war are not verified in the present case. In this event it is his *duty* to be a conscientious objector.

Third, he may subscribe to the opinion held by a number of theologians that a just war is in practice impossible under modern circumstances. This is so, not only because of the use of unjust means, such as lying propaganda, chemical warfare, and the murder of civilians. It is also and mainly so because war can be justified only when there is no international society to adjust differences among nations. Since there is such an international society today, or at least all the necessary means for forming one, there can be no need or justification for war. These same theologians are the ones who deny, or gravely question the possibility of a genuine "war of defense" in modern circumstances. A Catholic convinced of the truth of these views might be a conscientious objector on the basis of them.

Finally, a Catholic may oppose war on the grounds that it is not Christ's way and that he chooses to follow the higher way that Christ has given us. The conscientious objector need not be troubled by the slurs of his or her co-religionist or the assertion that this position is not truly Catholic. He should not be moved by the falsehood that Catholics cannot be pacifists. Pacifist means peacemaker. Now the greatest of all peacemakers was Christ Himself — who reconciled humanity to God and broke down the walls of division that had once divided people. Moreover, the Savior makes pacifism one of the points of His basic code contained in the Beatitudes: "Blessed are the peacemakers, for they shall be called the children of God."

One wonders, therefore, by what authority certain Catholics would argue that pacifists, or peacemakers, are not legitimate followers of Christ. It is also difficult to understand how a Catholic can say, as many do, that the Church is opposed to pacifism and even condemns it. Precisely where might one find such a condemnation?

It is true that certain Catholics condemn pacifism, but they are not the Church. *Ubi Petrus, ibi ecclesia*: Where the Holy See takes her stand, there is the position of the Church. The Pope is the authentic voice of the Church.

And in the modern world, the greatest, the most uncompromising, the most insistent of all pacifists are the occupants of the See of St. Peter.

"I bless only peace," said Pope Pius X to the Austrian ambassador who sought for a blessing on the imperial arms and this statement admirably sums up the whole position of the modern papacy. Caught in the awful storm of war, they nevertheless talk only of *peace,* and refuse to say one word that would encourage war, whatever may be the pretended cause.

Although both sides try to force the Pope's words to favor their own position, none of the papal statements can be forced to imply an approval of war. When war is glorified as the means of saving democracy, or liberty, or Christianity, they who have the first duty of defending Christianity speak of the deeds which patriots applaud as "murder," "slaughter," "havoc," and "destruction."

Everyone knows of the popes' neutrality. But it is too often overlooked that there is something in their neutrality besides the unwillingness to favor one side rather than the other. There is the steadfast, heroic refusal to speak a syllable that might be construed as approval of war.

The Catholic Worker (May 1943)

Nations and the Moral Law

How strange that Catholics, who in peace time unanimously attribute all the ills that afflict modern society to its rejection of Christ, should in wartime declare that differences among nations may be settled without reference to His teaching.

Now to exempt nations and governments from the obligation of the Gospel law is not only unfortunate; it is also contrary to the clearly defined teaching of Christ and His Church: "Go, therefore, and make disciples of *all nations* . . . teaching them to observe *all* that I have commanded you" (Mt 28:19-20).

Pope Leo XIII, basing himself on these words, said in *Immortale Dei,* his encyclical letter on the Christian constitution of states: "To the Church has God assigned the charge of seeing to and legislating for all that concerns religion; *of teaching all nations.*" In the same letter he speaks in praise and longing of the "time when states were governed by the principles of Gospel teaching."

In *Pacem Dei,* his encyclical letter written at the close of World War I, Pope Benedict XV, after expounding Christian principles of charity goes on to add: "All that we have said here to individuals about the duty of charity, we wish to say also to the peoples who have been delivered from the burden of a long war. . . . *The Gospel has not one law of charity for individuals and another for states and nations,* which are indeed but collections of individuals."

To the Church alone, adds Pius XI in his peace encyclical *Ubi arcano Dei consilio,* belongs the capacity "to see that, when *public* and private morals have been reformed and established on more holy principles, *all things* shall be fully subjected to God, who beholdeth the heart, and shall be inwardly informed by His teachings and laws, with the result that in all things, the minds of all men and women, private individuals and rulers, and even the public institutions of civil society, shall be penetrated by the sense of religious duty and Christ shall be all in all."

Such statements, which might easily be multiplied, are clear enough: states and nations are under Gospel law. If you object that many states are not in fact Catholic, or even Christian in a loose sense — and therefore cannot be expected to acknowledge their religious duties or accept the teachings of Christ, at least as interpreted by the Catholic Church — it must be replied that such states do not by their religious neglect escape responsibility to God.

Those therefore who, pointing out that the proper end of the state is the common good of its citizens, go on to conclude that this end is material only and not also moral, fall into one of the liberal errors condemned by Leo XIII. "Those who are in authority owe it to the commonwealth not only to provide for its external well-being and the conveniences of life, but still more to *consult the welfare of men's souls* in the wisdom of their legislation," Leo said in *Libertas humana,* his encyclical on freedom.

The state, then, has a grave responsibility toward the souls of its citizens and their spiritual welfare: and because of this it must acknowledge the authority and truth of the one true religion established by God Himself. The state that turns away from Christianity, or fails to make those inquiries into the true religion demanded by religious sincerity, is not less reprehensible — rather, is far more reprehensible, since it has superior opportunities for inquiry — than the individual who refuses to seek the light, or who having even found it, prefers darkness rather than the light.

The Catholic Worker (June 1943)

War in Scripture and Tradition

To a Catholic, every social and economic problem is, in the first place, a spiritual problem. This indeed is a first principle of Christian sociology.

I know that there are certain pious phrases that almost all Catholics use when speaking of war — that it is a scourge of God, for instance. But they scarcely mean these things or even understand them. Pope Pius XII, in letters and radio addresses, pointed out the spiritual implications of the Second World War. And I have heard good Catholics refer to these utterances as "impractical," "unrealistic," and even as a kind of pious fiddle-faddle.

In a time of great spiritual need, too many Catholics think and act exactly as do the multitude who have no belief in spiritual powers. At the same time, they are not slow to claim spiritual sanction and authority for the perfectly secular, nationalistic, and sometimes un-Christian views that they maintain.

In all seriousness let us go to divine revelation for the light that we need in this time of darkness. The Old Testament especially contains a complete theology of war. Indeed, the one passage that I am about to quote is a brief but sufficient statement of the reason and cause of war. In it we can learn more of World War II than in the ingenious theories propounded in the newest books or in the latest dispatches from the special correspondents of *The New York Times*. Here is the text from the Book of Judges (2:11-12, 14-15):

> And the children of Israel did evil in the sight of the Lord, and they served Baalim. And they left the Lord the God of their fathers, who had brought them out of the land of Egypt; and they followed strange gods, and the gods of the people that dwelt round about them, and they adored them. And they provoked the Lord to anger. . . . And the Lord being angry against Israel, *delivered them into the hand of plunderers: who took them and sold them to their enemies, that dwelt round about. Neither could they stand against their enemies. But whithersoever they meant to go, the hand of the Lord was upon them . . . and they were greatly distressed.*

The passage which is begun by these words clearly shows that war is punishment inflicted on peoples for turning away from God. It is the penalty for infidelity and disobedience. That nations suffer from war, therefore, shows that they have turned aside from the service of God to the service of creatures.

It is impossible to believe that a nation is fighting for Christianity when it refuses to live in accordance with the laws of Christianity. If we had been Christians, there would be no war. And our arrogant self-righteousness, in the midst of our delinquency, is not the attitude best suited for turning aside the wrath of God. "God resisteth the proud, and giveth grace to the humble" (Jas 4:6).

When people appeal only to the mercy of God, forgetful of His justice, they make of the divine mercy a cloak for their own negligence and misconduct. Let us not forget that God is just, and that, as the passage from Judges shows, He is angered by infidelity even to the point of delivering His chosen people to the awful suffering of war.

That our country is now engaged in war means that we are being punished by God; that we are being punished means that our ways — our ways, as well as the ways of Germans and Japanese — have been evil.

"But," you will say, "can we so simply apply a doctrine from the Old Testament to conditions today?" A Catholic can scarcely ask that question: truth is one and eternal. Circumstances change, but the essential truth of things remains forever the same.

"Still," you will argue, "what angered God against the Israelites was idolatry — the whole passage from the Book of Judges is concerned with that particular sin. Now idolatry is indeed a serious offense; it sets at naught the very first and fundamental commandment. When a whole people becomes idolatrous, there is certainly reason that it should be punished by war. But we are not idolaters. In our worst excesses we do not go that far. Even when disobedient to the divine decrees, we for the most part acknowledge that there is but one true God."

One who would make such an objection would simply reveal that he does not understand what is meant by idolatry. We have our false gods, too. And if the manner of our idolatry has changed, the thing itself has remained the same.

Idolatry proceeds from the love of creatures — the merely natural, selfish love of creatures which causes men and women to turn aside from wholehearted love for the Creator.

Idolatry is love for creatures carried to its extreme; it is but the extremity of love. Thus people are said to be slaves and worshipers of what they love. "He that loves a creature," says St. John of the Cross in *Ascent of Mount Carmel,* "becomes as low as is that creature, and in some ways, lower; for love not only makes the love equal to the object of his love, *but even subjects him to it.*"

The love of creatures, then, is the occasion and the cause of idolatry. If unlike the heathens, we do not fall into childish and superstitious expressions of our idolatry, nevertheless in our hearts we still retain the root of the evil. Can anyone be blind to the frenzied pursuit of the vanities and pleasures of this world that goes on among those who claim to be fighting for God? Here is the idolatry that causes war!

Let this not be considered a forced interpretation of the Scriptures. Twice St. Paul, going much further, describes as *idolatry* the inordinate desire and love for creatures. "Mortify therefore your members which are upon the earth: immorality, uncleanness, lust, evil desire, *covetousness (which is a form of idol worship)*." Again: "For know you this and understand, that no fornicator, or unclean person, or *covetous one (for that is idolatry)* has any inheritance in the kingdom of Christ and God" (Col 3:5, Eph 5:5).

These words do not mean, according to St. Thomas, that idolatry and covetousness are identical. The apostle wishes us to note a similarity between these two offenses, and his words are therefore to be understood as a comparison. "As an idolater *subjects himself* to another creature, so also does the avaricious man," Thomas writes in *Summa Theologiae*.

The difference between them lies in the mode of their submission, Thomas continues. The idolater "subjects himself to the other that he may give it divine worship, whereas the avaricious person subjects himself by desiring it immoderately for its own use."

Can we say, then, that we are not idolaters and that the words of the Old Testament spoken on this score do not apply to us? On the contrary, we are being punished exactly as the Jews of old — for infidelity, for earthliness, for devotion to the false gods of this world. Indeed, our idolatry is the more malignant in that the very Son of God has come since the time of the Judges to teach us the secret and the mystery of the cross.

The New Testament reaffirms the teaching concerning war from the Old Testament. St. James asks the identical question that we have asked: "From whence are wars and contentions among you?" And he answers at once: "Are they not hence, from our concupiscences, which war in your members?" (Jas 4:1)

Concupiscence is simply the Latin for *desire*. Our concupiscences are our desire. Only, since our nature has been touched by the poison of original sin, these desires have been turned awry; so that now, instead of seeking satisfaction in their true good, which is God, they pursue restlessly the "fleeting and failing things of earth."

Therefore, the concupiscence that causes war is simply the inordinate desire for earthly goods — and desire becomes inordinate the moment that people seek their joy in these goods apart from God.

Pope Pius XI, in *Ubi arcano Dei consilio,* applies the text of St. James to conditions in our own day. He enumerates and describes in some detail, following St. John the Evangelist (cf. 1 Jn 2:15-17), the concupiscences that bring about war.

There is "the lust of the flesh," which the Holy Father explains is the "desire for pleasure." The "lust of the eyes" is "the desire for gain," and the "pride of life" is "the desire of dominating others" and of obtaining worldly honors. "It is from this intemperance of desire," concludes the Pope, "sheltering itself under an appearance of public good or love of country, that come the rivalries and enmities that we see between nations."

The Old Testament says that idolatry is the cause of war, St. James says the cause is concupiscence. The difference is only apparent. The explanation and connecting link between the two teachings is supplied by St. Paul when he calls covetousness a form of idolatry, and a form not unfamiliar to the modern world. Concupiscence, covetousness, idolatry. Describe it as you will, here at any rate is the true and the deepest cause of war.

Modern popes, in their great peace encyclicals, carry the same teaching forward to explain the dissension and misery in our contemporary world. In *Ad beatissimi Apostolorum,* Benedict XV enumerates four causes of war, and deeper than any of the others, he says, is "the feverish striving after the empty goods of this world."

We have already quoted from Pius XI the words which attribute war in our day to the fact that "all strive insatiably to attain the fleeting and failing things of the earth." He adds in *Ubi arcano Dei consilio,* that "it is of the very nature of material things that when sought unrestrainedly, they bring with them every sort of evil." Finally, the whole doctrine is summed up, with unsurpassed brevity and simplicity, in an address given by Pope Pius XII: "Forgetfulness of God is the fundamental cause for the ills which are distressing humanity."

Such is the teaching of the Scriptures and of Christian tradition concerning the causes of war. Let us at once draw from it some practical conclusions or corollaries:

First. It is customary to speak of war as a necessary evil. But the most terrible thing about war — worse by far than any of the gruesome stories that come from the front — is that it is a wholly unnecessary evil.

A Christian cannot subscribe to the stale and stupid fatalism that looks upon war as inevitable; nor may the words of Christ concerning "wars and rumors of wars," which refer to conditions before the destruction of Jerusalem, be twisted, as is sometimes done, into meaning that it is impossible to destroy war and therefore useless to work for such an end.

War comes from man's failure to love God with his whole heart; it comes from his freely turning away from God toward the creatures of the world. It is not the effect of huge, overpowering forces that carry men and women along with them willy-nilly; such a view is directly contrary to Christian teaching concerning personal freedom. It results from ignorance or neglect of a truth that is found on almost every page of any Christian devotional book. In *The Imitation of Christ,* the truth is expressed like this: "He that desireth the perfect joy that is everlasting, setteth little price by temporal joy. And he that seeketh any worldly joy or doth not in his heart fully despise it, showeth himself to love but little the joy of Heaven."

Secondly: If the cause of war is primarily moral and spiritual, then the cure for it must likewise be primarily moral and spiritual. The cure cannot be anything that is applied to the mere externals of human life or society, nor can it be any merely human means, however efficacious.

Spiritual and supernatural means must be brought into play. "For though we walk in the flesh, we do not war according to the flesh" (2 Cor 10:3). The trouble is in the human heart, which is turned toward creatures. An opposite movement must be begun and the heart directed to its Creator. Therefore the prophets cry out in troubled times: "Turn to the Lord with all your heart" (1 Sam 7:3).

Further, the popes never place *war* even among the natural means to be used for bringing about a new order of justice and charity and peace. After the outbreak of World War I, Pope Benedict XV protested in his encyclical *Ad beatissimi Apostolorum:* "Surely there are *other ways and means* whereby violated rights can be rectified. Let them be tried honestly and with good will, *and let arms meanwhile be laid aside.*" Again he said in a 1915 exhortation, still more insistently: "Nor let it be said that the immense conflict cannot be settled without the violence of war."

Similarly, in 1939, after the beginning of World War II, in his Christmas message, Pope Pius XII said of the problems that had brought it on that they "were not unsolvable" but that a solution had been prevented by "deep and apparently irremovable distrusts." That is what we have just said: the love of earthly things leads to distrust and division and, finally, if it is not checked, to destruction.

Pope Pius XI advises us, if we wish to get to the roots of the modern trouble, to consider these words of our Lord: "All these evil things come from within" (Mk 7:23). From within what? Obviously, from within the heart. Jesus had just said: "Understand you not that everything from without, entering into a man, cannot defile him. *Because it entereth not into his heart.* . . . The things which come out from a man, they defile a man" (Mk 7:18-20).

To eliminate war, not only must the conduct of leaders be reformed, *but also the hearts of those whom they lead must be purified of the dross of earthly affections.* "Prepare you hearts unto the Lord, and serve Him only" (1 Sam 7:3).

Weapons of the Spirit

The Law of Love

This text is notable for Father Hugo's careful reading of the Beatitudes, as well as for his comments on the plight of blacks in the United States and his prediction that war will one day be outlawed as slavery was.

⚜

Love is law, not a counsel. It includes our enemies. Further, it includes all men and women. Catholics are too prone to make national and racial distinctions. We criticize Hitler's prejudice against the Jews. Such criticism, however, is scarcely better than hypocrisy as long as we continue to segregate Negroes and discriminate against them.

Again, we sometimes limit the extension of Christ's body to the members of the Church. Such is not Catholic doctrine. It is not even Catholic doctrine to limit the Church to what we call the soul of the Church, that is, all those who are united to God by charity. *In the intention of God,* the Church includes all men and women.

For this reason Pope Leo XIII in 1899 consecrated the whole human race to the Sacred Heart of Jesus. Christ's empire, explained the sovereign pontiff, "extends not only over Catholic nations, and over those duly washed in the waters of holy baptism, who belong of right to the Church even though erroneous opinions keep them astray or dissent from her teaching cuts them off from her care — it comprises also all those who are deprived of the Christian faith, so that the whole human race is most truly under the power of Jesus Christ."

There is no political or racial limits to the law of love. Nor does war suspend or interrupt its binding force.

It may be pointed out against these views that nowhere in the Gospels is war explicitly condemned. Neither is there in the Gospels any condemnation of slavery. Indeed, no less than St. Paul accepts the institution of slavery, as is evident from his letter to Philemon. Yet who would deny that the law and spirit of the Gospel are opposed to slavery, or that slavery disappeared under the leavening influence of Christianity? In fact, we claim this as one of the great triumphs of the Christian religion.

There is an even greater triumph ahead: outlawing war. Let it be added that it is not only the spirit of Christianity that is opposed to war: the letter seems clear enough, too. Christ has given definite legislation on the matter, and it is difficult to understand how Catholics can say that He has not.

"Blessed are the peacemakers," He said. And in so doing, He made pacifism one of the eight basic principles of action contained in the Christian Manifesto, the Sermon on the Mount. One could not desire a more explicit manifestation of the divine will than this.

The exact relationship between the Gospel law and ethical principles in this matter of war can be studied by considering parallel cases. Reason and the Mosaic code say: "Thou shalt not steal." Jesus, while not reversing this, went much further. He said: "Do not lay up for yourselves treasures on earth, where rust and moth consume, and where thieves break in and steal; but lay for yourselves treasures in heaven, where neither rust nor moth consumes nor thieves break in and steal" (Mt 6:19-20).

What Our Lord wants is interior detachment from worldly goods and gold; people who have this will surely not steal, for they lack the desire for money.

Again, of old it had been said to men and women, both by reason and the decalogue: "Thou shalt not commit adultery." Jesus transforms this by a demand for complete inward purity: "But I say to you that anyone who even looks with lust at a woman has already committed adultery with her in his heart" (Mt 5:27-28).

Here also He wants detachment, mortification of carnal desires, single-hearted devotion to God. He wants people not to move by the breadth of a hair in the wrong direction. And those who follow Him are in no danger of committing adultery.

So also it had been said to them of old: "Thou shalt not kill," and again, "An eye for an eye and a tooth for a tooth." But Jesus goes higher: "A new commandment I give unto you, that you should love one another" (Jn 13:34). Once more, if we would listen to Him, there would be no hatred or bitterness among people, no murder or revenge; *and no war.*

The new law, then, while not reversing the old, nevertheless renders certain ordinances of the latter obsolete, or better, superfluous. It establishes a more perfect norm of conduct, a norm that certainly includes that given by reason and the decalogue, but rises beyond these to loftier heights. To a Christian — that is, to one who really has the mind of Christ — it is superfluous and unnecessary to say: "Thou shalt not steal," "Thou shalt not kill," "Thou shalt not commit adultery." He lives by a higher law that includes these but goes beyond them.

The higher law that he follows is that of love; and living by this, he may rule his conduct by the axiom of St. Augustine: "Love God and do what you will."

The Gospel of Christ with its law of universal love has brought us beyond the time when discussion of the mere natural justice of war should be a live issue. Those who have the mind of Christ would think rather in terms of the kingdom of Christ. They should judge war according to its ability to promote the interest of this kingdom of love. That the ethical

164

discussion is still the almost exclusive point of interest where there is any concern about the moral and spiritual implications of war at all, simply reflects the fact that the world, after having admired Christ for two thousand years, has not yet tried Christianity.

It is not that there is any opposition between the Gospel law and ethical truth; not even that there is conflict between ethical teachings on the just war and the law of evangelic love. It is only that once possessed of the nobler possibilities given to us by Christ, it is at once unnecessary and an act of infidelity to Christ to go back to the cruder notions and methods and ideals of the natural person.

"For the whole law is fulfilled in one word: *Thou shalt love thy neighbor as thyself.* But if you bite and devour one another, take heed or you will be consumed by one another" (Gal 5:14-15). This means that wars result from man's refusal to observe God's law of love; if it were observed, then there would be no wars, just or unjust. But if it is not observed, then there will be contention and mutual destruction. God's plan, and His legislation, would not simply outlaw war, they would exclude the possibility of war.

Unending warfare is the result of continuous failure to observe the first and greatest commandment: it is the result of man's failure to accept *and practice* the Sermon on the Mount. We have been too prone to look on that sermon as a pretty exercise of poetry, a mere decorative piece of Christianity. It is, however, the basic code of the Christian life; it is God's legislation governing man's conduct on earth. If men and women had followed it, there would be no war. Because the vast majority have disregarded it, there is ceaseless war.

But shall those who desire to observe the Gospel in its fullness be forbidden to do so because the infidelity of the many covers the earth with corpses? Surely, if any merely human authority would seek to prevent the Christian from realizing the fullness of the Christian life, he may call up that principle given us by the Apostles, "We must obey God rather than men" (Acts 5:29).

Suppose that this objection is made: "But there can be a just war of defense; when unjustly attacked, an individual or a nation has a right and even a duty to defend himself; a ruler has a duty of providing for the defense of his citizens. And in such cases warfare does not offend against charity. At any rate, St. Thomas does not think so. For he holds in *Summa Theologiae* that is licit to oppose one's enemies in order that they may changed from their evil course, and also to pray that temporal evils will befall them for their correction."

Certainly we have neither the desire nor the intention to impugn the principle of just defense; no doubt there is a right, even an ethical duty at times to repel force with force. In all this discussion it should be kept in mind that the right of self-defense is not in question at all, nor is the duty of dying for one's country.

What is questioned is whether there is a duty to kill one's brethren in Christ; especially as Christ has provided another way and other means for settling differences among His brethren. Ethical rights and duties — all that is clear enough. But what should be the supernatural behavior of a person who is called to be as perfect as the Heavenly Father is perfect?

Divinized by grace, the Christian is henceforth to live a divinized or godly life, for that is what is meant by a holy life. And his or her norm for this kind of life is the life of Jesus, who came on earth to teach men and women how to live. Can anyone imagine Jesus killing people? One of the rules given by spiritual writers to people seriously seeking to imitate Christ is that in all circumstances and difficulties they should ask themselves, "What would Christ do now?" Whatever we cannot imagine Him doing, then we ought not to do ourselves.

Mark well: We should not only avoid sin, we should seek to avoid whatever is un-Christlike. It is easy to think of Christ and how He would act even in the circumstances of modern life: for since His perfection required no particular set of external conditions, we can easily imagine Him moving among the scenes of modern life with His own unique perfection. But the imagination balks at the picture of Christ killing others.

Can you imagine Him who had compassion on the multitude bombing helpless civilians in a great city? Can you think of Him who cared for the lame and blind, heaping mass destruction on the aged and helpless, women and children? Can you think of Him glorifying or even sanctioning this kind of heroism? Can you think of him mowing down with a machine gun the men and women whom He died to redeem?

The Catholic Worker (June 1943)

The Evil of the Draft

This essay again highlights Father Hugo's logical style of argument, the legacy of his study of St. Thomas. It also marks the most explicit statement of Father Hugo's belief that opposition to war is a religious freedom issue. Because God made each person and destined them for a personal relationship with Him, then no authority, for whatever reason, may deny one the freedom to follow God's call. A much longer version of this essay was reprinted by Dorothy Day in The Catholic Worker on numerous occasions.

Universal military conscription alone is what makes modern war possible. More important even than technological advance for carrying on the wholesale slaughter characteristic of war today is the levying of modern mass armies. Were it possible to end this practice, war as it is known in the twentieth century simply could not exist.

Accordingly, in examining the ethical justification of modern war, there is no aspect of the question more important than that of the morality of conscription. Yet, despite this obvious importance, the subject has been little discussed and the morality of universal compulsory military service is commonly taken for granted.

Although we today seem to think that conscription always existed, in its modern form it is no older than the French Revolution. Of course something like it was known in ancient pagan nations like Greece and Rome, whose tendency to deify the state, plus their barbarism or semi-barbarism led them to adopt the ideal of "the nation in arms."

Sparta, in which every child was brought up to be a soldier or to assist in war, or simply left to die if not fitted for this, is the typical example of ancient compulsory military service and of the nation in arms. However, even in pagan nations, such service tended to disappear with advancing civilization so that Greece and Rome, at the height of their cultural achievements, were overcome by more barbarous peoples who saw in force, not art or learning, the measure of greatness. In Christian times conscription vanished almost entirely, and, with certain isolated exceptions, was unknown for a thousand years before the French Revolution.

Here is the argumentation upon which conscription depends for its morality. I quote from a report of the ethics committee of the Catholic Association for International Peace: The state's "primary purpose — the very reason for its existence — is the welfare of its citizens. But it is unthinkable that it continue in existence and be in a position to discharge its essential function, unless it be vested with the right to conscript the wealth and services of its citizens, according to the ability of each, in peace and in war, in so far as the public good demands it.

"When therefore, the state calls its citizens to arms in a just defensive war, or in preparation for such a war, it is acting fully within the limits of its strict rights. It is but exercising its natural prerogative of taking legitimate steps necessary for justified or even obligatory, self-defense. Now to the state's right to exact, corresponds the citizen's duty to render. The individual citizen is now no longer free to choose whether or not he will serve in the nation's armed forces."

167

Mark the words exactly: Because of the state's right to exist, it "is vested with the right also to conscript the wealth and services of its citizens." By means of those two apparently innocent but ambiguous words, "and services," conscription has been made morally acceptable. There is its ethical foundation. Is it really solid?

Taking these words —*and services*—exactly as they stand we do not at present quarrel with the conclusion: a state, we may concede, has indeed the right to conscript the wealth and services of its citizens. Only despite appearances, this is not an accurate description, therefore not a convincing justification of compulsory military service. In reality a state when it conscripts soldiers demands far more than what properly belongs to it, lays claim to something far beyond the wealth and *services* of its citizens.

Human beings, composed of body and soul, can be considered either in their bodily life, as an *individual*, or in their spiritual life, as a *person*. Looking on them as individuals, we see them primarily in their material component, their bodily life and work, their physical, economic and social activity. From this point of view, they are part of the community and therefore under the authority of the state. The state, therefore, whose end is the temporal welfare of its citizens, has power within limits over their temporal possessions and activities.

But men and women are not only individuals, material units in the state. He or she is also *a person,* a rational and spiritual substance, a complete agent of action, free and responsible in his or her own right. As persons, they are not part of the state, but are rather themselves a whole, a universe within themselves, independent of the state and above it.

Hence St. Thomas Aquinas teaches in *Summa Theologiae* that "man is not subordinated to the community in his total being and in regard to all matters." Accordingly, if we consider men and women as persons, *the community exists to serve them.* The reason is of course that human personality is spiritual and superior to all material interests.

Yet this is not the only reason, nor would it be sufficient to prevent people, in practice, from being absorbed by the state. The human person also has a supernatural end: and as the heavens are exalted above the earth, so is man's supernatural destiny above the terrestrial interests and temporal end of the state.

As a person, a man or a woman is destined to be united immediately to God. That is why St. Thomas says that in certain matters — that is, in the innermost core of personality — he is bound by obedience only to God. Because of eternal interests, therefore, one may be at times exempt from obedience to the state.

Further, there may be times when one is bound in conscience to disobey, that is, when the welfare of the soul or the interests of God are threatened. Pope Leo XIII writes in *Sapientiae Christianae:* "It is a sin to disobey God for the sake of pleasing men; it is wrong to break the law of Jesus Christ in order to obey the magistrate or under pretense of civil rights to transgress the laws of the Church: 'We ought to obey God rather than men' (Acts 5:29). The answer which Peter and the rest of the Apostles were wont to give to the governors when they laid unlawful commands upon them must always be made once for all on occasions. There is no better citizen either in peace or war than the Christian who is mindful of his or her duty; and he ought to suffer everything even death itself, rather than forsake the side of God and of the Church."

Moreover, the end of the state is not only inferior to that of the person, belonging to an altogether lower order, but it is also subordinate to the latter: society and the state are bound to help people realize their supernatural destiny. In the providential plan, the state's task is to care for those earthly interests whose real although hidden purpose is to assist, instruct, and try people in the practice of virtue, thereby conducting them to the their supernatural end and beatitude.

If people must obey the state within the limits of the latter's authority, the state may nevertheless not interfere with the rights of the person. This is precisely the reason for the Church's condemnation of communism. Pius XI writes in *Divini redemptoris,* his encyclical on atheistic communism: "Man cannot be exempted from his divinely imposed obligations toward civil society, and the representatives of authority have the right to coerce him when he refuses without reason to do his duty. Society, on the other hand, cannot defraud man of his God-granted rights. . . . Nor can society systematically void these rights by making their use impossible."

And if conscription as it exists today is to be ethically justified, it can only be because a state has the right to conscript, not only the *services* of its citizens, but also their *persons.* Conscription invades the domain of personality. And unless the state can be truly said to have complete sway over men and women — over their interior lives and rights, over their supernatural actions and choice of a final end, as well as over their external life and activity — then this method of raising soldiers, so intimately bound up with modern war, is without moral foundation.

It is only by such confusion, by such swamping of the spiritual by the material, such a persistent failure to understand the spiritual things, that the popular mind is enabled to accept conscription as a duty. Were people more spiritually-minded, more proficient in perceiving the realities of the spiritual world, they would be troubled by these huge concessions to the state — concessions which are part of that pagan conception of society whereby the human person is entirely absorbed by the state and subordinated to its terrestrial aims.

If you consider people as individuals, in their external life and activity, they exist for the sake of the whole, as the hand exists for the entire body. From this point of view, being a part, he is obliged to act for the good of the whole, even though this would involve great sacrifices, like the giving up of wealth and even life itself; as it may be necessary to sacrifice an arm to procure the health of the body. The individual as such has the same relation to the community that the bee does to the swarm or the ant to its colony.

This is why materialism and paganism so quickly and inevitably lead to slavery. Seeing only a man's material life, they judge his value solely in reference to the social whole, so that his personality, his freedom, his spiritual life, are completely disregarded and he is absorbed wholly in the life of the community.

When we take account of people's unique spiritual life, together with the dignity and rights that go with it, then the material measurement and analogy no longer hold. In this case their value cannot be assessed as that of a material part in relation to a whole, existing only for the good of the latter.

Consequently, although people must give up their natural goods, even life, for the sake of the country should this be necessary, they are never required nor are they permitted to give up their spiritual and supernatural rights and gifts for this reason.

Thus people are not required to give up chastity for the sake of the state. Moreover, they are not permitted to do so and, should such a command be given to them, they must obey God rather than men. The same holds true of other spiritual goods. To give up what is spiritual for something material, to abandon a supernatural good for one that is merely natural and even material, this would be a frightful inversion. The state has not the right to require it, and should it be required, the citizen has neither a duty nor a right to obey.

Right order requires a due subordination of ends: what is material must serve the spiritual, what is natural must serve the supernatural. The state, being of the natural order, is infinitely inferior to the supernatural good which the human person is bound to pursue. Accordingly the state violates the rights of person when it fails to provide, within its own sphere, the assistance which people need to seek after their supernatural end. It also violates these rights when it places in the way of its citizens hindrances to the attainment of their supernatural end, compels them to live in conditions opposed to their soul's welfare, or in any other way jeopardizes by its policies their true and eternal good.

Conscription hinders people from following their God-given vocations. It takes them at the best time of their youth, the time allowed them to prepare for their life work, pulls them out of their normal activities, postpones their education, in many cases putting a stop to it altogether, and prevents them from taking advantage of whatever opportunities might be given for pursuing their careers.

In order to appreciate how deep an injury this is, recall to mind the meaning of vocation. It is a call from God to some particular lifework, as a means of glorifying Him here below and of meriting happiness with Him in heaven. Knowing all the secret and unrealized potentialities of each person, God apportions to each his or her place and function in society, and also, on a higher plane, in the Church, the Mystical Body of Christ.

Everyone has his or her own unique and necessary place in each of these communities: in human society there is a need of a division of labor, in the Mystical Body there are "diversities of ministries." The work given to each one — manifested to them by their special abilities, the providential direction of their life, and the opportunities placed in their path — is their true and rightful vocation, their own way of serving God, of doing God's will, of working out their own souls' salvation.

Military conscription forces men and women to leave off, perhaps wholly to abandon, their true vocation. It forces them to depart, in many cases permanently, from the path intended for them by God, the path in which they were to find happiness, salvation, and the graces necessary to obtain these ends.

Depriving people of their vocations involves still graver evils. Conscripts, most of whom would ordinarily be married, are compelled by the state to accept a condition of celibacy for which they have neither call nor preparation nor the "graces of state" which are needed for this higher and more difficult mode of life.

Even when the conscription is temporary, this is a great hardship and *an occasion of sin*. Already, the unnatural exigencies of modern life force many young people to defer their marriage years beyond what is good for them, exposing them to inward strain and great outward temptation. Conscription makes the difficulty much greater. These young people have a *right* to get married if that is their calling; they also have a *need* to do so; and a *duty* as well, if failure to satisfy this need places them in danger of sin.

In other words, this is a right which very intimately involves their spiritual well-being and eternal salvation. The matter of vocation St. Thomas says is one over which human authority has no jurisdiction and the citizen is under no obligation to obey.

If it were a question merely of material good, no doubt the state could compel great sacrifices for the sake of the common welfare. But not even the state has the right to place people in the way of sin, at the same time depriving them of the ordinary aids needed for living a life of virtue.

The condition of enforced celibacy demands that people observe a rigorous chastity, such as is obligatory for priests and religious. In other words, they are made to live according to the obligations of a state in life which is not properly theirs and which becomes in fact an occasion of sin. Indeed, in the case of married conscripts, the injustice is much more flagrant.

The state itself recognizes the impossibility of the situation into which it forces its conscripts by the provisions it makes for keeping up their morale — provisions which are a further wound to the personality. Entertainments in which the passions are incited, lust aroused, and an artificial outlet provided for concupiscence, are supplied to maintain the conscripts in the mental and emotional condition needed in "good soldiers."

The immense cynicism of the godless state is shown in the fact that it will bring suggestive and obscene entertainment, not only to training centers, but also to the very battle-fronts all over the world where men and women are living in the very shadow of death and may at any moment be sent to stand before their Creator and Judge. First to put the young men and women in an occasion of sin, then to provide carefully prepared temptation, finally to lead them out to be slaughtered — this is the devilish procedure of the modern war, the manner in which the state of today seeks to assist its citizens to procure their eternal salvation.

Worse yet, realizing full well the impossibility of celibacy in conscripts, the state makes ample provision for contraceptives. Catholics may blink their eyes at this, seeing in it merely an accidental adjunct of a great crusade. Army authorities know differently, and they have therefore made available to the manufacturers of contraceptives materials which are not otherwise available outside the war industries. The practice of contraception, the encouragement of fornication and adultery — these are necessary means of keeping up "morale" in a conscript army.

In the case of married conscripts, the break-up of the family and the violation of family rights are likewise more obvious and more flagrant. An already existing home is dissolved. Husband and wife are both compelled to accept an enforced celibacy, being thus deprived of an intimate right and at the same time subjected to the abnormal strain and extraordinary temptations that go with such a state.

Moreover the father's influence is removed entirely from the home. Already modern industrialism had created a grave family problem by compelling fathers to work away from their homes and thereby throwing almost the whole burden of rearing the children upon the mother. This is certainly an undesirable situation and one responsible for much mischief.

In God's providential plan both husband and wife are meant to cooperate in the rearing of children; by depriving the latter of either parent there is removed from them an influence which the other parent cannot supply. In this matter also, male and female, father and mother, complete each other.

With shocking indifference to the sacredness of family life, the spiritual well-being of spouses, and the moral and religious upbringing of children, the state by its policy of conscription removes the father from the home entirely. It does not even stop to ask the number of children, but in large families as well as small ones, throws the burden of rearing entirely upon the mother. With its utterly materialistic outlook, it thinks that it is making sufficient compensation when it gives a money allowance for the care of each child.

It must be insisted that concern for family life is not mere sentimentality. As the person is above the state so that the state may not interfere with one's essential life, so also the family is prior to the state, which therefore may not interfere with the family's natural rights.

In his encyclical on marriage, *Casti connubii*, Pius XI writes: "No human law can abolish the natural and primitive right of marriage, or in any way limit the chief and principal purpose of marriage ordained by God's authority from the beginning. 'Increase and multiply' (Gn 1:28) Thus we have the family — the society of man's own household; a society limited indeed in numbers, but a true 'society' anterior to every kind of state or nation, with rights and duties of its own, totally independent of the commonwealth."

These principles have received a very telling, although most unfortunate, corroboration in the wave of juvenile delinquency that has spread over the country following our entrance into World War II. The whole moral and spiritual welfare of individuals and nations is involved in the life of its families. To tamper with it or with marriage, as conscription does, cannot but have disastrous results.

For the state to interfere with normal family life and force the members of families into situations that expose them to great moral danger is to commit an act of tyrannical and irreligious injustice.

We do not forget that the governments provide for chaplains for the people in the armed forces; nor do we underestimate the good that is done by these chaplains. The heroic devotion of so many of them is an inspiring story.

However, we are not concerned here with the achievements of individuals; we are trying rather to assess objectively the moral dangers of a particular situation. And it must be said that the army accepts chaplains, not as ministers of religion, but as *morale officers*. As such, they are burdened with many duties that have nothing to do with religion: this is the price that they must pay in order to provide divine services for their people.

Furthermore, as morale officers their function as ministers of a Catholic and transcendent religion is obscured or lost altogether by the fact that they are expected to subordinate their ministry to the furtherance of the national cause. Although Catholic chaplains in particular, through the administration of the sacraments, are able to give great aid to souls in spite of the restrictions laid upon them, they are as helpless as the others to change those basic conditions which make army life a morally unhealthy environment.

Their achievements, however heroic when individually considered, are at best palliative. This is particularly true when they are expected to provide religious services acceptable to all sects and shades of belief — a situation which prevents Catholic priests from communicating those specifically Christian and Catholic moral and ascetical teachings which are so indispensable for the practice of virtue.

It is necessary also as part of the indictment of conscription, to take account of the other training given to soldiers: propaganda to hate and instructions in brutal methods of inflicting death.

"Until he [that is, the soldier] hates the enemy with every instinct and every muscle, he will only be afraid. . . . Hate must become first nature to a soldier." That is a sample of instruction handed out to soldiers in World War II. People must be made utterly callous in regard to taking human life, all their moral repugnances must be broken down.

To quote a U.S. major speaking to a group of Allied soldiers he is instructing: "The average Englishman and American, unfortunately, suffers from remorse. You must overcome that, or it will slow you down at a crucial moment and cause your own death. Shooting a Jerry is like swatting a fly. Keep thinking that, shoot a few, and you'll sleep like a baby even after the bloodiest shambles."

Such excellent instruction naturally bears fruit, as is shown by such words as the following, spoken by an Allied pilot who had shot down 32 planes. "It's strictly fun. . . . I like to knock the enemy down and the only question that ever flashed across my mind is whether he'll be blown or fried (exploded in mid-air or burned up)."

Surely the barbarous cruelty attributed to the Nazis is no worse than this. Such a statement, which might be matched by others of the same kind from newspaper reports any day during the war, reveal the moral corruption that results from the profession of arms: "Out of the fullness of the heart the mouth speaketh." This is a sample — no better or no worse than hundreds of others of the same kind — of what military training does, and is intended to do, for youth.

There is no exaggeration in saying that military training forms and confirms youth in evil (the confirmation of the devil), corrupts them to the heart, glorifies every evil passion and gives ample opportunity for their expression.

Conscription — this will be our general conclusion — especially in the case of women and of unmarried men, brings the state into direct opposition with the Christian and truly human conception of personality and family life.

Because the person is above the state and the family prior to it, compulsory military service must be rejected as unjust, evil and un-Christian. The democracies by adopting it have aped in detail the very tyrannies whose vile principles they have claimed to oppose. They have thereby shown that there is in fact no difference in principle between themselves and the totalitarian dictatorships. Convenience, material interest, expedience, power, national honor at any price, military necessity — these are the things and not moral principle — which fix the abominable code that is observed by all participants in the modern war system.

As for conscription, the ethical theory which is its foundation-stone is that moral relativism. This theory, which is inseparable from state absolutism, holds that society and the state are the source of rights, that rights enjoyed by individuals are conferred by the state and that the state may therefore revoke any of all individual rights at will.

This is the direct opposite of that other ethical system which, based on reason and natural law, provides a starting point for the supernatural teaching and practice of Christianity. For the latter system teaches that human rights are rooted ineradicably in human personality and in the inescapable duty of every person to seek his or her final and supernatural end in God.

The Catholic Worker (November 1944)

After the Bomb

In Father Hugo's prophetic reaction to the dawning of the nuclear age, his analysis of "tribal morality" seems especially poignant, given the rising up again in our own time of new animosities, wars, and atrocities committed in the name of creed, race, and country.

≈⊙≈

They are over at last. All these years of terrible death — of slaughter, rather. The end of the war, although bringing also fresh causes for sorrow, is reason for genuine thankfulness — quite apart from all the jingoistic glorying in victory.

Yet it does bring causes for sorrow, at least to lovers of God and mankind, because the war has not chastened us, has not taught us the lesson that God would have us learn from it, has not brought repentence for the frantic pursuit of temporal goods, which is the cause of war. With the coming of peace, too many see only an opportunity — as one editorialist put it thankfully — to go back and live as they please again, that is, to return to the kind of living that causes war. Yes, there is much reason for sorrow.

Nevertheless we should be thankful. For the cessation of hostilities at any rate — for the end of the insane killing, for the coming of peace, even such as it is.

"Such as it is." At the end of First World War. Pope Pius XI wrote, in *Ubi arcano Dei consilio:* "No one can fail to see that neither to individuals nor to society nor to the people has come true peace after the disastrous war. The fruitful tranquility which all long for is still wanting. Peace was indeed signed between the belligerents, but it was written in public documents, not in the hearts of men. The spirit of war reigns there still, bringing ever-increasing harm to society."

Cannot the same be said after the Second World War? Arms have been put down, documents have been signed. But where there is so much bitterness, hatred, sullen submission, and desire for revenge, can there be said to be true peace? Even so — for the cessation of hostilities we should be thankful.

But not for the victory. Let us not thank God for that. National pride urges that we should: but then national pride has sung *Te Deums* for many victories that must have been odious to God. *Te Deums* were sung for the victories of Napoleon; they were later sung for the victories of the Prussian militarists. No doubt *Te Deums* were also sung for the victories of Hitler. Would it not have been the "patriotic duty" of Catholics thus to give thanks?

It is the religion of militarism which believes that God is with the big battalions. It is the same religion (proper to modern nationalism) which regards victory as the unfailing mark of divine favor. Do we not every day see that God does not invariably give temporal prosperity to the just, but rather afflicts them grievously, while very often allowing sinners to thrive?

To thank God for the victory is to claim God's approval of the victory. It is to assert that He willed the victory — not only permissively as He wills evil, but positively and directly as He wills good. It is also to assert that He approved and willed the means whereby the victory was won: flame throwers, jellied gasoline, burning oil to destroy enemies like rats in a hole, incendiary bombs, the terror bombing of civilians, the obliteration bombing of great cities, and, finally, the use of the atomic bomb, by which the war was so dramatically shortened and won. Did God positively will all these things? Is it not blasphemy to say so?

Here, however, let us confine our attention to the atomic bomb. What is to be said of it? That its use against those Japanese cities, regardless of the pretense, was a great crime, surely the greatest crime, committed against humanity by humanity. It was the culminating crime of that fierce and frantic nationalism that is rapidly making the earth uninhabitable. Above all, from the Christian point of view, the most terrible crime committed by a Christian nation against the Mystical Body of Christ.

True patriotism — which is to love one's country within the order fixed by God not excluding the other nations which form part of the same order — does not require that we give thanks to God for a victory obtained by violating His laws. True patriotism requires us rather to acknowledge the crime, to weep over it, to do penance for it. And so great a crime will require much penance, patriots!

As long as there is crime, unrepented and even unacknowledged, on our national conscience, how can we hope for God to bless our country? And shall we be guilty of the further blasphemy of thanking God for our crimes as though they were His responsibility? Shall we demand that He approve them and claim His favor for them? To do penance for the victory — that is, for the means whereby the victory was won — this would be more appropriate than thanksgiving for it.

Of course there are some, even Catholics, who see no evil in the use of the atomic bomb — who, in fact, look upon its use as good since it hastened the end of the war and saved many American lives. Such a view only reveals, however, how our consciences have been corrupted by war.

There is no sound moral argument to justify the use of the atomic bomb: those ethical principles which are brought forth in the attempt to effect such a justification are revealed, upon examination, to be themselves immoral. The theological principle of double effect, which is used in times

177

of war to justify the indirect and unintended killing of the innocent, has no relevance where the deliberately intended effect is to kill noncombatants and terrorize an entire civilian population.

We have now arrived at that advanced stage of spiritual development in which the very system of morality to which we appeal is positively immoral. Let us consider some of its arguments and principles.

The chief argument set forth to defend the use of the atomic bomb is that given by President Truman when he first announced its discovery and use to the nation. He justified it by emphasizing the crimes of the Japanese. Yet, even as he spoke — remarked Dorothy Thompson — his voice sounded hollow. Well it might. For this moral principle is the immoral principle which says that the end justifies the means.

So also *The New York Times.* By their own cruelty and treachery, our enemies had invited the worst we could do to them. This same crooked thinking was to be found among Catholics. For example, it was a Catholic editor who, seeking to resolve the doubt and torn between "patriotism" and the statements of certain theologians who condemned the bomb, settled the matter in his own mind and for readers by the observation that critics of the atomic bomb seemed to forget that it was used in a just cause. Such is the ethics of nationalism.

Another argument used to defend the atomic bombing is traceable to what may be called the tribal morality. This is the code found among barbarians and primitives, reappearing in modern militaristic nationalism. Its ethical teaching may be summarized in the axiom, "Love your friends, and hate your enemies." In this code anything is justified against an enemy — morality and decency need be observed only toward friends, that is, toward the members of one's own tribe.

Thus we are supposed to consider it a crime, as indeed it was, when the Germans bombed London. And all the American press showed their righteous horror and indignation at that time. But when the Allied airmen obliterated Hamburg and Berlin and dozens of other German and Japanese cities, this was part of a great crusade, morally justified and supremely heroic. To question its morality would open one to the suspicion of being "unpatriotic." Again, it was a crime for Germans and Japanese to starve and abuse prisoners in their camps. On the other hand, it was an act of great patriotic virtue, doubtlessly very pleasing to God, when our flyers murdered countless, thousands of helpless noncombatants with the atomic bomb.

The same tribal morality lies behind the assertion, meant as an ethical defense, that the atomic bomb saved American lives. As though American lives were the only lives worth saving, as though they were intrinsically more precious than other lives, as though any measures are justified to save American lives, including the cold-blooded slaughter of those whose only crime is that they are not Americans, as though Germans and Japanese were not be included within the unity of mankind and the higher and holier unity of Christ's Mystical Body, where there is "neither Greek nor Jew," where national differences are of no importance.

Again, tribal morality is implicit in the statement, so frequently made, that, if we had not first discovered and used the atomic bomb, they would have used it against us. And we are horrified, certainly not without reason, at what would have happened to us if they had found it first.

For them to have used it would of course have been a crime. Nor would we have had any trouble seeing the enormity of their crime. It would have been against *us*. On the contrary, in dropping the atomic bombs, we were using a legitimate means of saving American lives and ending the war.

A third justification for atomic bombing was offered by a theologian. He said that such means are justified because modern conditions have changed the character of war and rendered obsolete the old distinction between combatants and noncombatants. In total war, all the people of the belligerent nations are more or less involved, and are therefore to be considered combatants and may accordingly be killed by those who fight in "a just cause."

It does not, apparently, occur to this theologian that there is an alternative to his view. Namely, that effacing the distinction between combatants and noncombatants, with the elimination consequent upon this step of all humanity from war, is itself a condemnation of modern total war and an admission that talk about just warfare under modern circumstances is a tragic joke.

These are some reasons why the atomic bombing of Hiroshima and Nagasaki must be condemned as a crime. And not only as a crime, but also a great crime: the greatest crime ever committed by a nation against humanity and the Mystical Body.

Why is the crime so great? Even the numbers killed by the atomic bombs make it great, absolutely great, in comparison with the most terrible methods used by the Germans and the Japanese. Nothing that they did could approach the magnitude of this slaughter. But it is not only the amount of physical destruction and death that make it so great. The attendant circumstances increase its horror.

There is the fact that this was done, not by Nazis or barbarian militarists, but by a nation that claimed to be acting in the very name of civilization itself.

There is the fact that it was done deliberately and coldly by people who had in conscience condemned the Nazi principles that alone could justify such an act.

All the crimes of the Nazi horror camps do not add up to this. What a fearfully ironical commentary it is on the trials of war criminals. One set of criminals executing another.

There is the fact that it represents, in the best Nazi tradition, the abuse of scientific truth. We were horrified at the way in which the Nazis brought out scientists and perverted science to serve their ends. Yet we did not fail to learn from them, even to "out-Nazi" them. And how proud we are (the tribal morality again) of the scientific learning and co-ordinated research on our side that produced this horror.

There is the fact that, acting in the name of civilization, our country has given an example to other nations for all time. We have set a precedent to all the future international gangsters. They will point to the conduct of the American idealists. They will adopt the same pose of virtue — as they drop their atomic bombs, in all likelihood, on us.

Finally, there is the fact that our nation is responsible for loosing on the world a horror so enormous that all coming generations will live under a constant fear.

No doubt as the apologists of the atomic bomb affirm, the principles of atomic energy can be used for good. In fact, they have already been used for good, Almighty God has been using them for good these countless centuries.

President Truman said that the atomic bomb harnesses the basic energy of the universe. Of course, the scientists who discovered this energy did not put it there. God put it there in the beginning. Sometimes we forget this. So great is the childish pride of scientists at their discoveries that it almost seems as if they had created, at least in their own opinion, the energies of nature, and not merely discovered what had been present in the universe for uncounted aeons, silently working for man's benefit and God's glory.

The discoveries of scientists are much more a witness of the wisdom of God than their own wisdom. And to His goodness and love. When you think of the immense energies of the atomic bomb, remember too that these energies have been here from the beginning of the world and have been used by God to sustain our life on earth.

But "My ways are not your ways and your thoughts are not My thoughts," God says to us (Is 55:8). Never was this truth clearer than now.

That power which God, out of love, has been using all these ages in secret beneficence, people use, even in the very act of discovery, out of hatred, to destroy.

In truth, Lord, our ways are not Your ways! And oh, unhappy we that they are not! What a revelation in the iniquity of mankind! One thinks of those terrible words of the Gospel concerning men and women — still true in spite of all the oceans of grace that have meanwhile flooded our world: "But Jesus did not trust Himself to them, in that He knew all men, and because He had no need that anyone should bear witness concerning man, for He Himself knew what was in man" (Jn 2:24-25).

The Catholic Worker (September 1945)

A Christian Manifesto on War

Written in 1981, with tensions high between the United States and the Soviet Union, with the nuclear disarmament movement gaining ground in the U.S. and Europe, and with the U.S. bishops beginning work on their unprecedented letter on war and peace, this manifesto was distributed worldwide and translated into several languages. It is by far the most radical and the most apocalyptic of Father Hugo's pacifist tracts.

Christians of the World, unite! Men and women of all religions, let us unite! All men and women of good will, let us unite! Too long have we been scandalously divided over differences of belief. However weighty these may appear, they shrink into insignificance when compared to the threat currently launched against what we all cherish, namely, the very order of Creation itself, given to us all by the Maker of us all.

Like maniacs, those occupying the seats of power are planning to destroy, indeed annihilate, whole populations, the very earth its fruitfulness, its capacity to sustain life. A total war is declared against the Creator whom we all love, honor and worship.

What we do must be done without violence, as befits followers of the God of peace. But it must be done. Let us march forward in our struggle as Jesus moved inexorably toward Jerusalem, on a donkey, revealing thereby His intent to establish without violence and in love His Father's kingdom of peace.

Not even as a last resort can violence be approved; any more than Jesus would then consent to violence. "Put your sword into its sheath," He said to Peter at the last, critical moment (Jn 18:11).

If we act without violence, we need nevertheless to act with determination. Let us prevent money collected by governments for the public good to be used against the common good of the race. Let us refuse to allow our

181

tax money to be converted into diabolic machines for the slaughter of our brothers and sisters all over the world.

Let us halt the plundering of this planet earth to proliferate these deadly machines. Let us turn around the ominous tendency in our society to concentrate control of material resources in those centers of power where they are readily converted into the cruel instruments of death and destruction blandly and hygienically described by those trafficking in them as "military hardware."

Let our workers, the common men and women of the world, refuse to create these machines destined for the extermination of their fellow workers. Let us block the continuing effort to pervert our youth by training them to operate these engines of horror.

More than that, let us outlaw conscription. This ignominious institution, hypocritically invoking the name of democracy, has made universal the vilest and most degrading slavery that the world has ever known, a slavery that condemns its victims to maim and kill their fellow humans by the most cruel means imaginable. Let us end the rash exploitation of nuclear power, which contaminates and renders uninhabitable this fair earth, God's gift to all.

Let us once and for all refuse to give allegiance to any god of battles, serving rather the God of peace. "All who take the sword shall perish by the sword" (Mt 26:52).

Too long have we delayed. Now at last, on the brink of universal ruin, we cannot avoid seeing the absolute need to love all our fellows (at the least!) as we love ourselves, desiring and seeking for them the basic needs of a truly human life, if we are ourselves to survive to give homage to the one Father of all.

Is this matter hopeless? We can only begin to practice hope, G.K. Chesterton observed, when things seem hopeless. Dorothy Day, one of the great peacemakers of our time, remained ever hopeful, even in the dark days of World War II, confident in the ultimate potentialities of the common people and in the providence of our Father in heaven. She liked to cite these words of William James:

> I am done with great things and big things, great institutions and big success, and I am for those tiny, invisible, molecular moral forces that work from individual to individual, creeping through the crannies of the world like so many rootlets or like the capillary oozing of water, yet which, if you give them time, will rend the hardest monuments of men's pride.

In a Christian society it is love that penetrates the crannies of the world: "God's love has been poured into our hearts through the Holy Spirit which has been given to us" (Rom 5:5). Charity is God's love moving through the world in His friends.

The little ones of the world, beloved by God from Old Testament times are now the only ones who can hobble the leaders in their madness. Let the voices of these little ones swell from their villages and neighborhoods into a thunderous roar demanding peace, and survival.

From their rank, too, let more leaders rise up like Mahatma Gandhi, Martin Luther King, Dorothy Day and Archbishop Oscar Romero. These, and others inspired by them, can teach the techniques of nonviolent action.

Nonviolent resistance, nonparticipation, nonsupport, protests, fasting, civil disobedience, conscientious objection can be effective weapons in the service of love. For any law that is immoral, since it cannot reflect the goodness of God, is without moral force.

Scripture confirms our hope: "God chose what is foolish in the world to shame the strong, God chose what is low and despised in the world, even things that are not, to bring to nothing things that are, so that no human being might boast in the presence of God" (1 Cor 1:27-29).

Finally, let the little people form a great chorus of prayer. As Tennyson said, "More things are wrought by prayer than this world dreams of. Wherefore, let thy voice rise like a fountain . . . night and day."

Many would like to do more than pray. Indeed, we do need to do more than pray. Jesus bestowed a special blessing on peacemakers (Mt 5:9).

A basic teaching of Christianity is that God wills the happiness and salvation of all peoples. He is the "one God and Father of us all" (Eph 4:6). Because of this Jesus told His disciples: "Go therefore and make disciples of all nations" (Mt 28:19). To love your neighbor as yourself means opening your hearts to all, regardless of race, nationality, sex or religion.

To live according to this universal love we must therefore learn, accept and practice what is surely the most difficult truth of Christianity: "Love your enemies and pray for those who persecute you, so that you may be the children of your Father who is in heaven and who makes His sun rise on the evil and the good, and sends rain on the just and the unjust" (Mt 5:44-45).

We are to become "like God" (cf. Mt 5:48). This is indeed the great distinctive teaching of Jesus as He brought the Old Law to perfection: "Think not that I have come to abolish the law and the prophets. I have come not to abolish them but to fulfill them" (Mt 5:17). Love extended even to enemies is this fulfillment.

Here also is the fulfillment of the deep desire of all human beings to live in peace among themselves. Religion, then, should lead nations to peace. Paul places peace among the gifts of the Spirit (Gal 5:22).

Religion that is not political, said Gandhi, is not religion. That is to say, authentic religion does not seek the welfare of this or that party or group to the disadvantage of the other, but rather works for the common good of all. Peace is the final good of a community. "Peace is my farewell gift to you," said Jesus. "I do not give it to you as the world gives peace" (Jn 14:27).

This is the only way in which we can hope to establish universally the kingdom of God, which is the Sermon on the Mount transposed into political actuality: Willingness to suffer rather than to inflict suffering, to die rather than to kill, which is what Jesus meant when he said, and afterwards carried out in practice — "The kingdom of God suffers violence, and the violent bear it away" (Mt 11:12). Jesus had described Himself as "meek and humble of heart" (Mt 11:29). In His death He passed the fullest limit of humility.

The needed prayer for peace is much more than the addition of a few petitions or more verbal prayers added to routine devotions. It can mean only prayer in the sense of Jesus as He explained to the disciples why they had been unable to heal the afflicted boy (Mt 17:21). What is needed is the prayer of deep faith.

"The appointed time is very short" (1 Cor 7:29). God will have the last word: it will be either the kingdom of God or extinction. "For God sent the Son into the world, not to condemn the world, but that the world might be saved through Him; he who does not believe is condemned already, because he has not believed in the only Son of God" (Jn 3:17-18).

The form given of the prayer that we need has been given to us by Jesus Himself: "Our Father who art in heaven, hallowed be Thy name. Thy kingdom come, Thy will be done on earth as it is in heaven" (Mt 6:9-10).

A Christian Manifesto on War

The Impractical Weapons of the Spirit

The truth is that practical people are shallow and do not see the reality of things at all. They are the ones who live in a world of unrealities.

In their dealings they have not to do with things but the surface of things: their concern is with tables, statistics, papers and documents of all kinds, money, checks, ledgers, votes, filing cards. Their experience and skill is confined to computing in such surface dimensions, but they know nothing of the realities beneath; they have lost contact with such things as earth, sky, land, property, freedom, human nature, life.

This is why all their analyses are false, their predictions unfulfilled, their efforts to control the forces at work in society a dismal and continuous — nay, increasing — failure. Their world is like the two-dimensional world of old paintings; they live entirely among smooth and shining surfaces; they have no sense of depth, of the third dimension.

All the essential truth of things, therefore, is unknown to them; they have no knowledge of the demands of human nature, the purpose of human life, and the end of human society and the high destiny of people. Discussion of such things is lost on them: their minds work in terms of economic "schemes," financial legerdemain, legal shifts and political maneuvers.

It is to such minds as these that the teachings of the popes seem "unreal." But those who have, or seek to have, "the mind of Christ" — who have had some glimpse, however inadequate, of the unseen world of spiritual reality — will understand the power of the means that are now to be described.

"The spiritual man judges all things" (1 Cor 2:15). Hence, he knows that the use of spiritual weapons, like the cross of Christ, which indeed gives value to these spiritual weapons, "is foolishness *to those who perish,* but to those who are saved, that is, to us, *it is the power of God*" (1 Cor 1:18).

I do not choose these weapons at random, relying upon a fancied insight of my own. I choose them from the armory recommended by two of the greatest modern popes, Leo XIII and Pius XI, who considered them useful for modern needs.

The first weapon is the Rosary. This prayer, I would remind the reader, is not given here as a private devotion, not (as some would have it) as a half-superstitious practice for doddering old women. Both Pope Leo XIII and Pius XI seriously desire us to consider and use the Rosary as a means of overcoming and rooting out the evils of our day — the evils that are at the bottom of our economic and social problems of war.

In *Laetitiae Sanctae,* Leo XIII enumerated the three basic ills of modern society for which the Rosary will prove a potent remedy. "These are — first, the distaste for a simple and laborious life; secondly, repugnance to suffering of any kind; thirdly, the forgetfulness of the future life."

By meditating on the Joyful Mysteries we will learn to know and love the poverty and humility of Bethlehem; the simplicity, unworldliness, and hiddenness of Christ's life at Nazareth; the perfect domestic life, proceeding from the highest virtue, of the Holy Family. In a word, we would learn to esteem a simple and laborious life, which would counteract the first evil we have mentioned.

By the Sorrowful Mysteries we would learn to love *and imitate* the sufferings and death of Our Lord; we would be disposed to seek a life of hardship and penance, to accept suffering patiently and even joy fully, in this way being "crucified to the world" (Gal 6:14). And there is the remedy for the second evil.

By the Glorious Mysteries we are taught to place our hopes for happiness in heaven, in the knowledge that we will rise to a new life hereafter and thus, even now, to turn aside from the fleeting joys of earth and fix our desires on the new life in Christ Jesus by raising our minds to "the things that are above" (Col 3:2). In this way the third evil, forgetfulness of God and of the future life, would be removed.

The Christian life has its own special activity: it lives by faith, by hope, by charity. The soul who can exercise these activities, and frequently does so, is alive and healthy spiritually. Now the Rosary, says Pius XI in *Ingravescentibus Malis,* gives us practice in these three virtues, therefore increasing them and extending their influence: in this way increasing the radiation of divine truth and grace.

By meditating on the Joyful Mysteries we exercise our faith in the great fundamental truths of religion — namely, the Incarnation and the earthly life of the God-man — and we are led to make them the foundation of our own lives. In the Glorious Mysteries we exercise hope, for we look ahead to our own resurrection and entrance into heaven with Jesus. Being thus strengthened, we are able to lay aside the desire of mere earthly joys. By the Sorrowful Mysteries we become practiced in divine love, contemplating the One who loved us unto death. We learn what is meant by love and we are inspired to rise to the generosity necessary to sacrifice ourselves wholly for Him.

The second weapon recommended by the popes is devotion to the Sacred Heart. We might have expected this: not only the popes, but Jesus Himself has urged this devotion as most efficacious for our modern world. Attention is called to it here, once more, not as a private devotion that will greatly assist the individual soul, although it will assuredly do this, but as a social remedy, a weapon fitted to destroy all the evils of our day, including war. The reason for this social value is that it has a peculiar power to restore moral order to a world that is out of joint.

Devotion to the Sacred Heart is not the weak, sentimental thing that it is frequently made by those who, refusing to rise to the heights of love which it requires, reduce it to the maudlin caricature of love that is so popular today. True devotion to the Sacred Heart, it is no exaggeration to say, besides energizing individuals with divine life, would of itself reform and restore human society.

Such true devotion demands, first of all, Pope Leo XIII taught in *Annum Sacrum,* a consecration to Christ: a consecration, for each of us, of ourselves, our talents and achievements. The initial act of all love and loyalty, and the most characteristic expression of them, is consecration.

For this reason the Pope consecrated the whole human race to the Sacred Heart of Jesus; and since his time an act of consecration has become the most ordinary method of expressing love to the Sacred Heart. Alas, this act too often is a mere formula of words; if people were to make it from the heart, it would at once transform their lives and their society.

If people were really consecrated to the Sacred Heart, all earthly goods would be utilized according to necessity, never for the pleasure or mere vanity; they would be used only in so far as they promote the reign of Christ.

The kingdom of Christ is not impossible to realize; all that we need to establish it is the same zeal and energy and self-sacrifice that nationalistic greed and ambition calls up for its military expeditions. People need to do only what they are doing already, only their efforts would be consecrated to the God of love, instead of to the god of war.

Pope Pius XI, who completes his predecessor's teaching on the Sacred Heart just as he did with the doctrine of the Rosary, adds that reparation must be joined to consecration. In *Miserentissimus Redemptor,* he explains that reparation is the performance of penitential works and patient submission to suffering as a satisfaction made to God for sin.

Through pain Jesus redeemed humanity from sin — by submitting to pain He took upon Himself the punishment of sin. It is the law of redemption that sin should be thus compensated by pain — our pain as well as Christ's, ours given value by the fact that it is offered in union with His to the Eternal Father.

The reasons for this law are clear: By penance and suffering we rectify that abuse of creatures which is the cause of sin, we purify ourselves of this abuse, we restore harmony as best we can to the universal order that we have broken up by sin, and finally, we give evidence of our contrition by thus renouncing the things whose love caused us to offend God.

Consecration and reparation — these are the central characters of devotion to the Sacred Heart. Nothing sentimental here! What is asked of us is nothing less than complete, heroic loyalty to the King of Kings, a surrender of self to His cause, a willingness in His interests to face a life of hardship, sacrifice and unselfish effort.

It is no exaggeration, therefore, to say that devotion to the Sacred Heart, rightly understood and practiced, would at once transform the world, bringing fulfillment of the prayer Jesus taught us: "Thy will be done on earth as it is in Heaven." And it is only through this rule of the rightful King of Kings that the world will enjoy justice and peace and love.

You ask why, if these weapons of the spirit are so powerful, has not the kingdom of Christ already been established. The story of Samson, symbolic of deep spiritual truth, will tell us why. Samson, too, had enormous strength, but to keep it he had to remain a Nazarite, that is, unshaven. When he allowed his affections to alight upon a daughter of his enemies, she betrayed him, had him shaven, and thereby rendered him powerless.

We Christians are likewise strong, and with the strength of God. We can accomplish, if we will, incredible feats of strength and daring. Yet, like Samson, we must remain Nazarites. We must remain detached and untouched by the world. When we allow our affections to alight upon this, our enemy, then we are compromised and made impotent.

If Christianity seems powerless to the "realistic" or "practical" critic, this is because the worldliness of Christians have robbed them of the ability to use their strength. Moreover, as Samson was blinded by the Philistines after he had lost his strength, so also are worldly Christians blinded by their attachment to this world — blind to the power that they might exercise, blind to their responsibility, blind to the malice and ravages of sin, and, worst of all, blind to their own blindness and infirmity.

For worldliness, as St. John of the Cross teaches in *Ascent of Mount Carmel,* both blinds and weakens the soul. Finally, Samson's returning strength, because of his blindness, could be used only for destruction. Similarly, the opportunities of spiritually blind Christians, instead of being a benefit to all, will bring damage to their fellows and destruction to themselves.

Weapons of the Spirit

Our Lady, Queen of Peace

True devotion to Our Lady, the most pure Virgin, *Virgo purissima,* is an integral and necessary part of the Christian peace effort. Let it be noted that Our Lady's importance here, as in the plan of salvation generally, is doctrinal and not sentimental. Being part of the *order of means* fixed eternally by Almighty God to obtain all graces and spiritual benefits, her assistance is surely necessary to obtain the peace of God.

To call her Queen of Peace is not just to add to a picturesque but empty enumeration of meaningless titles. To call her Queen of Peace is to designate a prerogative, a dignity, a power, conferred on her by God Himself. This title directs our attention to the fact that only through her will the world be filled with peacemakers, will her Son's kingdom of peace be established on this earth.

A queen is one who rules. If Mary is Queen of Peace, she rules over peace — its treasury is in her hands. To seek entrance into the kingdom of peace is to enter her domain; to work for the coming of the kingdom of peace is to place one's self under her authority.

In his *True Devotion to the Blessed Virgin Mary,* St. Louis Grignon de Montfort, quoting St. Augustine, shows why Mary has a principal part in spreading the Gospel of peace. "The world was unworthy to receive the Son of God immediately from the Father's hands. He has given Him to Mary in order that the world might receive Him through her."

By Mary and through Mary can men and women overcome the heavy handicap that hinders them in their work for individual and social happiness. If they are now, as they are, not fit to possess happiness and peace, they need not despair. They can become fit. Our Lady will show them how it is to be done, how they may set about purifying and preparing their souls. This is the great and arduous preliminary task that must be done before the world can receive peace, the "pearl of great price."

Because Mary is our mother, she not only tells us what we must do, but helps us to do it, supporting every step. Her Immaculate Conception, high as it was, was the result of divine grace. As our mother, she will see that we in turn obtain the grace needed to become her pure children.

"It is with her, in her, and of her, that He (the Holy Spirit) has produced His masterpiece, which is a God made man," St. Louis Grignon de Montfort writes. But this does not end the work of the Divine Artist. If Christians are to be like Christ, conformed to Christ, "other Christs," this also is the work of the Holy Spirit and He accomplishes it, as He forms the God-man, through Mary. St. Louis Grignon de Montfort teaches that it is through Mary that He "goes on producing [Jesus] in the persons of His members daily to the end of the world."

People can realize the high ideals of the Sermon of the Mount, they can walk according to the pattern of life set down there by Jesus, only if they are *other Christs.* What is required is no mere human righteousness or respectability, it is divine holiness; we are to become perfect as our heavenly Father is perfect.

To achieve such conduct, Christ must act in us and through us. It must be, with us, as it was with St. Paul, that *we no longer live but Christ lives in us.* Then will we also be able to say, with St. Paul, that we can do all things through Him who strengthens us. Jesus in us will make us poor in spirit, meek, loving toward our enemies, ready to turn the other cheek, rejoicing in tribulation. Jesus living in us will also make us peacemakers.

In this way can we have a Christian society, for in this way will we have true Christians. Only in this way, let us add: only if Jesus lives in us will we be able to rebuild the world on the plan set forth in the Sermon on the Mount. Only then will we realize that dream of Pope Pius XI, "the Peace of Christ in the reign of Christ."

In bringing Jesus to birth in us, Mary also enables us to attain to that climactic achievement of the Beatitudes — peacemaking — which, by making us children of God, thereby unites us in true brotherhood to Him who, while the only-begotten Son of God, was also the "first-born of many brethren."

The Gospel of Peace

The Leaven of the Beatitudes

While the word "nonviolence" does not appear in the New Testament, the idea it expresses is contained in the Beatitude, "Blessed are the meek, for they shall inherit the earth."

Meekness is the Christ-like response to anger, hatred, violence; it is their antidote, reaching out with love. It is the readiness to suffer privation, in faith, with patience and equanimity. It contains within itself the healing needed to affirm truth and transform hatred into love.

Jesus has told us: "*Blessed* are you when men revile you and persecute you and utter all kinds of evil against you falsely on My account. *Rejoice and be glad,* for your reward is great in heaven." Elsewhere, He goes on to say that these persecutions may include death, but He adds, "Do not fear those who kill the body, and after that have no more than they can do" (Mt 5:11-12; Lk 12:4).

St. Paul cites even the Old Testament in support of this teaching: "If your enemy is hungry, feed him; if he is thirsty, give him a drink; for by so doing you will heap burning coals upon his head and the Lord will vindicate you." The apostle then adds on his own: "Do not be overcome by evil, but overcome evil with good" (Rom 12:20-21, Prv 25:21-22).

Moreover, the Old Testament, despite all its accounts of savage violence perpetuated in the name of Yahweh, records at least two instances of Jews gaining nonviolent victories over their enemies — that of Gideon (Jdg 6) and that accomplished under King Jehoshaphat (2 Chr 20).

The supreme scriptural example of meekness was Jesus Himself. Harried by His enemies, He "was silent and made no answer" (Mk 14:61). He spoke only to bear witness to the truth, thereby "incriminating" Himself and bringing about His own death.

Nonviolence, with its willingness to suffer rather than inflict suffering, is what Gandhi once called the "fundamental law of humanity." Without such nonviolence, neither people or peoples will never learn to live together in peace.

190

Nonviolence also, it is self-evidently clear, is the reverse and underside of God's primary and universal law, "Love the Lord your God with your whole heart, your whole mind, your whole soul, and with all your strength." And your neighbor you shall love, not only "as yourself," but "as I have loved you" (Jn 15:12). God by His law has made nonviolence the indispensable means for achieving universal peace.

Onesimus was a valuable young slave that ran away from Philemon, a convert of Paul, with whom he now sought refuge. Paul brought him into the Christian community and made him his own helper. According to the law Onesimus was subject to severe punishment. But Paul, according to law also, and because of a personal scruple about acting without the consent of Philemon, returned Onesimus to his master.

All this we learn from St. Paul's Letter to Philemon, the shortest of his epistles, but very precious. It marks the first time, so far as we know, that Christianity came into direct personal confrontation with slavery. A universal institution in ancient pagan times, slavery was the economic basis of society and was taken for granted even by Christians.

Elsewhere St. Paul urges slaves to be obedient to their masters. And St. Peter, in his first letter, wrote a long and eloquent exhortation to such obedience. Now a slave emerges from the crowd as a human person and a Christian, whom Paul in his letter speaks of as "my child," saying also to Philemon that, "in sending him back to you I am sending my very heart." He even puns a little with the name Onesimus, which means "useful," recalling that for a time Onesimus had been useless to his master but was now useful to them both.

Looking back at these events from our vantage point, we may wonder how Christians could ever accept slavery. Yet in America also we took it for granted until 1865, and its effects are with us still. Only in 1948 did the United Nations issue the *Universal Declaration of Human Rights*. Until then even the Church had not made such a pronouncement.

In Onesimus we are looking at close range upon the inevitable collision of Christianity with paganism; and it was a happy event that revealed the crack in slavery through which the leaven of Christianity could enter and begin to work. Eventually the influence of the Gospel, direct and indirect, would undermine and destroy this degrading and inhuman institution.

It was therefore a historic and providential moment when Paul, confident in the charity and generosity of Philemon, yet still without directly challenging slavery, wrote that he was sending Onesimus "back forever, no longer as a slave but more than a slave, as a beloved brother."

Of the reception of Paul's letter, we know nothing for certain except that it was not angrily destroyed or rejected, but given over to the Christian community at Colossae from whence it passed into the New Testament. Some say that Onesimus lived to become Bishop of Ephesus and himself collected Paul's letters. This was the death knell of slavery in Christian society.

A slave, in becoming a brother or sister becomes economically useless (that pun again!). He can therefore no longer be a slave. This is what Paul now realized and was taking this unique opportunity to say. It provided a living instance of what he articulated clearly elsewhere for the Christian community: "There is neither Jew nor Greek, there is neither slave nor free, neither male nor female; for all are one in Christ Jesus" (Gal 3:28).

Some may find this slow leavening process of the Gospel unsatisfactory, observing that it makes possible and even seems to justify, a guilty gradualism, forever postponing what should be done today at once. "Justice delayed is justice denied." But the very process of altering human minds and hearts, we know by much experience, is inevitably slow, although it presses for progress constantly and does not justify procrastination.

This is the way — gradually, but persistently — that the Gospel works because this is the way that Jesus worked, reaching out to enter and possess minds and hearts. This is His only method: "Behold I stand at the door and knock" (Rev 3:20). Even His greatest signs can be accomplished only in accordance with truth, that is, by *metanoia,* changing minds.

Through the mind he seeks to enter and take the heart, yet waits for human liberty to respond. "I am . . . the truth" (Jn 14:6). We, and not Jesus or the Father, are guilty of excessive gradualism if we are not prompt and vigorous in kneading the leaven of the Gospel. The motto that Newman chose for his life when he was made a cardinal was, "Heart speaks to heart."

Clearly the leaven of the Gospel has had little effect in curbing the violence of war, and the growth of the evil has taken place primarily in the West, the home of Christianity. While there has indeed been great technological and scientific progress, inflating the arrogance of the great ones of this space age, the quality of moral and spiritual relations among peoples has scarcely advanced, despite full dress diplomacy, beyond paleolithic times.

The ultimate barbarity of war now threatens whole populations and the very planet. Now and as long as life continues on this planet we live under the constantly growing threat of a mushroom cloud spewing sparks of annihilation. Divisions, rivalries, greed, and hatred expand and glacierize. A leaven is not enough; flame is needed.

"I came to cast fire on the earth!" (Lk 12:49). If Jesus has told us that the kingdom of God is a leaven (Mt 13:33), He also gives us this image of fire. Augustine transposes it into a practical axiom for the kingdom with the words, "One loving spirit sets another spirit on fire."

The love which Jesus said makes His followers perfect even as His heavenly Father is perfect — like God — is not to be brushed aside as a remote idea. At this crucial moment of human history it is necessary for survival. Only through the flame of such love can humanity survive and peoples prosper. Else there will be a different flame. God will have His way in the end. Will the mushroom cloud interpret Scripture?

The day of the Lord will come like a thief, and then the heavens will pass away with a loud noise, and the elements will be dissolved with fire, and the earth and the works that are upon it will be burned up. Since all these things are thus to be dissolved, what sort of persons ought you to be in lives of holiness and godliness, waiting for and hastening the coming of the day of God, because of which the heavens will be kindled and dissolved, and the elements will melt with fire! But according to His promise we wait for new heavens and a new earth in which dwells the justice of God (2 Pt 3:10-13).

At this late date, with ultimate destruction threatening, may we still hope that the kingdom can be built up through the radical Christianity of the Gospel?

Radical Christianity, the only authentic kind, and differing vastly from the tepid mix which is euphemistically called the religion of common sense, is briefly comprised in the Beatitudes. "Blessed are the peacemakers" is in fact the consummation of all the others; for peace is the supreme good sought in every human effort, personal, social, and political. It is the crowning fruit of the Beatitudes.

Still, the central peak and climax is the fourth Beatitude. It would concentrate all the energies of our being into hungering and thirsting for holiness, in God's plan the ultimate goal of human experience (Mt 5:6). "O God, I seek Thee, my flesh faints for Thee" (Ps 63:1). This holiness, a divine attribute, is the perfection of love, "for God is love" (1 Jn 4:8). Vatican II sets forth the pursuit of such perfect love as the universal vocation of all humans, all occupations, all states of life. The whole universe is oriented Godwards.

Because love of neighbor is inseparable from the love of God, the fifth Beatitude is all but predictable: "Blessed are the merciful, for they shall obtain mercy" (Mt 5:7). God Himself is thus the human exemplar; love and mercy, as well as holiness, are divine attributes, but all are to be shared with His human creatures.

Those also are blessed, said the sixth Beatitude, who pursue this goal of holiness with absolute singleness of purpose as "the one thing needful." "Blessed are the singlehearted, for they shall see God" (Mt 5:8). Such concentrated love is to be the goal for attaining the blessings and promises of the other Beatitudes. It includes love of enemies, which is indeed the keystone of this universal overarching love, bringing the Old Law to fulfillment.

In order to desire holiness, the first three Beatitudes are presupposed and indispensable. Dredging and self-emptying are imperative — "dying" to self — that each disciple may be filled with truth and love, "with the whole mind and the whole heart."

"Blessed are you poor," is how St. Luke reports the first Beatitude (Lk 6:20). This shows that the purification needed is to be accomplished by voiding the heart of the love for earthly treasures, the invariable cause of division, strife and war (Jas 4:1).

St. Matthew in delivering this as, "Blessed are the poor in spirit," has been blamed at times for weakening the teaching. On the contrary, Jesus is here telling us that poverty is not merely outward but also inward, and must reach into the very roots of action.

This is the meaning of radical, and it is precisely in their roots that Jesus desires to take hold of our lives by entering the deepest recesses of the heart through the motive (motor) force of action. As the corresponding promise indicates, this is indeed the narrow gate into the kingdom: "for theirs is the kingdom of heaven."

The second and third Beatitude, according to St. Luke, extend the first. "Blessed are you that hunger now, for you shall be satisfied. . . . Woe to you that are full now, for you shall hunger." All the good things of the world are spurned as "rubbish," to borrow St. Paul's word (Phil 3:8). The affluent consumer society is repudiated in advance. The world's idols are toppled.

Obviously, for its success, the Christian revolution depends on the thoroughness of the change, the *metanoia,* effected by carrying out these three Beatitudes.

At this juncture we hear from St. Matthew the blessing bestowed on the meek, whose observance is of critical importance for peacemaking. Indeed, the Beatitude of the peacemakers, to reveal its inner meaning, may be transposed as, "Blessed are the breakers-down of barriers." It is not enough to be peace-loving or peaceable.

The blessing is given to peacemakers. These, besides being ready to abandon a bovine contentment, will also relinquish a merely natural happiness — ready, that is, to die to self (Lk 9:23). Implied here is willingness to put up with privation and loss patiently, without anger, with equanimity and unfailing love: choosing, as Gandhi will say, to suffer rather than inflict suffering. Such are the meek — breaking down the barriers to reconciliation, regardless of the consequences to themselves. Of these Jesus says, "Blessed are you who weep now, for you shall laugh. . . . Woe to you who now laugh, for you shall mourn and weep" (Lk 6:21, 25).

Nonviolence is thus inescapably the method and practice of peacemakers. You do not crush or exterminate those whom you serve by the works of mercy. Moreover, despite allegations to the contrary, nonviolence is not all passive. Peacemakers make war with truth and love, the unconquerable weapons of the Spirit (Eph 6:10f).

From this height we may see all the Beatitudes in perspective; now we are prepared to comprehend the word spoken to the peacemakers and its exalted promise: "Blessed are the peacemakers, for they shall be called the sons of God" (Mt 5:9).

"Universal peace for those who love Thy law, no stumbling blocks for them!" (Ps 119:165). The peace of Christ, "not as the world gives" (Jn 14:27), arises from fulfilling the fundamental law of love. St. Thomas Aquinas observes that peace, like love, is twofold. Inner personal peace is attained only by loving God wholly: "In His will is our peace." Peace among people — all peoples — ignited by His love, is then scattered abroad by His friends, reconciling variant interests and desires.

The final promise attached to the Beatitudes, and bestowed especially upon peacemakers, is that they will be "like God," His sons and daughters, who in loving Him, come to resemble Him. They accordingly fulfill the words to be spoken just a few verses further on: "You, therefore, are to be perfect just as your heavenly Father is perfect" (Mt 5:48).

An epilogue: a description of the collision between peacemakers, as they recapitulate the Beatitudes, with the enemies of God and of peace.

"Blessed are you when men revile you and persecute you . . . on My account. . . . Leap for joy!" (Mt 5:11; Lk 6:23). Jesus Himself pointed out the wrenching irony of this opposition when He said, "I have shown you many good works from the Father. For which of these do you stone Me?" Yet He went on, Son of God and Prince of Peace though He was, to die on the cross. Understandably He said to His followers: "Do not fear those who kill the body but cannot kill the soul; rather fear him who can destroy both body and soul in hell" (Mt 10:28).

Your Ways Are Not My Ways, vol. II

VII
Virgins and Lovers:
Is the Church Obsessed with Sex?

Celibacy and Sex

Throughout his career, Father Hugo was thrust into theological disputes over questions of sex and sexuality. This is perhaps no surprise for he was a preacher trying to evangelize Western culture in the latter half of this century, a period which was shaped decisively first by the theories of Freud and by a so-called "sexual revolution."

Early on, Father Hugo sparked criticism for using sexual comparisons to speak about the relationship between God and individual souls. Later, in 1968, he wrote one of the early theological defenses of "Humanae Vitae," Pope Paul VI's controversial encyclical letter condemning artificial birth control. In both cases, Father Hugo argued that the teachings of Christ and the most ancient authorities and mystics of the Church were on his side.

Well in advance of many in the Church, Father Hugo had sketched the working outlines of a truly Catholic understanding of human sexuality. In his writings, sexuality is assumed to be basic to human personality, an essential element in the spiritual and bodily nature of human beings.

The key to sexuality is love, Father Hugo would say. Humans were created out of love by a God who is love and were made with a vocation to love. Father Hugo taught that sex was among the most powerful of the gifts given to us by God for expressing love. In the marriage relationship, authentic sexual love opens the couple to the full creative power of that gift, while at the same time knitting them more closely together and giving them a glimpse of the vision of God.

In this first selection, Father Hugo outlines his general understanding of human sexuality and defends the Church's laws regarding priestly celibacy. In the consecrated life, he says, the great "good" of sex was being offered up in a spirit of sacrifice for the sake of following Christ totally.

᠁

In recognizing and promoting celibacy the Church is charged with over emphasis, even with having a hang-up on sex, also with teaching dualistic doctrine that regards the body and its function as tainted with evil. Yet there is no trace of Manichaean dualism in the true Christian attitude toward sex.

Christianity emphasizes sexuality as a good intended to lead us to God. Moreover, it seems hypocritical at a time when the very atmosphere we breathe today is sex-saturated, to charge with overemphasis the one institution that seeks to harness these vital and good but explosive energies for the benefit of all humanity and the glory of God.

Now there would be no problem and no debate except that Jesus chose to remain celibate and virginal in carrying out His Father's will. If He is the perfect human being, as affirmed by the Second Vatican Council, then it is He who has introduced celibacy and virginity as an acceptable, even recommended alternate life style among His followers.

Indeed, since He invites all to follow Him, there will always be at least some who will be inspired to carry out this invitation in the manner that He himself exemplified. Yet He himself also limits this tendency with His words, "He who is able to receive this, let him receive it" (Mt 19:12).

Let us note here what a radical innovation appears with Jesus, Son of God and Son of Man, "the firstborn of many brethren," coming on the world scene as a celibate (Rom 8:29). Nothing in Jewish history would have led us to expect this, or enables us to explain it. It was all but unheard of that a Jew, man or woman, would choose such a course, and as an act of worship. He was thus doing something not only unusual but in the circumstances preposterous and utterly at variance with what the Jews were accustomed to viewing as the will of God.

Nevertheless the way was prepared in the Old Testament at least by Jeremiah, whose unmarried state imaged the complete fidelity of Yahweh to His espoused people.

John the Baptist also, the last and greatest of the Old Testament prophets, remained celibate and virginal. He was the forerunner and "friend of the Bridegroom" — Jesus — who in turn was the surrogate of Yahweh and therefore the Bridegroom of the Virgin Church.

In Isaiah, the marriage of a young man and a virgin symbolized the Messianic nuptials of Yahweh and Israel (Is 62:5). Mary, the Mother of Jesus, had already disclosed herself as a virgin. She symbolizes the virgin Church, committed wholeheartedly to God. The transition to the New Testament thus begins with three virgins — John, Mary and Jesus.

Was there any reason apart from symbolism why Jesus should remain celibate? We may observe, in answer, that only celibacy and virginity would enable Him to reciprocate fully, according to His human powers, and in the manner of Jeremiah, the total fidelity of God to His people.

As St. Paul says, "The unmarried man is anxious about the affairs of the Lord, how to please the Lord. But the married man is anxious about worldly affairs, how to please his wife, and his interests are divided. . . . The married woman is anxious about worldly affairs, how to please her husband" (1 Cor 7:32-34).

If Jesus had married, Paul would not be able to say of Him that He "did not please Himself" (Rom 15:3). Nor would Jesus have been able to say, "I do always what is pleasing to Him" (Jn 8:29). The total fidelity He wished to give His Father in response to God's own unbroken fidelity pressed the virginal and celibate life upon Jesus.

Celibacy offers the opportunity to seek unreservedly the pearl of great price promised by Jesus to those willing to give up all they possess (Mt 13:46). As a lifestyle acceptable and pleasing to God, it implies the freedom to follow this prompting of the Spirit in preference to the noblest human callings.

It does not imply any evil in marriage, the body, or sexuality. A bride in choosing her spouse does not reject other suitors as deformed, evil or undesirable. She obeys the impulse of love. Indeed, the more attractive the rivals left behind, the greater the love she shows for her beloved.

Celibacy allows those "able to receive it" the chance to choose God over the supreme sample of marital bliss, in which the generality of men and women spontaneously and eagerly seek the greatest measure of human happiness available in this life. Celibacy is not a rejection of love but an entrance into perfect love, the greatest act of love possible to mortals, inviting them to concentrate their love-power totally, not on one individual, but on God and His people.

As sacramental marriage sublimates sexual union, celibacy is the opportunity to explore to its limits the challenge of Jesus. "Whoever of you does not renounce all that he has cannot be My disciple" (Lk 14:33). As bride and groom are the living sample of God's love for his people, celibacy reveals the utmost limits of human love for God.

It is insufficient to explain St. Paul's acceptance of celibacy, and his urging it on others, only because of the imminence, as it seemed then, of the Lord's coming. If this were all it was, how could Paul, "a Hebrew of Hebrews" (Phil 3:5) become so quickly and thoroughly enamored of virginity and celibacy?

In fact Paul was intoxicated with the love of the Lord, whom he had not known "in the flesh," however, but only as "designated Son of God in power according to the Spirit of holiness by His resurrection from the dead" (Rom 1:4). The apostle gathers up the whole moral and ascetical practice of Christianity into the paschal mystery, seeing it as a dying to flesh, that is, to natural tendencies and desires, in order to live and walk with the risen Christ.

198

If we are to be ready to die with Christ, celibacy or virginity will seem a secondary sacrifice. And Paul can say, "I should like you to be as I am" (1 Cor 7:7), although he acknowledged that he had "no command of the Lord" on this point (1 Cor 7:25). With real depth of conviction also, recognizing the brevity of life for all and expecting the Second Coming, Paul also writes, "The appointed time has grown very short; from now let those who have wives be as those who have none" (1 Cor 7:29).

He further joins the married to the celibate and virginal in the central mystery of Christian living: "Husbands, love your wives as Christ loved the Church, and gave Himself up for her" (Eph 5:25). As a sacrament, matrimony brings to the couple the power of the paschal mystery of the Lord's death and resurrection to support and sanctify their lives together. Moreover, Paul thinks of the virginal life as the better way, because of its undivided attachment to the Lord. John asserts that all who are received in the kingdom are as virgins in their chaste fidelity (1 Cor 7:32, Rev 14:4).

In sacramental marriage, for which chastity and celibacy are but a preparation, a measure and a buttress, the Church thus resolves the ambiguity of sexuality, establishing it as a channel of divine life, thereby joining it also to the Eucharist and the other sacramental rites, the holiest gifts that the Church distributes to sanctify her people. Here is the final answer to those who would accuse Christianity of Manichaean dualism in its handling of sexuality.

All this does not prove that celibacy is necessary in order to assume the priesthood of Christ. But it certainly is shown as appropriate for those sharing in the priestly role of Him whose whole life "was a cross and martyrdom," and who was both priest and victim in His culminating cosmic sacrifice on Calvary.

Whether it should be made obligatory for those who are called to the priesthood is another matter. On the basis of contemporary experience many would assert that it is not even feasible. Assuredly, taking the vow of itself does not exempt the celibate from the present human condition, within which "all have sinned and fall short of the glory of God," and "if you live according to the flesh you will die" (Rom 3:23, 8:13).

The celibate will heed the counsel of Prospero to the young lovers of *The Tempest*: "Look thou be true; do not give dalliance/Too much the rein; the strongest oaths are straw/To the fire in the blood; Be more abstemious,/ Or else good night your vow!"

To put it differently, celibacy is not feasible if it is not received and observed in the deep mainstream of evangelic and Christian spirituality. So far this has not happened. The mainstream has trickled down only into a few oases here and there. To make it available for all, and it must also reach the families from whom candidates are expected. The clergy, led by their bishops, rather than allowing themselves to be overwhelmed by material duties, need to drink deep of these living waters and channel them to the whole Church.

The mainstream of the Christian and evangelic spirituality we speak of has its origin in the Beatitudes. Celibacy and virginity fall within the scope of, "Blessed are you that hunger now, for you will be satisfied." But celibacy can survive only if this Beatitude is taken together with those meeting it on either side, "Blessed are you poor. . . . Blessed are the poor in spirit" (Lk 6:20, Mt 5:3).

This is not mitigation but, literally, a radicalization that extends poverty into the roots of all human actions. These Beatitudes raise the minds and hearts of those who know them beyond earthly goods and samples.

All the Beatitudes must therefore be taken together, as indicated by that other one mentioned by Matthew: "Blessed are the single-hearted, for they shall see God" (Mt 5:8). The first three Beatitudes empty the heart only to fill it with the perfection of love which is the meaning and content of the holiness for which all are to hunger and thirst. Only in such radical Christianity can celibacy thrive.

Your Ways Are Not My Ways, vol. II

Wedded Bliss

Matrimony, the usual calling of the Christian laity, is a sacrament. Religious profession is not. Christ and His Church have paid their supreme compliment to the married by placing their union among those sacred signs which extend the action of Christ and draw us into the mystery of His death and resurrection.

Still, as the result of a double standard, Catholic spirituality until the present has been all but exclusively preoccupied with those living in religious communities. Marriage, issuing in the family community, should in fact be the center of concern. It is the basic unit of society and the primary cell of the Mystical Body of Christ. The health of the whole Church depends on its spiritual well-being.

All members of the Church, including clergy and vowed religious, receive primary spiritual formation at the fountainhead of the family. In relation to the family the work of religious communities is supplementary and supportive. Indeed, some religious communities have been established to assist families, for example, in educating children, in caring for orphans or the disadvantaged, and in working with those problems, especially involving youth and old age, which come from broken or distressed marriages and families. Even the early monastic orders taught the domestic arts as well as religion in the communities where they lived.

The entire teaching and fruit of the Gospel, up to the highest holiness — which, remember, is the perfection of love — belongs to the laity and the married. Thus, there is nothing second-rate in the holiness of those who live in the world.

As Cardinal John Henry Newman said, "But it is even a greater thing, it requires a clearer, steadier, nobler faith, to be surrounded by worldly goods yet to be self-denying; to consider ourselves to be stewards of God's bounty but faithful in all things committed to us."

Marriage is also the source of sexual morality; for the procreative love of marriage, mirroring the creative love of God, is integrated with sexuality as its conjoined instrument and expression. Use of sex which serves neither marital love nor procreation is outside the boundaries set by the Creator to govern sexuality. Marriage is a carefully protected treasure-house.

On this matter Jesus did not say much, but what He did say is decisive. "You have heard that it was said, 'You shall not commit adultery.' But I say to you that everyone who looks at a woman lustfully has already committed adultery with her in his heart" (Mt 5:27-28). While this teaching is given from the point of view of male-dominated society, the words certainly reject the exploitation of sex so common in our society from the female side as well.

The Lord's concern with a deeply interior chastity is also evident from those further comments, which while by no means applying only to sexual morality, include it no less than other areas of possible moral misconduct, such as avarice. "If your right eye causes you to sin, pluck it out and throw it away; it is better that you lose one of your members than that your whole body go into hell" (Mt 5:29).

In these few words the whole modern degradation of sex is condemned. Nor are they a Manichaean rejection of the body; they mark, as part of Jesus' own radical demand for interior purity, an expression of the divine will, a delimitation by God through His Son, of the use of what He Himself created.

The meaning of sex in the Christian life cannot be understood, therefore, solely in relation to the natural law governing human inclinations. To do so would be to impoverish it. Indeed, the law of nature concerning sexuality must itself be studied in relation to sacramental marriage, which is its matrix.

And if only the Catholic Church regards marriage as sacramental, it nevertheless remains true that the plan of God — "the mystery of Christ" — envisions universal salvation. Therefore, all marriages are at least potentially signs of the covenanted love of God with mankind.

The sacrament of matrimony is designed to seal the mutual loving fidelity of the spouses as well as to safeguard the life, in both its physical and spiritual dimensions, issuing from it.

Marriage fidelity mirrors Yahweh's own faithful love for His people, while procreation extends the divine creative activity. Jesus does not tell us only to observe the rudimentary demands of morality. He urges us not to take the least step in the wrong direction. And that first step is in the outreach of our desires.

Your Ways Are Not My Ways, vol. II

Visions of Loveliness

Some early censors were scandalized by the retreat movement's comparisons between sexual union and the beatific vision, or vision of God. Responding to such criticisms, Father Hugo in this selection stresses that the use of nuptial imagery to talk about each soul being the bride of Christ dates back to the earliest Christian interpretations of the Biblical Song of Songs and remains a staple of the writings of Christian mystics down through the centuries.

✦

All love is perfected in union. In its fullest sense, it is union, so that sexual union, being the climax and consummation of the highest human love, is the very noblest of God's creatures; there is nothing in all creation which provides a more apt or truer analogy for the contemplation of God.

God Himself indicated this analogy; its source is the Holy Scripture. Passages as the following from the Canticle of Canticles, not only point out the comparison but describe it with some intimacy of detail:

Show me, O thou whom my soul lovest, where thou feedest, where thou liest in the midday. . . (Sg 1:7).

Thy cheeks are beautiful as the turtledove's, thy neck as jewels. . . (Sg 1:10).

Behold thou art fair, my beloved, and comely. Our bed is flourishing. . . (Sg 1:16).

His left hand is under my head, and his right hand shall embrace me. . . (Sg 2:6).

In my bed by night I sought him whom my soul loveth (Sg 3:1).

Jesus, when He appeared, described Himself as "the Bridegroom" (Mt 9:14-15, 25:1-2; Mk 2:18-20; Lk 5:34-35). A bridegroom is a man having a bride. Who is the bride of Jesus? Obviously, He was speaking in a spiritual or mystical sense. He was fulfilling the prophecy of the Canticle. So, Catholic nuns speak of themselves as brides of Christ. But not nuns alone — every Christian soul is the bride of Jesus.

St. Paul does not fail in turn to point out this analogy: "Husbands, love your wives, just as Christ also loved the Church" (Eph 5:25). Again, he says, "For I have betrothed you to one spouse, that I might present you as a chaste virgin to Christ" (2 Cor 11:2).

Without knowledge of this imagery, the Catholic mystics could not be understood at all. One unacquainted with it might be shocked, for example, at the poems of St. John of the Cross:

Oh, night that guided me,
Oh, night more lovely than the dawn,
Oh, night that joined Beloved with Lover,
Lover transformed in the Beloved.

Upon my flowery breast,
Kept wholly for himself alone,
There he stayed sleeping and I caressed him,
And the fanning of cedars made a breeze. . . .

I remained lost in oblivion;
My face I reclined on the Beloved.
All ceased and I abandoned myself,
Leaving my cares forgotten among the lilies.

True, St. John of the Cross, is a mystic. Nevertheless, the relationship he speaks of is that of every Christian to God. Accordingly, it is not to mystics alone, but to every Christian, that the Church addresses these words in the very ceremony of baptism: "Observe the commandments of God that when Our Lord shall come to his nuptials, thou mayest meet Him together with all the saints in the heavenly court, and live forever and ever."

The only thing peculiar to the mystics is their vivid realization of the nature of the soul's relationship with God, and their actual possession, following great fidelity to grace, of a very perfect degree of union with Him. St. Bernard describes this union in his commentary on the Canticle:

> For although the *Spouse,* as a pure creature, is less than her Creator, and hence also loves less, yet if she loves with her whole being, her love is perfect and wanting in nothing. It is love of this kind that constitutes the *spiritual marriage* of the soul with the Word.

Mark that the saint speaks of the spiritual marriage *of the soul* — not of the mystic — with the word. He goes on:

> Happy the spouse to whom it has been given to experience an embrace of such surpassing delight! This spiritual embrace is nothing else but a chaste and holy love, a love most sweet and ravishing, a love perfectly serene and perfectly pure, a love that is mutual, intimate, and strong, a love that joins two not in one flesh but in one spirit, according to the Apostle's testimony: *"He that is joined to the Lord is one spirit."*

The Church, moreover, gives her approval to this language. Here, for example, are the words she addresses to the newly-wedded bride in the Nuptial Blessing, clearly indicating the symbolic and spiritual character of the marriage union:

> *Deus qui tam excellenti mysterio conjugalem copulam consecrasti, ut Christi et Ecclesiae sacramentum praesignares in foedered nuptiarum. . .* (O God, Who has made marriage sacred by a significance so sublime that in the nuptial union Thou wast pleased to forecast the mystical union of Christ and the Church. . .).

Other spiritual masters use the same language. St. Francis de Sales, describing the attractiveness of the Bridegroom to the Bride, writes:

> The sacred spouse wished for the holy kiss of union: Oh, said she, let Him kiss me with the kiss of His mouth (Sg 1:2). But is there affinity enough, O well-beloved spouse of the well-beloved, between thee and thy loving one to bring to the union which thou

desirest? Yes, says she: give me it; this kiss of union, O Thou dear love of my heart: *for thy breasts are better than wine, smelling sweet of the best ointment.*"

The same saint makes quite explicitly the comparison between sexual union and the Beatific Vision:

In fine, the heavenly King, having brought the soul He loves to the end of this life, assists her also in her blessed departure, *by which he draws her to the marriage bed of eternal glory. . . .*"

We touch here, in truth, the very heart of Christianity, the essential relationship that it establishes between God and the soul, a relationship that marks it off from merely natural religion and a merely rational code of upright conduct.

The Christian relationship of soul and God is one of love. The end of Christianity, the final goal to which everything else in the Church is ordered, is to unite the souls of the faithful to God in the love of eternal friendship. Therefore, the essential supernatural relationship between God and man is one of personal, intimate, eternal love.

Now in order to bring home to our minds this essential relationship of love between God and the soul, the Scripture employs two analogies   it represents God as Father and Christians as His children, and it also represents God as Bridegroom and the soul as Bride.

These, then, are the two ways given to us by God Himself for studying His love, for learning its exigencies, for discovering the manner in which it is to be expressed. Each of these analogies is useful, yet each by itself is insufficient. Hence God has provided the two together.

The relationship of child to parent reminds us that our love of God is one of dependence as well as of tenderness, and must therefore be accompanied by filial fear and reverence. The analogy of Bridegroom and Bride, teaches us, as no other method could, that the love of God is one almost of equality, since we have been elevated to the supernatural plane by grace. It is a love of deep and intimate and lasting affection, as between spouses.

Of these two analogies, the more perfect is that of the Bride and Groom. Better even than the other it shows us the real nature of love — the perfection of the union that should exist between God and the soul, since the union between husband and wife is the most perfect known to human love and friendship.

Clearly, to forget this essential relationship is to remove the heart from

Christianity and to eliminate from Christianity Christ Himself, His teaching, His way of life, the End that He has fixed for our striving. The special command that He laid upon us is that we should love God with our whole heart, that is, exclusively, as a faithful bride loves the bridegroom. And the highest gift and power that He gave us — charity — is that which binds us to God by Love.

A Sign of Contradiction

Unsafe Sex

Here, Father Hugo puts sex in the context of his idea about the created world being filled with "samples" of God's glory. Like every other created sample in our world, sex is a "good," desirable in its own right and is a means to bring us closer to God. In the same way, sex can also be abused and disordered, as Father Hugo describes in this passage, which speaks eloquently of what he describes as the "pagan" degradation of sex in contemporary Western culture.

Here we return to the ambivalence of all created samples, to the recognition of their double aspect — as goods at once desirable and yet to be taken up with restraint, even at times relinquished altogether. The samples please with their taste but do not long satisfy. Too much of them ends in revulsion and emptiness.

So sexuality joined to love offers the highest joy known to mortals. Yet it can also swing back to contempt and satiety. It can be harmonious and unifying but also disruptive and ruinous. It can end in unhappy marriages, broken homes, seduction, rape, sadism, suicide, and murder. There is in it the potentiality of a beast, arising from animal nature, to be tamed, else to destroy.

Sex follows the negative potentiality, regressing to the condition of beast, precisely when people fail to acknowledge the created limitations of sexuality as a sample, exploiting it as an ultimate good, rather than seeing it as a new opportunity to glorify God.

Marital love as a created sample allows us to see how, on the one hand, it can lead to God as a sacramental sign, and on the other, without being rejected as evil, may nevertheless be limited by the restraints of faithful love, as well as by celibacy, to a great act of preferential love.

Like all other created samples, nuptial union itself can be abused. An old Latin saying has it that the best, corrupted, becomes the worst. Because of the strength of sexual passion, deeply rooted in nature's own desire and determination to survive, and even more poignantly because of the urgent need for deep and satisfying love by all human beings, which on earth is most nearly realized in marital union, this kind of love may become idolatry.

In poetry and song, as in the declarations of lovers, it is frequently described in the language of worship. By pagans, sexual ecstasy was actually regarded in ritual prostitution as an act of worship.

In our more sophisticated world of paganism, as we constantly see in the all but universal exploitation and violation of sex, it is still commonly taken as a supreme good and substituted for the eternal joy of loving God. The sample replaces the Reality. The creature usurps the place of the Creator.

"Romeo is the god of my idolatry," said Juliet as their excess of love led this couple inexorably into tragedy. And she speaks for all who in their lives substitute the sample for the reality of God, thereby making it an idol.

We may compare sexuality to the mighty force of a river that is controlled and damned up for human use. Besides sustaining life itself and the crops that become food for populations, it may also provide them with light and heat and power. On the other hand, it causes disaster when the water runs unharnessed over the banks or bursts the dam. The levee that holds this human force under control is chastity, reinforced by the sacrament, indeed, by all the sacraments. Chastity here means, not simply the relinquishment of sexual activity as in celibacy. Nor does it mean only the avoidance of sexual disorder.

In the typical instance of spouses, it means, as the marriage ritual has put it — fidelity to one embrace. For the unmarried, chastity means abstention until a couple is ready to assume the responsibility, together with the rights, of matrimony. Mutual affection by itself does not entitle them to experiment with marital love or to tamper with the sources of life.

These several modes of chastity are intended by nature, and therefore by the Author of nature, to contain and concentrate these huge energies into channels that will most benefit all men and women, together with their children, while reaching out also to glorify God by diffusing His goodness and multiplying His holiness.

Your Ways Are Not My Ways, vol. II

VIII

The Sense of Suffering:
The How and Why of Human Pain

Why Must I Suffer?

In approaching Father Hugo's writings on the Christian meaning of suffering, it is important to remember that he is not really engaged with either the existential question of why "bad things happen to good people" or the theological mystery of why a good God permits evil. His concern is rather with how, in their sufferings, Christians can find God revealed and be united with the sufferings of Christ for the redemption of the world. His writings on suffering can be viewed, in fact, as a summation of his writings on Christian spirituality, presenting in the starkest terms the abandonment of the will and the self-offering that one must undertake to know the living God. One of Father Hugo's most widely distributed works was a booklet titled "Why Must I Suffer?" a modern and very personal retelling of the biblical Book of Job. It is addressed to someone suffering with debilitating illness.

❦

You have been overtaken by one of the least desirable of life's gifts. You are sick, and you are not very happy about it. You are inclined to be resentful, even bitter, and if you think that God has anything to do with it, you scold Him.

A question intrudes itself upon your mind, And, especially if your illness is a severe one, or lasts very long, or incapacitates you seriously, this question will recur with maddening insistence: "Why? Why must I suffer? Why must I be so afflicted? Why must I endure such pain? Why must I put up with this discomfort, this long tedium? Why must I be forced to lay aside my normal activities, my work and recreation? Worse yet, why must I be a burden to others? And worst of all, why must I put in these long, lonely hours separated from my friends and loved ones? Why? Why? Why?"

The question to some seems unanswerable. Almost all tend to scold God for their trials, others are embittered and turn definitely against Him. They cannot answer the taunt of the atheists: "If your God is good, why does He make you suffer?"

Let it be said at once that it is a good thing you are a Christian. If you were not, there would really be no answer to the question for you. The pagan cannot explain suffering. To him it is cruel, stupid, unnecessary, meaningless, without any possible value whatsoever. He judges by his own human reason with its limited range of view, and he forms his thoughts concerning sickness and suffering from the immediate unpleasant effects which he sees it has on human life. He has no second sight, no means of penetrating beyond its appearance to possible hidden meanings and purposes.

For this reason he is likely to become embittered. For this reason, too, those who follow no higher guide than reason are prone to be impressed by the atheistic objection that a God who is good could send no suffering. If the pagan wishes to avoid bitterness and despair, he will marshal the efforts of science and discovery. Then he will speak hopefully of a better but distant day in which science (he says) will abolish disease and, with it, pain and suffering.

But this view, to those who remember how suffering came into the world, and even to those who look frankly at human life now, seems far too rosy. No doubt science will make many more discoveries to cure disease, alleviate suffering, and perhaps greatly lengthen human life. But to remove sickness and suffering from human life altogether, that is a feat of more doubtful attainment.

In any case, supposing (for the moment) that science would at some distant date completely abolish sickness and pain, that would not relieve you now, nor would it help millions of your contemporaries, to say nothing of the hundreds of millions of sufferers tho have lived much of their lives in pain before you.

What about *you*? What about *them,* as we await the millennium promised by science? Meanwhile, it is perhaps not without relevance to remember that this science, while talking glibly of ending suffering, invented the atomic bomb: to end suffering, too, for any number of men, but not in a manner devoutly to be wished.

Of course, there is also the attitude of those who refuse to talk or think about such things as suffering or death. They say that we must avoid such gloomy thoughts. But they are probably healthy and strong — they have not been afflicted as yet. When their day comes, as come it will, it will be seen whether they will be able to continue in the conviction that life is a bowl of cherries.

Meanwhile, their attitude is about as realistic as that of a man who, standing on a railroad crossing and observing a train bearing swiftly upon him, seeks to avoid the danger by turning his back to the engine. If we wish to keep our equilibrium in this world, if we wish to possess true peace and an indestructible joy, we must learn to face, quietly and calmly, and to accept with equanimity, even such dread realities as sickness, pain, and death.

━━━⟨◉⟩━━━

But now (we are supposing) you yourself are actually faced with the problem, and you are a Christian. But you are also human, and your mind now frames that inevitable: "Why?" If this is your first great trial, and you have not meditated on these matters before, perhaps your memory struggles to recapture fragments of divine truth which you have heard long since but have perhaps forgotten or neglected in days of pleasure and prosperity.

At this point, too, a friend intervenes, a devout person, who wishes to offer comfort. You cannot refrain from speaking aloud your question — so exclusively do pain and suffering occupy your attention — and you therefore ask, "Why has this befallen me?"

Your friend has a ready answer. "God sends us afflictions," he says, "in punishment for our sins. Therefore, if you are a good Christian, you will accept this trial in good part as a penalty for sin." Your friend adds a few more words of explanation, to soften the bluntness of this reply. Then he beams at you, expecting your countenance to show at once the relief brought by his words of consolation. But instead, perhaps, a feeling of bitterness surges up within you. You look at your friend: plump, complacent, condescending — and in good health. Why doesn't he suffer? Are you the only sinner? Is he telling you, with unconscious insolence, that you are a sinner deserving of dire punishment, whereas he by his virtuous life is being pampered by an indulgent Providence?

Perhaps your mind goes back to another sufferer, Job, a just man, sorely afflicted, and you recall those mourners who came to him and told him almost the same thing that your friend has told you: That suffering comes in punishment of sin, that he should therefore accept the punishment and acknowledge his sins.

Your friend is trying to palm off, as Christian spirituality, that stale and cruel error of Job's comforters. Job was not a sinner, but a just man. Yet he suffered nevertheless. It is true that God sends afflictions to the wicked in punishment for their sins. But it is not true that He afflicts only evildoers. In fact, the most exasperating question in this whole matter is, "Why does God afflict the just?"

Of course there is a sense in which we are all sinners, for we were born in original sin and have doubtless been guilty at least of venial faults later on. And therefore you, like others, are deserving of punishment. But that is the point: like others. Why, then, are so many of the others spared, while you are picked out for such severe suffering?

At the very least, there is no equity in such an arrangement. Providence is apparently not very careful to observe the niceties of justice. Many others have sinned more gravely than you, but they are not spending months, perhaps years, in a sickbed. There is many a flagrant sinner walking the streets in the best of health, while you, who have at any rate tried to observe the commandments, have been stricken and now repine as an invalid or semi-invalid.

And so you say to your friend, "But what have I done to deserve such punishment as this? Am I the only sinner? In fact, I have tried to live the good life. Such sins as I have committed have been sincerely repented of. But others live openly wicked lives and seem blessed with prosperity — at any rate, they are not afflicted as I am."

Your friend is a little disappointed that his words have not brought the comfort intended. It seems that you are not as good a Christian as he had hoped! But he is ready for the occasion. He goes on:

"There is not only a question of your own sins. You may also make reparation for the sins of others. In this way you satisfy divine justice, and thus prepare the way for and induce a new outpouring of divine mercy on your brethren."

This is true, and you know it. In the thought that your trial may be of value to others there is comfort. But not enough. Again, you are disposed to wonder why your friend, and others too, are not called upon to share this burden of reparation equitably. Are you to carry it all? No, this explanation of your friend cannot be the whole answer.

The need for reparation can explain why one should do penance occasionally, perhaps frequently. It will explain why Christians should be ready at times to bear afflictions, even severe afflictions. But it will not explain why a whole life is blighted and ruined. It does not give satisfying reason for the fact that months and years of one's life are wasted, that one is forced to endure sickness and pain for two, ten, twenty years, or more, meanwhile deprived of the most elementary satisfactions of human living.

The need of reparation, however real and serious, will not explain this — especially as it seems to be you and a relatively small group with you who are carrying the whole burden of reparation while the majority who talk so glibly about it, and are bound by charity to their neighbor as well as you, are allowed to continue in good health and live normal happy lives.

And so you shake your head, still dissatisfied. If there is any change as a result of these friendly counsels, it is that a deeper depression settles upon your heart. So it is sin, so it is justice. It is the just God, the avenging God, who rules your life. Where is the God of mercy, the God of benevolence, the

God of love? In your weakness and wretchedness, you had looked hopefully, if uncertainly, to Him. Was not the Savior ever gracious to the humble, the poor in spirit, the suffering, the sick? Has He not a word for you? No, you are being punished, or the race is being punished in your person. Your part is but to endure — although others smile continually in the sunlight. Such is the bitter consolation offered you.

And so you are disconsolate (and no wonder) and yet you do not know what to do. "Lord, to whom shall we go? Thou hast the words of eternal life" (Jn 6:68).

Well, your friend, the Job's comforter, has gone. Do not be so sad. Things are not as bad as they seem. The God of love is the One responsible for your trial, and the one to whom you should address your query. The merciful Jesus does have a word of strength and comfort for you in your affliction.

What your friend said was true, but only part of the truth, and what he omitted is the more important part. Even a pagan, guided only by reason, can understand that afflictions are a penalty for evildoing. But while this outlook may parade as Christian thinking, it is really deaf and blind to the real meaning of divine revelation on this subject of suffering.

And yet there is nothing specially mysterious or obscure in what God reveals concerning the trials of life. No doubt, since God is so far above us, His wisdom is in every case mysterious to our natural minds. But through His revelations on the one hand, and on the other through the gift of faith by which He enlightens our mind, He gives us all the necessary insight into His truth. And since suffering plays so large a part in our sanctification, it may be taken for granted that what He has to say on this score will be sufficiently plain — for those who have ears to hear.

For example, you learned, probably in your first school days, that you are a child of God, destined by your heavenly Father to an eternity of bliss with Himself. You learned that, to prepare you for this happy destiny, the Holy Spirit enters your soul and dwells there personally, adorning it with His precious gift of sanctifying grace, and other gifts designed to render it holy.

Doesn't that tell you anything? Doesn't it tell you that you must be changed, that you must be veritably transformed? To be a child of God, you must cease being a child of this earth. To be a citizen of the heavenly kingdom, you must relinquish your citizenship here. In a word, to enter heaven, you must become holy, for only the holy can see God.

No doubt you have often said that your are no saint, perhaps regretfully, perhaps boastfully. But you must become one if you wish to enter heaven: only saints dwell in heaven. To aspire to go to heaven and to desire to be a saint, to work to go to heaven and to labor after sanctity — these are really one and the same thing. To enter heaven we must become saints, and we must become saints while we are here on earth, before we begin the journey into eternity — in a word, before we die.

To make us saints, the Holy Spirit comes into our souls bearing sanctifying grace. This grace is the principle, the cause, the seed, the germ, the root, of sanctity. By itself it can sanctify us, but as the root must not only nourish itself but also send its vital energies coursing through all the branches of the tree, so grace is not to remain inert but must carry its work of sanctification into all our faculties — into our mind and heart, into our senses and imagination, too, into all our actions and deepest roots of action. And there's the rub.

Let us imagine a sculptor, first going into the quarry to obtain stone, and then forming it into a statue — we will suppose, the statue of a saint. When the statue is completed, the artist's friends and clients and other admirers gather to praise his work. A splendid achievement, indeed — this fitting representation of one of God's special friends. But at what a cost — what chiseling, what hammering, what carving, what grinding, what polishing!

Fortunately, the stone has no feelings. If it did, it would find this transformation into the image of a saint a very disagreeable experience. It might object and kick against even the glorious destiny marked out for it.

And could it, while still in the quarry, obtain some faint pre-vision of what is in store for it, perhaps it would say something like this, "No, thank you. Just leave me alone. I am quite content to remain where I am, very comfortable in the bowels of this hill!" But the sculptor is undeterred by such considerations — a beautiful conception has taken hold of his mind, and he gathers up his tools and goes to work.

If the stone has no feelings, we have. Accordingly we are going to feel it very much, and no doubt will object strenuously when the Divine Artist takes up His tools, which are all the creatures around us, and begins working to make us, not mere cold images of saints, but real living saints. We might be tempted to say, "No, no — dear Lord, just leave me alone. I am quite content as I am — I do not cherish any dizzy ambition to be a saint. Please don't cut and hew and grind and polish me!"

But God will not heed us, will not be hindered from His grand scheme of making us, even us, holy as He is holy, so that we may come close to Him and share His bliss. And really, He knows our minds better than we do. He knows that, although we say we don't want to be saints, we do want to go to heaven.

He sees very clearly the inconsistency in our thinking, which we do not see. And so He sets to work, with all kinds of trials, all kinds of hammerings and chiselings and cutting, to change us into saints that we may realize our dream of going to heaven with Him. If we do not get into heaven, we are going to be very unhappy — much more unhappy than we could possibly be now in the midst of our severest trials. But we cannot enter heaven unless (and until) we are holy.

In this process of transforming clods like ourselves into saints, God uses all kinds of trials. Not only sickness, but every suffering, every sorrow, every kind of pain, every deprivation, is used in purifying and sanctifying us.

And this is something for sick people to remember. Sometimes you talk as if sickness were the only trial and you the only ones called upon to endure pain. In fact, all are called upon to suffer (with only one dreadful exception, which we shall notice later on), for life on this earth is a time of probation for all. And there are sufferings much graver than sickness.

Many who are able to walk about have hearts that are aching with pain and minds oppressed with some intolerable burden. The very fact that they must go through the motions of normal living may make their grief all the heavier. They would like to lie down and get out of the fight for awhile, perhaps for good. They are inclined to envy you as you lie there in bed, in a state which you consider absolutely unenviable.

No less a person than St. Peter, in the first of his inspired letters, gives a useful comparison to show us why God sends suffering. He tells us to rejoice in our salvation, but he adds: "Though now for a little while, if need be, you are made sorrowful by various trials, that the temper of your faith — more precious by far than gold which is tried by fire — may be found unto praise and glory and honor at the revelation of Jesus Christ" (1 Pt 1:6-7).

Gold, before it can be used in some precious article — let us suppose, in some sacred vessel — must be refined. The dross must be removed, and this is done by fire — a very painful business were the gold not happily insensible to pain. Similarly, to become vessels of holiness, capable of receiving the divinity, we must be refined and the dross removed from our soul.

Here, too, the purification is accomplished as it were by fire — by the penetrating fire of tribulation — and we, also, are so very sensitive to pain. There is dross to be removed even from the just, hence their sufferings. So that dross does not mean only definite moral evil or sin but includes many faults and imperfections, negligence, and failures, which we ourselves are ready to excuse very easily as only human, but which God finds it necessary to remove before we can enter His all-holy presence.

Especially may attachments and vanities of the world be classed as dross, not evil in themselves, perhaps, but infinitely inferior to the precious gifts with which God fills and sanctifies our souls. It is these higher gifts that He would have us seek. And what better way is there to purify us of such attachments than by forcibly taking from us, in various trials, the pleasures to which we are humanly so prone to cling?

Why Must I Suffer?

Pruning: Reflections Under Trial
Father Hugo followed Jesus in using an agricultural practice, pruning, as a metaphor to help explain the suffering of the just.

When spring comes, farmers plow the ground and plant their seeds, and we all live in hope that they will have a good crop. Eagerly then we watch the plants bursting into flowers and fruitfulness. But also, before this happens, we see the farmer do something else, a very interesting and significant maneuver, although for those with no experience in cultivating the soil it may appear to be, in part at least, quite puzzling. To the already growing plants and trees he takes a sharp knife or shears or saw. He cuts off all the dead or false growths from his plants and vines and trees. Nothing puzzling about that: they are worthless and he will burn them.

But his next procedure is not so clear (to the nonfarmer). He begins to cut back, at times drastically it seems, the fruitful branches of the living plant. He calls this pruning. Why does he do this? The plants, if they had feelings and a voice might well ask this themselves.

"Hey, boss," they might say in fright as they watch him move determinedly toward them, "What are you going to do with those wicked-looking shears? Surely you're not going to use them on us! We have worked hard for you. We have produced much fruit. Of course we understand why you cut off those dead branches — they were lazy and produced nothing for you, but we are making you rich!"

Nevertheless the farmer continues to come, threateningly it seems, toward them. Yet he is not going to "punish" them, but rather "reward" them by making them more fruitful. That's what pruning does. It reveals a law of nature: from death comes life. This is not a law that the farmer discovered by logic or by thinking about it. He learned it by experience and

215

observation. It is a law hidden mysteriously in the depths of nature: out of death comes life, dying we live. Everywhere we see it in operation throughout nature: in all vegetation nature dies, but in the spring it rises again to life.

Jesus observed all this and therefore watched this law working in His Father's creatures, and when He began to preach He applied it also in the spiritual and eternal life which He implants in His followers with His grace. He tells us this Himself: "I am the true Vine and My Father is the Vinedresser. Every branch in Me that bears no fruit He cuts away and every branch that does bear fruit He prunes to make it bear even more" (Jn 15:1-2).

Jesus thus knows this secret of life and fruitfulness from His Father's creation. And they use it on us — as well as on plants and trees. The Church is the vineyard, God is the Vinedresser, Jesus the Vine, and we are the branches grafted by baptism into the Vine.

The Farmer comes into the vineyard with His pruning shears (these are the troubles and afflictions of life). He sees some fruitless branches — false friends who produce nothing for Him and turn away from Him. He cuts these off in rejection. This is logical. We expect it. In fact, we often wonder why the wicked seem to prosper and why God does not cut them off and punish them.

But what He does next, to His friends — that is, to those who have sought to please Him — does not seem logical at all for One who is said to be so wise.

He begins to use those cruel shears on us. And we do have voices and sensibilities. And so we complain and whimper and weep and we ask why God can be so hard on us. We have not yet learned the secret of pruning. It seems unreasonable. Indeed, St. Paul will call it the foolishness of the cross. Yet it is the law of life: Dying and behold we live! This is the way St. Paul himself states it in one place (2 Cor 6:9).

God afflicts the evil in punishment but He tries His friends, the just, because He is so pleased with them. They have brought forth much fruit for Him and He will now enable them to produce more that they be given a greater harvest in eternity.

If we believe in our Father's providence — that He cares for the swallows that sell for a farthing and is even concerned about the grass in the field (Mt 10:29-31) — then we can realize that anything, or anyone, may be an instrument in the hand of the Divine Vinedresser. Mishaps, disasters, losses, sickness, suffering, persecutions: God can use them all fruitfully. As He does so, He is waiting for us to make a supreme act of faith, even amid our tears, and say, "God is doing this to me. These trials are His pruning knife. He is doing it in love, to multiply for me the fruits of holiness, that I may grow in love."

To do this is to live by faith. Jesus taught us this "secret" just before He Himself would be pruned, drastically indeed, by His Father, the Vinedresser, in His passion and death. This was His way of multiplying life, His own eternal life, in His friends and followers throughout the whole world. Further He wants us to join in this great surge of production, filling up, as members, His sufferings for His body, the Church.

Pruning: Reflections Under Trial

For the Sake of Joy

Father Hugo here examines the scriptural precedents for the suffering of the just

But the just are caught between both blades of the pruning knife, between that which punishes and that which increases life and fruitfulness.

For the just are also sinners and cannot be wholly exempt from the penal blade of the knife. "All have sinned and have need of the glory of God" (Rom 3:23). All inherit the primal guilt of mankind, and all are drawn invariably by the consequences of this guilt to personal sins. Even the just are told to say, "Pray for us sinners." "For though the virtuous man falls seven times, he stands up again" (Prv 24:16).

For the just man, too, therefore, the pruning knife may be used in punishment, but punishment that is drawn into the higher purpose of purification. "The path of the virtuous is like the light of dawn, its brightness growing to the fullness of day" (Prv 4:18). St. Thomas observes that while the works of the just, as a consequence of sin, have a penal character, in their case it becomes medicinal. Job illustrates this purifying action of God on the just.

There are other examples in the Old Testament. Tobit was acceptable to God, yet he was blinded by a stupid accident and his useful career interrupted. Judith encouraged her people in affliction, recalling how the saints of old had been tried.

"Let us rather give thanks to the Lord our God who, as He tested our ancestors, is now testing us. Remember how He treated Abraham, all the ordeals of Isaac, all that happened to Jacob in Syrian Mesopotamia while he kept the sheep of Laban, his mother's brother. For as these ordeals were intended by Him to search their hearts, so now this is not a vengeance God exacts against us, but a warning inflicted by the Lord on those who are near His heart" (Jdt 8:25-27).

The purpose of purification in affliction is described by Sirach with graphic example that will turn up again in the New Testament. "My son, if you aspire to serve the Lord prepare yourself for an ordeal. Be sincere of heart, be steadfast, and do not be alarmed when disaster comes. Cling to Him and do not leave Him, so that you may be honored at the end of your days. Whatever happens to you, accept it, and in the uncertainties of your humble state, be patient, since gold is tested in the fire, and chosen men in the furnace of humiliation" (Sir 2:1-5).

In the New Testament, St. Peter repeats this lesson, again comparing the just man to gold in which the dross is refined away by fire: "This is a cause of great joy for you, even though you may for a short time have to bear being plagued by all sorts of trials, so that, when Jesus Christ is revealed, your faith will have been tested and proved like gold — only it is more precious than gold which is corruptible even though it bears testing by fire — and then you will have praise and glory and honor" (1 Pt 1:6).

The Letter to the Hebrews (1:3) shows that God's motive in sending trials is His transforming love. This letter also provides the most complete and explicit treatment, comprising most of chapter twelve, of His medicinal or purifying intent. The author, like Judith, having encouraged the faithful by recalling the trials of Old Testament saints, concludes:

> With so many witnesses in a great cloud on every side of us, we, too, then should throw off everything that hinders us, especially the sin that clings so easily, and keep running steadily in the race we have started. Let us not lose sight of Jesus, who leads us in our faith and brings it to perfection. For the sake of the joy, which was still in the future, He endured the cross. . . . In the fight against sin, you have not yet had to keep fighting to the point of death.
>
> Have you forgotten that encouraging text in which you are addressed as sons? "My son, when the Lord corrects you, do not treat it lightly. But do not get discouraged when He reprimands you. For the Lord trains the ones He loves and He punishes all those that He acknowledges as His sons." . . . God is treating you as His sons. Has there ever been any son whose father did not train him? (Heb 12:1-7).

The father, seeing the undesirable traits in his son — whom he loves — corrects him to remove those flaws. So also God treats His "sons," to remove the faults marring the holiness befitting them. So much so that, "If you were not getting this training, as all of you are, then you would not be sons but bastards." And the reason: "Our human fathers were thinking of this short life when they punished us, and could only do what they thought best. But He does it all for our good, so that we may share in His own holiness" (cf. Heb 12:8-10).

The transformation intended by God cannot be other than a shattering experience for the "old man" as he becomes new: the old man, in shriveled confinement within his own excellence, with his proneness to vanity, sensuality, selfishness, indeed to all the deadly sins and to the false goods to which they deceptively lure him. This is the man destined to be a son of God, called to be perfect as the Father is perfect, to become "like Him," to share in His holiness. No metamorphoses in nature, remarkable as they are, can be compared to this.

Love Strong As Death

Destiny Draws You On

Our new life will manifest itself in the activity of charity, or love, by which we are drawn ever more powerfully to the things of God and ultimately to the embrace of God Himself: Through the growth of grace, we will mature as Christians, which means that we will become saints, practicing, as our new mode of activity, all the virtues that mark the lives of the saints.

This is our future, a glorious one indeed. But it means, on the negative side, that we must no longer be satisfied with mere human desires and aspirations. We must no longer content ourselves with mere natural satisfactions — we must in fact be ready to renounce natural pleasures and, in order to possess God ever more fully, break off our attachments and affections for the goods of this earth.

Herein is revealed the purpose of sufferings sent by God: for it is precisely by sufferings that our attachments for the pleasures and the good things of the world are severed. Perhaps we consider ourselves well-off as we are, willing, could we be but spared pain, to forego that glorious future planned for us in heaven as children of God.

Let us remember, however, that the pleasures of this world are transient — and bring no very satisfying happiness even while they last. But anyway, we have received grace and are under a law of spiritual growth. Of course, unlike physical laws, grace does not work in us of necessity: you can reject the grace of God if you want to and live for the transient and unsatisfactory pleasures of the earth. Then you would be like the stone that doesn't want to be transformed by the sculptor into the likeness of a saint, like the gold that objects to being refined and used in a sacred vessel, like the egg that won't become a bird, or the seed that refuses its destiny as a tree.

Still, in the case of you who are sick — you can hardly live for the things of the world. You are, by your very illness, being forcibly deprived of them. The law of spiritual growth is already operating in you. Your destiny is drawing you on. You may as well submit. Indeed, we must all submit. If the egg were not hatched, the birdling would die unborn. Either live or die — these are the alternatives, and if we choose to live we must submit to the laws of life. In the spiritual order, too, we must either live or die. If we refuse life and the laws which govern life, then we will die. For the love of the world, brief and unsatisfactory, also leads to sin, and the "wages of sin is death" (Rom 6:23).

And so, we have scarcely begun to enjoy this world when we must begin to give up its pleasures. We have no sooner started to live than we must learn to die: just as the happiness of the caterpillar, grubbing about the earth for food, is interrupted by the law of growth which turns him into the dead-looking chrysalis.

Our life here on earth, with its arduous duties, with its self-denial and unending trials, is itself a kind of death, a mortification or dying, and may therefore be aptly compared to the chrysalis. The mortification takes place in us continuously, and in a twofold way: in voluntary detachment, by which we sever our affections from the goods of earth, as also in the outward acts of self-denial which express this inward detachment and unworldliness. Secondly, in the trials and sufferings which forcibly deprive us of earthly joy and are therefore a knife by which Providence Himself cuts the attachments we have for things of the earth.

And yet as the chrysalis is but an intermediate state, from which the graceful butterfly will soon emerge, so the mortification of this life is also but an intermediate stage from which we too shall emerge "new creatures" capable of entering upon and enjoying the glory of heaven. "Through many tribulations we must enter the kingdom of God" (Acts 14:22).

Why Must I Suffer?

Everything to Gain

You may be tempted at this point to object, or at least to ask, "Why is God so determined that we should sacrifice our affections for the things of the earth? Why does He demand that we ourselves relinquish them through voluntary self-denial and be ready to give them up quietly when He takes them from us forcibly in various trials? The things of the earth are good —

God has Himself made them, and they could not be otherwise. Why then must we be so severely mortified in their regard?"

Assuredly, the things of the earth are good! And it is not thought that they are evil which makes it necessary for us to deprive ourselves of them or which causes God to deprive us of them. Still we should always bear in mind that the love of earthly things, good in itself, leads to evil, and that at times swiftly and disastrously.

In any event, these earthly goods are a lesser good. They are a good of the natural order, and it is our duty, as sons of God, to devote all our energies to the pursuit of the divine good of the supernatural order. Everything else that we do, every creature that we use or touch, should be brought into line with our quest for this higher good.

A father provides toys for his children. But if, after a prolonged absence, he returns home and finds his children so absorbed in their toys that they hardly look up to greet or embrace him, their own father — surely then he will be hurt and annoyed. We tend to become so absorbed in the goods of this world that we treat our Heavenly Father with coolness or indifference. Should we expect Him to be otherwise than indignant? Or should we not expect Him, with Fatherly tenderness, to anticipate and prevent such delinquency by teaching us, even though not without pain, the right use of creatures?

But perhaps another objection will occur to you. You admit, we will suppose, that the pursuit of worldly pleasures and attachments to worldly goods are a dross which God must purge from the soul to sanctify it fully.

But the most painful suffering of all is not the deprivation of pleasure or bodily well-being. It is rather the separation from loved ones — from friends, family, brothers, sisters, parents, children, wife, husband. Can such separation and loss-by-estrangement, by some necessity or duty of life, and worst of all, by sickness and death — can such separation and loss be in any sense good or work toward good? Does not God want us to love our neighbor and family? How then can He wish to break off such affections as these? And yet evidently He does, since, whatever the circumstances of our loss of loved ones, we must regard it as within the compass and control of God's universal providence.

In answer to this, it must be observed that even our love of friends and family must be purged and elevated in order to harmonize with our new status and character as sons of God. First of all, it is evident that there are many faults in human love: Many intrusions of selfishness, vanity, sensuality. They may not corrupt such love wholly, but they blemish and spoil it, as bad spots spoil a piece of luscious fruit. We sometimes speak of the love of spouses or of parents or of children as if it is always unquestionably good, but such is not the case.

To become fully virtuous and holy, our love for others must be purged of such imperfections, and this will be done by the cleansing action of the fire of affliction.

But even apart from these incidental, though sometimes deep, disorders, there is the other need, following at once from our supernatural status, of supernaturalizing all our activities and affections. In other words, since we are Christians, we should not love creatures for themselves, because of their natural goodness, even though this goodness is unquestionable and was given to them by God Himself.

We must love them on account of God, with a reflected love, seeing them as participants of God's goodness and referring their use to Him. We see the moon, not by its own light, but by light reflected from the sun. Just so, we must learn to love creatures, not as though they were suns, that is, as though they were good of themselves and sources of goodness, but rather as reflecting the goodness of God.

This is why Catholic teaching defines charity as a virtue by which we love God Himself and our neighbor on account of God. In this manner the saints love creatures. But imperfect souls tend to love creatures for themselves, humanly or sensually. If we are to grow to the maturity of holiness and supernatural love, our love must be transformed and divinized.

Now for the accomplishment of this holy end, nothing is more useful than mortification and suffering. For by such mortification the natural bond of affection is broken and the soul is therefore prepared to receive and to exercise a love truly divine.

"They alone are able truly to enjoy this world, who begin with the world unseen. They alone enjoy it, who have first abstained from it. They alone can truly feast, who have first fasted. They alone are able to use the world, who have learned not to abuse it. They alone inherit it, who take it as a shadow of the world to come, and for that world to come relinquish it."

Now this supernatural love, this love of charity, by which our affections should envelop all creatures, includes also, first of all, our neighbors, our fellowmen. Them also we should love — not for themselves merely, and assuredly not for what they give to us — but on account of God: as the images of God and as our brethren in the blood of Jesus Christ. Our love for them is also to be changed, transformed, divinized — capable, after a brief separation, of resurrection and survival for eternity.

Nor does this rule of charity exclude our own relatives, our family, our dearest ones: in truth it begins with them, for "charity begins at home." Our love for them also will be ennobled and transformed. Do not fear! In this process it will lose nothing, gain everything. It will become, not less intense, but more intense, not less satisfying, but more satisfying. It will come to resemble the pure and perfect love of Jesus and Mary for each other and of all the saints among themselves. And because of them, we will in eternity rejoin our dear ones with purified and elevated affections, ready to love them unselfishly and everlastingly. What we have to do is to take the precaution of seeing to it that we will get into eternity on the same side — and the right side! Another reason for submitting to this purification.

Why Must I Suffer?

Look to Glory

Stand firm, unyielding stone, while the Divine Sculptor, using the sharp sufferings of life, chisels and carves you into a veritable saint. Yes, by means of this heavy sorrow, you, a child of earth, are being changed, into a true child of God.

The trial so hard to bear is in truth an act of love, the caress of a divine Spouse, who desires to raise you to His level that your union may be the more intimate.

And if, in the midst of the sufferings, you find it difficult to think of anything besides this intolerable burden of pain, try to do so nevertheless — try to look to the glory ahead. Say with St. Paul, "For I reckon that the sufferings of the present time are not worthy to be compared with the glory to come that will be revealed in us. . . . For our present light affliction, which is for the moment, prepares for us an eternal weight of glory that is beyond all measure; while we look not at the things that are seen, but at the things that are not seen. For the things that are seen are temporal, but the things that are not seen are eternal" (Rom 8:18, 2 Cor 4:17-18).

Why Must I Suffer?

The Eucharist of Our Lives

The Holy Eucharist was a recurrent motif in Father Hugo's teaching. The disciple, he taught, should identify with the Master who was sacrificed on Calvary. In a similar way, the disciple should identify with the elements offered in the Mass, to be transformed into the very Body and Blood of Christ. Father Hugo's reflections on Christian suffering brought Him to a profound conclusion about the Christian believer's Communion with the Lord Jesus.

☙❧

It may be a coincidence, but it is surely a significant one, that the two analogies we have been studying, the sowing of the grain of wheat and the pruning of the vineyard, point to the materials used in the Eucharist: bread and wine. And in the Eucharist the mystery of Christ in His death and resurrection is made present that we may be united with Him in dying and rising to live with Him.

The grain of wheat that dies is Jesus, it is also ourselves: We join Him in the eucharistic bread that is offered. The Vine is also Jesus, and we are the branches: He is pruned, so are we: And we join Him in the wine on the altar. Through the signs of bread and wine we also share in His risen life: "We proclaim the death of the Lord until He comes" (1 Cor 11:26).

Love Strong As Death

Epilogue
The Art of Living

The following appears on Father Hugo's memorial card, under the title "The Cross the Measure of the World: The Art of Living, According to the Gospel." It can be seen as his spiritual last testament.

I

God, apart from sin, apart even from His own prevision of sin, has destined His human creatures to share in His own divine nature through grace, thereby calling them to relinquish, in the sphere of human freedom, that is to say, in our desires and motivation, a merely natural mode of existence: after the model of Jesus.

Thus mortification, dying to self, follows at once from our destiny to see and love God face to face. Atonement, with the virtue of penance, relating to justice, is therefore contingent upon the occurrence of sin, but is necessary for the restoration of God's original plan.

II

In gratitude to God for our human lives, we should do nothing with our physical powers, or put nothing into our bodies, that does not contribute to the Glory of God through our health and human welfare.

In brief: "Who loves his life loses it, and who hates his life in this world [for My sake] will keep it for eternal life" (Jn 12:25).

Sources

The selections in this book were culled from more than forty years worth of Father Hugo's writings and preaching. In some instances the selections have been condensed and adapted from much longer works and certain minor editorial changes have been made in the interests of ease of reading and consistency of style. Father Hugo's most important writings are listed below.

Applied Christianity, New York: Catholic Worker Press, 1944.

A Christian Manifesto on War, privately printed, 1981.

"Dorothy Day: Apostle of the Industrial Age," *Pittsburgh Catholic,* December 12, 1980.

Dorothy Day: Driven by Love, homily at Marquette University, Milwaukee, Nov. 5, 1981.

The Gospel of Peace, New York: Catholic Worker Books, 1944.

"Health and Spiritual Renewal," *Pastoral Life,* 1968.

Homily Keys (sermon summaries), privately printed, 1971-75.

In the Vineyard, New York: Catholic Worker Books, 1942.

Love Strong As Death: A Study in Christian Ethics, New York: Vantage Press, 1969.

Nature and the Supernatural: A Defense of the Evangelic Ideal, for private use; duplicated by the author, after February 1949.

The Prayer Word or Mantra, pamphlet, privately printed, undated.

Pruning: Reflections Under Trial, pamphlet, privately printed, undated.

St. Augustine on Nature, Sex, and Marriage, Chicago: Scepter Press, 1968.

A Sign of Contradiction: As the Master, So the Disciple, typed and duplicated by the author, 1947.

This Is the Will of God, privately printed, undated.

To the Pagans, Foolishness, typed and duplicated by the author, undated.

Weapons of the Spirit, New York: The Catholic Worker Press, 1943.

Sources

Why Must I Suffer? Kenosha, Wis.: Marytown Press, 1952.

You Are Gods! typed and duplicated by the author, undated.

Your Ways Are Not My Ways: The Radical Christianity of the Gospel, vol. I, Pittsburgh: Encounter with Silence, 1986.

Your Ways Are Not My Ways: The Radical Christianity of the Gospel, vol. II, Pittsburgh: Encounter with Silence, 1984.

Index

A

A Christian Manifesto on War (Hugo) 181, 184
A Sign of Contradiction (Hugo) 95, 96, 99, 115, 206
abortion 40
active life 76-78, 129-130, 133
Ad beatissimi Apostolorum (Benedict XV) 161, 162
addiction 62-64, 100
adultery 164, 172, 201
affective prayer 91-92
aggiornamento 122
alcohol, alcoholism 62-64
alms, almsgiving 39, 51, 52, 128, 140, 146
Alphonsus, St. 61, 73
Ambrose, St. 111
American Ecclesiastical Review 19
anarchism 119, 120
Angela de Foligno, Blessed 60
Annum Sacrum (Leo XIII) 187
Anthony, St. 79
Apollinarism 112
Apology for the Monastic Life (Chrysostom) 24
apostolate 125-149
Apostolicam Actuositatem (Vatican II) 134
Ascent of Mount Carmel (John of the Cross) 40, 91, 159, 188
aspirations 26, 88, 92, 219
Athanasius, St. 111-112
atomic bomb 13, 177-179
attachment 14, 15, 22, 43, 57, 58, 60-64, 94, 129, 130, 135, 188, 199
Augustine, St. 11, 34, 37, 73, 85, 105, 111, 114, 145, 164, 189
Auschwitz 13
authority (in the Church, in society) 18-21, 90, 104, 105, 110, 115-120, 152-
     158, 165-169, 172, 173, 89
Ave Maris Stella 36

B

Balthasar, Father Hans Urs von 18
baptism 25, 27, 28, 44-46, 49, 50, 85, 86, 163, 203, 216
Beatitudes (see also Sermon on the Mount) 38, 39, 41, 155, 163-165, 183, 190,
     193, 194, 195, 200
Belloc, Hilaire 22

Benedict XV, Pope 152, 156, 161, 162
Bernard, St. 78, 84, 204
big business 118
bingo 96, 99-104, 126
birth control (see also contraception) 95, 121, 151, 196
bishops, Catholic 19, 110, 111, 113, 118, 150-154, 181, 200
blacks 163
Bonaventure, St. 111, 138
boredom 76
Boyle, Bishop Hugh C. 13, 18
The Brothers Karamazov (Dostoevsky) 55, 63
"burnout" 76, 78

C

Cano, Melchior 112
capitalism 144, 147
Casti connubii (Pius XI) 29, 173
Catholic Action 14, 59, 132, 134, 136
Catholic Association for International Peace 167
Catholic Church, U.S. 16, 19, 93, 127, 150
Catholic education 127
Catholic identity 17, 18, 19
The Catholic Worker (movement) 11, 14, 118-120, 143, 146-148
The Catholic Worker (newspaper) 16, 22, 119, 126, 129, 132, 134, 135, 138, 140, 142, 143, 144, 156, 157, 166 175, 181
celibacy 53, 155, 171, 172, 196 -200, 206, 207
chaplains 174
Chardin, Father Teilhard de 122
charismatic renewal movement 11, 20
charity 22, 25, 26, 29, 41, 60, 106, 125, 129, 130, 135, 144, 156, 162, 163, 165, 183, 186, 191, 206, 211, 219, 222
Charles Borromeo, St. 111
chastity 53, 170, 172, 196-200, 201, 207
Chautard, Dom Jean-Baptiste 136
Chesterton, G.K. 25, 182
children 24, 27, 29, 30, 31, 33, 38, 41, 42, 43, 44, 45, 55, 63, 80, 91, 119, 128, 129, 130, 155, 158, 166, 173, 183, 189, 190, 200, 205, 207, 219, 221, 222
Cicognani, Archbishop Amleto 19
City of God (Augustine) 34
civil disobedience 141, 152, 169, 183
Claver, Sister Peter 143, 148
The Cloud of Unknowing 82, 83
Collodi, Carlo 31

communion with God (see also union with God) 31
communism 169
concupiscence 58, 160, 161, 172
Confessions (Augustine) 114
Congar, Father Yves 18
Connell, Father Francis J. 19
conscience 89, 116, 119, 122, 141, 150-154, 169, 177, 180
conscientious objection 12, 120, 133, 141, 150-152, 153, 169, 183
conscription (see also draft) 55, 146, 167-175, 182
conservatives 99, 121
contemplation, contemplative life 77, 79, 98, 202
contraception (see also birth control) 21, 40, 120, 122, 172
conversion (see also *metanoia*) 192, 194
covetousness 160, 161
creation 29, 71-73, 220
cross (of Christ) 29, 36, 46, 48, 51, 53, 58, 64, 65, 67, 82, 107, 109, 114, 135,
        137, 138, 140, 160, 185, 195, 199, 216, 218
Cyril of Alexandria, St. 112

D
Day, Dorothy 11, 12, 13, 16, 22, 116, 118, 140, 142-149, 166, 182, 191
"Dear Abby" 77
Dei Verbum (Vatican II) 122
detachment 14, 17, 34, 39, 58-61, 63, 65, 70, 94, 109, 135-137, 140, 142, 164,
        219- 220
devil 98, 109, 118, 175
discernment 85
disobedience (see also obedience) 35
distractions 83, 84
divine filiation 27, 31, 44, 212
divine presence 133
Divini redemptoris (Pius XI) 169
divorce 151
docility 117
Doherty, Catherine de Hueck 80
Donatism 123
Dooley, Dr. Thomas 51
Dostoevsky, Fyodor 55, 63
draft (see also conscription) 16, 166
drugs 62, 64
duty 14, 21, 27, 28, 30, 39, 56, 69, 70, 89, 96, 103, 106, 112, 113, 119, 120,
        151-157, 165, 166, 167, 169-171, 175, 176, 221

E

eating 61, 64
England 139, 151, 152
Eucharist 33, 80, 199, 223-224
evil 15, 29, 32, 34, 36, 55, 57-62, 87, 88, 100, 107, 109, 125, 128, 133, 135,
    136, 144, 151, 158-162, 165, 175, 177, 183, 185, 186, 190, 192, 196, 198,
    206, 208, 215, 216, 221

F

Faber, Father William F. 75, 107, 139
faith 17, 19, 20, 21, 25, 29, 31, 32, 37, 44, 45, 49, 51, 53, 55, 71, 83, 85, 86, 93-
    95, 100, 101, 104, 106, 115, 116, 121, 125, 131, 133, 138-140, 143, 145,
    146, 148, 163, 184, 186, 190, 201, 212, 214, 216, 217, 218
family 21, 22, 27, 29, 52, 53, 69, 77, 95, 103, 106, 130, 143, 147, 152, 155, 172,
    173, 175, 185, 200, 221, 222
Farina, Father Louis 20
fasting 61, 128, 183
Fenton, Father Joseph Clifford 19
flesh, theological concept of 31, 32, 37, 42, 44, 58, 83, 84, 125, 136, 139, 160,
    162, 193, 198, 199, 204
Francis of Assisi, St. 22, 116
Francis Borgia, St. 113
Francis de Sales, St. 15, 27, 56, 57, 58, 59, 60, 63, 91, 102, 111, 113, 133, 204
French Revolution 167
fundraising 103

G

gambling 64, 96, 100, 102, 103
Gandhi, Mohandas 78, 118, 183, 184, 190, 195
Garrigou-Lagrange, Reginald 61
Germans, Germany 65, 67, 68, 150, 159, 178, 179
The Gospel of Peace (Hugo) 131, 133, 190
government 63, 100, 118, 140-141, 156, 167-175, 183
grace 12, 25, 26, 27, 29, 31, 40, 43, 45, 50, 54, 60, 66, 67, 70, 73, 74, 79, 83,
    86-88, 115, 134, 135, 138, 158, 166, 171, 181, 186, 188, 189, 204, 205,
    212, 213, 216, 219, 220, 225
Graham, Dom Aelred 121
Gregory, St. 56, 97, 111

H

"Health and Spiritual Renewal" (Hugo) 87, 89, 90
heaven 106
hell 73, 195, 201

Hennacy, Ammon 118, 119
Henry VIII, King 151
heresy 17-19
heroism 35, 56, 66, 68, 69, 117, 166
Hitler, Adolph 65, 68, 127, 163, 176
holiness, universal call to 13-16, 19-21, 23, 24, 27-30, 33-34, 41- 42, 54, 63-65,
     82, 86-88, 93-95, 99, 107, 112, 115, 117, 124, 125, 141, 142, 150, 189,
     193, 194, 198, 200, 201, 207, 213-219, 222
holy hour 80
Holy Saturday 45
Holy Spirit 24, 26, 29, 46, 48, 84, 88, 89, 90, 99, 115, 117, 122, 128, 137, 183,
     189, 212, 213
homilies 96-99
hospitality 76, 143, 144
Hugo, Cecilia 19
Hugo, Lawrence 12
Hugo, Mary (Caufield) 12
Huguenots 17
human dignity 31, 146
human rights 152, 168-170, 173, 175
Humanae Vitae (Paul VI) 196
humility 70, 115, 137, 184, 185

I

idolatry 159-161, 207
Ignatius of Antioch, St. 111
Ignatius of Loyola, St. 91
illness (see also sickness) 208, 220
The Imitation of Christ 16, 36, 51, 162
Immaculate Conception, dogma of 189
Immortale Dei (Leo XII) 156
In the Vineyard (Hugo) 59, 61, 64, 65, 70, 72, 75, 79, 127, 128, 137
Incarnation, doctrine of 33, 83, 186
infanticide (see also abortion) 40
Ingravescentibus Malis (Pius XI) 186
injustice (see also justice) 40, 125, 132, 146, 154, 172, 173
Inquisition, the 112, 113
interior life 29, 30, 57, 79, 94, 132, 136, 169
Introduction to the Devout Life (Francis de Sales) 57, 91

J

James, William 182
Jane Frances de Chantal, St. 79
Jansenism 17

Japan 150, 159, 177, 178, 179
Jeremiah (prophet) 197
Jerome, St. 112
Jesus Prayer 83
Joan of Arc, St. 113, 154
Job 210, 217
John of Ávila, St. 113
John the Baptist 99, 197
John Chrysostom, St. 24, 112
John of the Cross, St. 15, 22, 40, 56, 62, 63, 64, 66, 88, 89, 91, 111, 113, 137,
    147, 159, 188, 203
John XXIII, Pope 122
John Fisher, St. 152
John Vianney, St. (the Curé of Ars) 26, 92
Journet, Charles 37
Joseph Cupertino, St. 26, 56
joy 52, 53, 54, 64, 69, 70, 71, 73, 77, 81, 84, 102, 114, 137, 138, 149, 160, 162,
    186, 195, 206, 207, 210, 217, 218, 220
judgment 25, 32, 50, 87, 118, 123, 140, 142, 147-148, 153, 195
just war, theory of 145, 150, 155, 165, 178-179
justice 12, 41, 64, 107, 108, 111, 119, 125, 130, 138, 144, 146, 150, 154, 158,
    162, 164, 188, 192, 193, 211, 225

K

KDKA-AM (radio station) 104
Keats, John 72
kingdom of God 32, 35, 44-46, 52, 54, 60, 72, 85, 97, 108, 122, 126, 131, 140,
    148, 160, 164, 181, 184, 187-189, 193, 194, 199, 212
King, Martin Luther 183
Knox, Msgr. Ronald 32

L

Lacouture, Father Onesiums 14, 15, 18, 21
Laetitiae Sanctae (Leo XIII) 185
laity 24, 28-30, 93, 120, 171, 200, 201
Landers, Ann 77
law 25, 27, 28-30, 35, 39, 48-50, 54, 60, 63, 66, 70, 89, 95, 100, 105, 119, 133,
    140-141, 154-157, 163-169, 173, 175, 183, 187, 190, 191, 194, 195, 201,
    215, 216, 219, 220
Lectio divina 90, 98
Lent 61
Leo XIII, Pope 156, 157, 163, 169, 185, 187
Lewis, C.S. 123
liberalism 153

Liberius, St. 112
Libertas humana (Leo XIII) 157
liturgical renewal 11
liturgy, liturgical prayer 65, 67, 80, 81, 85, 97-99
love 128-131, 133-137, 141-148, 159-165, 180, 181, 183, 186, 187, 188, 190,
    193-196, 198, 200, 201, 202, 204-207, 219, 221, 222, 223
love of God 14, 25, 26, 29, 35, 44, 56, 57, 59, 60, 62, 67, 69, 79, 100, 102, 105,
    113, 127, 129, 131, 134, 135, 136, 137, 191, 193, 202, 205
love of neighbor 25, 56, 129, 130, 131, 145, 165, 183, 191, 193
Louis Grignon de Montfort, St. 111, 189
Louise de Marillac, St. 77
Love Strong As Death (Hugo) 36, 38, 55, 219, 224
Lubac, Father Henri de 18
Luis de Granada, Ven. 113
Ludlow, Robert 118, 119
Luis de León, Ven. 113
lukewarmness (see also tepidity) 56, 57, 74, 126, 135-136, 139
Lumen Gentium (Vatican II) 21, 31, 35, 45

M
Manichaeism 123, 196, 199, 201
mantras 81-82
marriage 12, 29, 30, 36, 45, 53, 54, 69, 95, 100, 122, 151, 155, 171, 173, 196-
    207
Maritain, Jacques 13, 107, 126, 154
Mary, Mother of Christ 12, 36, 37, 38, 74-78, 80, 81, 91, 138-140, 188-190,
    197, 223
Mass 15, 17, 20, 81, 84, 95, 97, 111, 223
materialism 93, 130, 170
Maurin, Peter 144
meditation 42, 79, 82, 91, 98, 123
meekness 70, 108, 137, 190
mental prayer 79, 85
Merton, Thomas 88
metanoia (see also conversion) 45- 46, 87, 192, 194
Miserentissimus Redemptor (Pius XI) 187
moral relativism 175
morality 21, 32, 131, 146, 153, 160, 167, 176, 178, 179, 180, 201, 202
Morality and War (Vann) 154
mortification 22, 60, 61, 70, 94, 106, 128, 137, 138, 140, 164, 220, 222, 225
Mozart, Wolfgang 70, 73, 141
Murray, Father John Courtney 19
Mystical Body of Christ 146, 171, 177, 179, 200

N

nationalism 13, 158, 176, 177, 178
naturalism 34, 94
Nazis, Nazi Germany, Nazism 65, 127, 153, 175, 179, 180
negative Christianity 64-66, 67, 70
Negroes (see also blacks) 163
neo-paganism 153
Nero, Emperor 120, 128
"new morality," the 21, 142
Newman, Cardinal John Henry 16, 29, 34, 58, 104, 105, 107, 192, 120, 201
The New York Times 158, 178
Noll, Archbishop John F. 12
nonviolence 181, 182, 183, 184, 190, 191, 195
nuclear power 182

O

obedience 20, 34, 35, 53, 86, 106, 115-120, 131, 141, 142, 152, 153, 154, 168-169, 172, 191
On Holy Virginity (Augustine) 37
Opus Dei 14
Origenism 112
original sin 35, 105, 160, 210, 217
Our Lady of Sorrows 37
overeating 62

P

Pacem Dei (Benedict XV) 156
pacifism 16, 21, 143, 145, 146, 155, 156, 163, 181, 182
paganism 17, 57, 94, 95, 99, 106-107, 123, 126, 129, 135, 170, 191, 207
papacy 155, 156
patience 70, 120, 137, 138, 190
patriotism 177, 178
Paul VI, Pope 46, 196
peace 12, 21, 36, 41, 64, 82, 83, 105, 119, 125, 126, 130, 137, 146, 150, 151, 156, 157, 161, 162, 167, 169, 176, 181-184, 188-191, 193-195, 209
peacemakers, peacemaking 41, 155, 163, 182, 183, 188, 189, 190, 193, 194, 195
Pelagianism 123
penance 46, 67, 69, 70, 86-88, 106, 107, 116, 137, 138, 177, 186, 187, 211, 225
perfection, Christian call to 15, 21, 23-30, 35, 38-42, 57-58, 60-63, 74, 76, 88, 106, 107, 127, 132, 148, 150, 162, 164, 166, 183, 185, 193, 195, 197-198, 200, 201, 204, 205, 218, 219, 223
persecution 41, 110, 112-115, 140, 183, 190, 195, 216
"pharisaism" 104, 106-107
Pinocchio 30, 31, 43, 45

"pious minimalism" 56
"pious naturalism" 17, 107
The Pittsburgh Catholic 149
Pius IV, Pope 113
Pius V, Pope St. 111
Pius X, Pope 156
Pius XI, Pope 13, 27, 29, 94, 113, 157, 160-162, 169, 173, 176, 185, 16, 187, 190
Pius XII, Pope 13, 157, 161, 162
positive Christianity 64, 65, 69
poverty 36, 39, 53, 94, 109, 131, 144, 151, 185, 194, 200
Powers, J.F. 16
prayer 15, 18, 42, 52, 70, 93, 94, 98, 99, 109, 128, 133, 142, 183-187
The Prayer Word, or Mantra (Hugo) 84
priesthood 11, 12, 27, 77, 94-99, 107, 199-200
progressives 93, 121
providence of God 47, 85, 86, 113, 182, 210, 216, 220-221
Pruning: Reflections Under Trial (Hugo) 215, 217
purgation 57
purity 25, 63, 41, 106, 164, 201

R

Rahner, Karl 89, 122
refugees 146
relaxation 81
"The Religion of the Pharisee, the Religion of Man" (Newman) 105
religious life (see also priesthood) 28, 53, 200
renunciation (see also mortification) 29, 36, 37, 50, 52, 53, 55, 56, 61, 65, 66, 67, 70, 138
repentance (see also *metanoia*) 14, 45, 46, 74, 87
Rerum Omnium (Pius XI) 27
respect for life 146
resurrection (of Christ) 36, 46-50, 53-54, 148-149, 186, 198-200, 222, 224
retreat movement 13, 202
reward 39, 40, 114, 135, 190, 215
Rite of Reconciliation 46
Romeo and Juliet (Shakespeare) 207
Romero, Archbishop Oscar 183
Rosary 185-187

S

Sabellianism 112
"sacrament of the present moment" 85
Sacred Heart of Jesus, devotion to 109, 163, 187

saints 13, 14, 15, 21, 22, 24, 26, 27, 29, 30, 56, 59, 60, 61, 70, 73, 90, 110, 203,
　　213, 214, 217, 218, 219, 222, 223
Salinger, J.D. 82
"samples," Father Hugo's doctrine of 12, 61, 71-72, 200, 206
Sapientiae Christianae (Leo XIII) 169
Schweitzer, Albert 51
science 98, 124, 130, 131, 145, 180, 192, 209
Scriptures, Sacred 16, 17, 43, 45, 53, 83, 84, 90, 107, 157, 183, 193, 202, 205
Second Vatican Council 12, 20, 21, 23, 31, 35, 45, 115, 119, 121, 122, 134, 193, 197
self-denial 64, 67, 69, 70, 135, 136, 137, 220
self-sacrifice 22, 37, 61, 65-70, 87, 89, 96, 97, 128, 135, 137, 142,170, 186,
　　187, 196, 199, 220
self-surrender 14, 35
Sermon on the Mount (see also Beatitudes) 15, 38, 39, 41, 42, 52, 54, 68, 150,
　　163, 165, 183, 184, 190
sexuality 11, 12, 21, 36, 62, 64, 122, 183,196-207
Shakespeare, William 199, 207
Sheed, Frank 13
Sheen, Bishop Fulton 80, 151
sickness 54, 208-211, 214, 216, 219, 221
silence 15, 20, 80, 99
sin 17, 25, 26, 31, 33, 34, 36, 43, 46, 56, 57, 59, 61, 63, 66, 73, 74, 85-88, 95,
　　105, 116, 117, 132, 136, 153, 159, 166, 169, 171, 172, 187, 188, 201, 210-
　　211, 215, 217-220, 225
slavery 163, 170, 182, 191, 192
smoking (see also tobacco) 15
social justice (see also justice; injustice) 142
socialism 147
The Soul of the Apostolate (Chautard) 136
Spellman Cardinal Francis J. 12
spiritual direction 87-90, 94, 107
St. Augustine on Nature, Sex and Marriage (Hugo) 21, 121, 124
suffering 25, 50, 55, 115, 128, 142, 144, 159, 184-187, 190, 195, 208-224
Summa Theologiae (Thomas Aquinas) 153, 160, 165, 168
supernatural life 14, 28, 32, 33, 34, 43, 60, 69, 75, 94, 115, 134, 137, 139

T

The Teaching of Christ (Wuerl, et. al.) 20
technology 13, 130, 145, 146, 167, 192
The Tempest (Shakespeare) 199
Tempier, Archbishop Stephen 113
temptation 43, 74, 85, 87, 90, 115, 124, 171-173
Tennyson, Alftred 183
tepidity (see also lukewarmness) 28

Teresa of Ávila, St. 15, 56, 79, 82, 89-90, 111, 113
theology 16, 25, 88, 90, 96, 99, 105, 120-124, 150, 151, 158
Theophilus 112
Thérèse of Lisieux, St. 13, 16, 20, 22
The Things That Are Not Caesar's (Maritain) 154
This Is the Will of God (Hugo) 25, 26, 27, 28, 30, 57, 68, 69, 74
Thomas Aquinas, St. 13, 25, 34, 56, 59, 77- 78, 98, 113, 121, 136, 145, 153-
154, 160, 165, 166, 168, 172, 195, 217
Thomas More, St. 27, 151, 152, 153
Thoreau, Henry David 141
Thompson, Dorothy 178
tobacco 62-64
Trinity, doctrine of 23, 31
Truman, Harry 178, 180
truth 23, 30, 38, 44, 49, 55, 60, 68, 83, 84, 90, 97, 108, 110-114, 119-127, 129,
132, 138-139, 142, 151, 153, 155, 157, 159, 161-162, 165, 180-186, 188,
190, 192, 194, 195, 205, 210, 212, 222-223

U

Ubi arcano Dei consilio (Pius XI) 94, 157, 160, 161, 176
union with God 25, 31, 94, 131, 168, 133, 202-206
United Nations 191
United States of America 35, 128, 144-145, 191
University of Oxford 113
unworldliness (see also detachment) 33, 59, 185, 220

V

Vann, Father Gerald 154
Vatican II (see Second Vatican Council)
Vincent de Paul, St. 77
virginity 37, 197-200
vocation 12, 13, 29, 33, 54, 56, 65, 77, 88, 89, 95, 106, 116, 155, 171, 172, 193,
196

W

war 12, 13, 16, 17, 39, 65, 67, 99, 125, 129, 130-131, 145, 146, 150-169, 172,
175-181, 185-187, 192, 194, 195
The Way of a Pilgrim 83
Weapons of the Spirit (Hugo) 162, 188
Why Must I Suffer? (Hugo) 208, 215, 220, 223
Willock, Ed 137
will of God 15, 37, 85-86, 133, 140, 142, 171, 177, 183, 184, 197
work 30
workaholism 76, 77

World War I 162
World War II 12, 16, 17, 118, 150, 154, 158, 162, 173, 174, 176-181, 182
worldliness 57-59, 95, 125, 135, 136, 188
Wright, Cardinal John J. 11, 20, 21
Wuerl, Bishop Donald W. 20

Y

You Are Gods (Hugo) 43
Your Ways Are Not My Ways (Hugo) 34, 45, 46, 62, 64, 73, 84, 85, 86, 108, 117, 118, 121, 133, 137, 142, 195, 200, 202, 207
youth 64-68, 78, 136, 137, 171, 175, 182, 201

Our Sunday Visitor...
Your Source for Discovering the Riches of the Catholic Faith

Our Sunday Visitor has an extensive line of materials for young children, teens, and adults. Our books, Bibles, booklets, CD-ROMs, audios, and videos are available in bookstores worldwide.

To receive a FREE full-line catalog or for more information, call **Our Sunday Visitor** at **1-800-348-2440**. Or write, **Our Sunday Visitor /** 200 Noll Plaza / Huntington, IN 46750.

Please send me: __ A catalog
Please send me materials on:
 __ Apologetics and catechetics __ Reference works
 __ Prayer books   __ Heritage and the saints
 __ The family   __ The parish

Name_____

Address_____Apt._____

City_____State ____Zip_____

Telephone (   ) _____

                A73BBABP

Please send a friend: __ A catalog
Please send a friend materials on:
 __ Apologetics and catechetics __ Reference works
 __ Prayer books   __ Heritage and the saints
 __ The family   __ The parish

Name_____

Address_____Apt._____

City_____State ____Zip_____

Telephone (   ) _____

                A73BBABP

Our Sunday Visitor
200 Noll Plaza
Huntington, IN 46750
1-800-348-2440
OSVSALES@AOL.COM

Your Source for Discovering the Riches of the Catholic Faith